Published by:

Wiley Publishing, Inc.

111 River St.
Hoboken, NJ 07030-5774

ISBN 978-0-470-60222-5
Editor: Naomi P. Kraus
Production Editor: Lindsay Conner
Photo Editor: Richard Fox
Cartographer: Elizabeth Puhl
Production by Wiley Indianapolis Composition Services

For information on our other products and services or to obtain technical support, please contact our Customer Care Department within the U.S. at 877/762-2974, outside the U.S. at 317/572-3993, or fax 317/572-4002.

Wiley also publishes its books in a variety of electronic formats. Some content that appears in print may not be available in electronic formats.

Manufactured in China

5   4   3   2   1

Fr

Las Vegas
day BY day™

2nd Edition

by Naomi P. Kraus & Kate Silver
with Mary Herczog

WILEY
Wiley Publishing, Inc.

Contents

A Note from the Editorial Director

Organizing your time. That's what this guide is all about.

Other guides give you long lists of things to see and do and then expect you to fit the pieces together. The Day by Day guides are different. These guides tell you the best of everything, and then they show you how to see it *in the smartest, most time-efficient way*. Our authors have designed detailed itineraries organized by time, neighborhood, or special interest. And each tour comes with a bulleted map that takes you from stop to stop.

Hoping to hit it big at the blackjack tables, visit the Dolphins at The Mirage, take in a Cirque du Soleil show, or just stroll The Strip? Planning a walk through Downtown, or dinner and drinks where you can rub shoulders with rich and infamous? Whatever your interest or schedule, the Day by Days give you the smartest routes to follow. Not only do we take you to the top attractions, hotels, and restaurants, but we also help you access those special moments that locals get to experience—those "finds" that turn tourists into travelers.

The Day by Days are also your top choice if you're looking for one complete guide for all your travel needs. The best hotels and restaurants for every budget, the greatest shopping values, the wildest nightlife—it's all here.

Why should you trust our judgment? Because our authors personally visit each place they write about. They're an independent lot who say what they think and would never include places they wouldn't recommend to their best friends. They're also open to suggestions from readers. If you'd like to contact them, please send your comments our way at feedback@frommers.com, and we'll pass them on.

Enjoy your Day by Day guide—the most helpful travel companion you can buy. And have the trip of a lifetime.

Warm regards,

Kelly Regan

Kelly Regan, Editorial Director
Frommer's Travel Guides

About the Authors

Naomi P. Kraus is a senior editor at Frommer's and has been visiting and covering Las Vegas for more than a decade. A graduate of the Columbia Graduate School of Journalism, she knows when to hit and when to stay . . . and is working on figuring out when to hold 'em and when to fold 'em. **Kate Silver** (ch. 6 and 10) spun the metaphorical Sin City roulette wheel for 10 years as a Las Vegas editor and is the former editor of *Las Vegas Life* magazine. A professional freelance writer, her work has appeared in *Playboy, People,* and *Spirit* magazines, and she contributed to *Pauline Frommer's Las Vegas.*

Acknowledgments

We'd like to thank David Gonzalez at MGM Mirage, Karin Tomcik at Cirque du Soleil, Sara Gorgon at Harrah's, and Heidi Baldwin at Kirwin Doak Communications for all of their assistance.

An Additional Note

Please be advised that travel information is subject to change at any time—and this is especially true of prices. We therefore suggest that you write or call ahead for confirmation when making your travel plans. The authors, editors, and publisher cannot be held responsible for the experiences of readers while traveling. Your safety is important to us, however, so we encourage you to stay alert and be aware of your surroundings.

Star Ratings, Icons & Abbreviations

Every hotel, restaurant, and attraction listing in this guide has been ranked for quality, value, service, amenities, and special features using a **star-rating system.** Hotels, restaurants, attractions, shopping, and nightlife are rated on a scale of zero stars (recommended) to three stars (exceptional). In addition to the star-rating system, we also use a **kids icon** to point out the best bets for families. Within each tour, we recommend cafes, bars, or restaurants where you can take a break. Each of these stops appears in a shaded box marked with a coffee-cup-shaped bullet 🍵 .

The following **abbreviations** are used for credit cards:

AE	American Express	DISC	Discover	V	Visa
DC	Diners Club	MC	MasterCard		

Dedication

This book is dedicated to our late Frommer's Vegas writer, Mary Herczog—a lot of this book was based on her material and without her legacy, it would not have had the same sense of fun and Sin City spirit. Working with Mary was like hitting a giant jackpot and we at Frommer's were all very lucky to know her.

Travel Resources at Frommers.com

Frommer's travel resources don't end with this guide. Frommer's website, **www.frommers.com**, has travel information on more than 4,000 destinations. We update features regularly, giving you access to the most current trip-planning information and the best airfare, lodging, and car-rental bargains. You can also listen to podcasts, connect with other Frommers.com members through our active-reader forums, share your travel photos, read blogs from guidebook editors and fellow travelers, and much more.

A Note on Prices

In the "Take a Break" and "Best Bets" sections of this book, we have used a system of dollar signs to show a range of costs for 1 night in a hotel (the price of a double-occupancy room) or the cost of an entree at a restaurant. Use the following table to decipher the dollar signs:

Cost	Hotels	Restaurants
$	under $100	under $20
$$	$100–$150	$20–$40
$$$	$150–$200	$40–$75
$$$$	over $200	over $75

How to Contact Us

In researching this book, we discovered many wonderful places—hotels, restaurants, shops, and more. We're sure you'll find others. Please tell us about them, so we can share the information with your fellow travelers in upcoming editions. If you were disappointed with a recommendation, we'd love to know that, too. Please write to:

Frommer's Las Vegas Day by Day, 2nd Edition
Wiley Publishing, Inc. • 111 River St. • Hoboken, NJ 07030-5774

15 Favorite **Moments**

0   0.5 mi
0   0.5 km

········· Monorail
········· & station

DOWNTOWN

ARTS DISTRICT (GATEWAY DISTRICT)

Fremont Street Experience

NORTH STRIP

MID-STRIP

SOUTH STRIP

McCARRAN INT'L AIRPORT

1. A walk on the Strip
2. Hotel hopping on the Strip
3. Spending an evening in Glitter Gulch
4. Embracing—and consuming—excess at a buffet
5. Giggling at the Liberace Museum
6. Getting a little culture at the Bellagio
7. Visiting the dolphins at the Mirage
8. Shopping the casino arcades
9. Marvel at Cirque du Soleil
10. Feel nostalgic and silly at *Jubilee!*
11. Changing the mood at the Atomic Testing Museum
12. Seeing a headliner
13. Eat with a star
14. Clearing your head in Red Rock Canyon
15. Stay in a fancy resort outside the city

Previous page: The Las Vegas Strip at night.

Elvis sang "Viva, Las Vegas," wishing there were more than 24 hours in the day to spend in the city that set his soul on fire. But some respond by saying, "Yeah, it's not my kind of thing." For me, that's like saying the Grand Canyon isn't your kind of thing. Sure, the latter is one of the great natural wonders of the world, but Las Vegas is *the* great unnatural wonder of the world. It's a life experience like no other. It has to be seen to be believed, and to see it is to experience it. And once you have, you may be singing along with the King, because even in a 24/7 kind of town there aren't enough hours to handle it all. My favorite picks should help you manage this sprawling mass of fun.

The Venetian is one of the Strip's best re-created locales.

1 Walking on the Strip. The heart of the city, a 13-block stretch of Las Vegas Boulevard South, is lined left and right with behemoth hotel casino resorts, all wonders of excess and each with its own particular absurd delight, from gaudy outside decor to attention-grabbing free attractions to a theme run amok. It's less spectacular during the day, but the lights at night are so head-spinning you might be too distracted to take it all in. Truth be told, it's too far to walk in one go, so plan to do it in stretches. *See p 42.*

2 Hotel hopping on the Strip. It's Vegas, after all, and even if you don't want to drop a dime (though isn't that partly what you came here for?), you'll want to see what's inside those flashy facades. The trend has been toward resort spas on steroids— what would be quiet good taste were it on a smaller scale—but there is still plenty, from ancient Egypt and Rome to medieval Venice to a scaled-down New York City to keep you agog. Remember, in other cities, hotels are built *near* the attractions. In Vegas, they *are* the attractions. *See p 42.*

3 Spending an evening in Glitter Gulch. The original heart of the city, the pedestrian-only section of Fremont Street comes as a relief after the overwhelming Strip. Sure, there's still sensory overload, but the scale is such that by comparison, it's practically small-town Main Street. Each casino is an easy distance from the next, the crowds seem less daunting,

Mustang Sally is among Glitter Gulch's most famous icons.

and you don't have to jostle for position to view the overhead Fremont Street Experience light show. *See p 58,* ⑭.

④ **Embracing—and consuming—excess at a buffet.** All-you-can-eat, low-cost buffets have long been a symbol of the city's bargain vacation status. Vegas is no longer a bargain, but the buffets remain, though similarly increased in price. Still, the sight of rows of prep stations, offering varieties of international and American cuisine, not to mention mounds of shrimp and prime rib, remains a sybaritic treat. And though prices have gone up, so has quality—and it's still cheaper than multicourses at a costly restaurant. The Buffet at Wynn Las Vegas is tops in appeal, though also in price. *See p 96.*

⑤ **Giggling at the Liberace Museum.** For a city that reinvents itself every 5 minutes, it's nice to see some level of appreciation for the past. And nothing says Vegas quite like a performer who appreciated the town's glitter and applied it to himself—literally. Marvel at the wonder and glory of the human performance project that was Liberace, not to mention his sequined clothing, rhinestone-coated piano, and

jewels—faux and fabulous alike. *See p 15,* ①.

⑥ **Getting a little culture at the Bellagio.** Vegas still remains too busy with the bang and the bustle to really dedicate itself to the quieter arts, but the Bellagio Gallery of Fine Art continues to defy the odds and offers excellent retrospective shows on everything from photography (Ansel Adams) to fine art (Monet). Ducking into a gallery from a casino is nearly an exercise in cognitive dissonance, but a little intellectual nutrition helps keep your balance in a city designed to throw you off same. *See p 16,* ③.

⑦ **Visiting the dolphins at the Mirage.** An unexpected oasis in the midst of the Strip's pleasurable madness. Visitors can watch these playful mammals swim and frolic in a meticulously designed environment; they'll even interact a bit thanks to cute and lively trainers, glorying in the best job in Vegas. Take as long as you like to enjoy the dolphins' company; if you are really lucky, they might even play ball with you. *See p 16,* ⑤.

Stuff yourself silly at one of the city's many buffets; it's a quintessential Vegas experience.

8 Shopping the casino arcades.
Vegas is a shopper's paradise only if you don't demand cute, quirky, and original stores. In other words, chains and other recognizable names rule the day, but rule they do, in shopping centers largely attached to the casino hotels and every bit as extravagantly designed. From Versace to Old Navy, there is something for every budget, and in the case of the Forum Shops, it's all set in an overblown Roman streetscape that adds fanciful (if not tasteful) glamour. Buy some shoes in between rounds of blackjack—maybe your winnings will pay for them! *See p 69.*

9 Marveling at Cirque du Soleil.
The tacky postvaudevillian variety shows that were once the standard for Strip entertainment have almost entirely vanished in favor of a great many offerings from the idiosyncratic human circus Cirque du Soleil. Truth be told, there can be too much of a good thing, and at five and counting (at least two more productions are ramping up at press time), not every one is worth the high ticket price. But the good ones certainly are, so much so that it's hard to choose. Right now, my favorite is *KÀ* at the MGM-Grand, a near-perfect blend of Cirque artistry, athleticism, visuals, and storytelling. *See p 45,* **12**.

10 Feeling nostalgic and silly at *Jubilee!* Classic, over-the-top (not to mention topless) Vegas revues are a dying breed, hedged out by special-effects-laden modern productions and just a modicum of good taste. But if you are nostalgic for some old-fashioned glamour and barely naughty fun, come see the pinnacle of what was once the dominant theatrical art form in town, the shameless and delightful *Jubilee! See p 115.*

You haven't really done Las Vegas properly if you haven't seen one of the city's famous showgirls; Jubilee! is the best place in town to check them out.

11 Changing the mood at the Atomic Testing Museum. With the Atomic Testing Museum, the city delivers something unexpected and otherwise unique. For 4 decades, Sin City's neighbor was the country's primary nuclear weapons testing ground. This admirable facility offers perspectives, technical and personal, on the science and implications of the work done there. *See p 15,* **2**.

An exhibit inside the Smithsonian-affiliated Atomic Testing Museum, one of the best museums in the city.

⑫ Seeing a headliner. Time was, all the names in show business did stands of varying lengths in Vegas. And though the decline of the Rat Pack left a longtime hole in the name-brand entertainment market, big deals such as Barry Manilow, Bette Midler, and Cher have taken up residency at various showrooms. Ticket availability varies, as do the performance schedules. If you can splurge on only one, make it Bette. *See p 113.*

⑬ Eating with a star. A Michelin-starred chef, that is. Any number of celebrity chefs have set up outposts in town, but only at Joël Robuchon at the Mansion (in the MGM Grand) can you dine on the work of the youngest chef in history to win three consecutive Michelin stars. It'll cost you, make no mistake about it, but it's also been hailed by the country's most prominent food critics as some of the finest French food on the continent. You won't regret spending the big bucks. *See p 90.*

⑭ Clearing your head In Red Rock Canyon. Less than 20 miles from the overstimulated artifice of Vegas is one of the great wonders of the natural world, an impossible set of sandstone monoliths stretching across an unspoiled vista. Take a car through the 13-mile (21km) scenic drive, or hike around on your own and marvel at what is possible given a mere 300 million years or so. *See p 19,* ①.

⑮ Staying in a fancy resort off the strip. There are so many Vegas hotel possibilities, but for a truly relaxing experience, you have to get off the Strip. For pampering luxury, I like the M Resort, an actual boutique property where the rooms are fabulously appointed, the spa and pool are great, and the staff is friendly. And it's just a short drive away from all the major Vegas action. If only they'd lose the "resort fee"—the sort of money-grubbing best left to one-arm bandits. *See p 128.* ●

The M Resort Spa & Casino offers a true boutique experience away from the hubbub of the Strip.

1

The Best **Full-Day Tours**

The Best **in One Day**

1 Luxor
2 Excalibur
3 New York–New York
4 MGM Grand
5 Paris Las Vegas
6 La Creperie
7 Ascend the Eiffel Tower for a view of the city
8 CityCenter
9 Bellagio
10 Bellagio Water Fountains
11 Caesars Palace
12 Mirage
13 The Venetian
14 Wynn Las Vegas
15 Wynn Las Vegas Buffet
16 Mountain/Lake of Dreams

Scale:
0 — 0.5 mi
0 — 0.5 km

··· Monorail & station

Previous page: Caesars Palace, a prime example of the Las Vegas theme hotel.

If all you know of Las Vegas is the Strip, that's okay—that's really all you need to know. This stretch of Las Vegas Boulevard South is the heart of the city—sometimes it's mistaken for the city itself. That's an understandable error, because here is what Vegas is all about: mammoth hotel casinos, glittering with electricity both real and metaphorical. See nothing else and you will see Las Vegas. START: **The main entrance to the Luxor.**

① ★ **Luxor.** With its glass pyramid-shaped main building (designed by noted architect Veldon Simpson), complete with a 315,000-watt light beam emanating from its peak, this hotel is an appropriate introduction to all things Vegas. There's a touch of historical accuracy (say howdy to those replicas of the Sphinx and Cleopatra's Needle), there's more than a bit of braggadocio (that light beam is allegedly visible from space), and it's all a bit weirdly wrong (not least because Luxor execs are doing their best to make the place more "chic" by obliterating the interior traces of Egypt in a 30-story pyramid). ⏲ *20 min. 3900 Las Vegas Blvd. S.* ☎ *888/777-0188 or 702/262-4000. www.luxor.com.*

② **Excalibur.** Though its interior's King Arthur mythology has been toned down over the years, this castle-shaped resort is still one of the largest in Vegas, and continues to give a sense of what the city was like at its kitsch-and-cash height. Note the battlements, the drawbridge, and even a moat, though the spoilsports ditched the larger-than-life Merlin that used to overlook the realm. ⏲ *20 min. 3850 Las Vegas Blvd. S.* ☎ *800/937-7777 or 702/597-7700. www.excalibur.com.*

③ ★★ **New York–New York.** Take the Big Apple's skyline, squash it down and turn it into a hotel exterior, and presto—you have this pinnacle of over-the-top fantasy Vegas. The Empire State and Chrysler buildings, a half-scale Statue of Liberty, and more are represented in brightly colored, semicartoon detail—and a roller coaster (whose

A marvel of modern design, CityCenter cost over $11 billion.

It's less Egyptian than it used to be, but you can still lose yourself in the Luxor's impossibly large atrium.

cars appropriately resemble NYC taxis) swooshes through it all. Ridiculous and fantastic all at once—even if the hotel execs deserve a Bronx Cheer for toning down the theme on the inside. ⏱ *20 min. 3970 Las Vegas Blvd. S.* ☎ *800/693-6763 or 702/740-6969. www.nyny hotelcasino.com.*

❹ **MGM Grand.** The biggest of the big, the MGM Grand's emerald interior (left over from its original incarnation as an homage to MGM's most beloved *Wizard of Oz*) is garish in the daytime, glowing at night, and enormous at all times. The biggest hotel in the U.S., it certainly is the greenest. A stately 100,000-pound (45,359kg) bronze lion guards the entrance beneath high-tech video screens. Once upon a time, this was the pinnacle of the ill-conceived—and hastily discarded—"Vegas is for families" campaign, but today it caters to more adult-oriented

tastes. ⏱ *25 min. 3799 Las Vegas Blvd. S.* ☎ *800/929-1111 or 702/891-7777. www.mgmgrand.com.*

❺ ★ **Paris Las Vegas.** More reproductions of famous landmarks (including a two-thirds replica of the Arc de Triomphe), though without much regard to actual geographical location, as the Hôtel de Ville is crammed on top of the Louvre. The $785-million resort is one of the few Strip resorts that still embraces its theme to the max and is no less chic for it. Vive la France! ⏱ *15 min. 3655 Las Vegas Blvd. S.* ☎ *888/ BONJOUR (266-5687) or 702/946-7000. www.parislv.com.*

Sidewalk creperies are everywhere in Paris, so continue your ooo-la-la mood and grab a traditional snack, with either sweet or savory filling, at ❻ **La Creperie.** *Inside Paris Las Vegas; see* ❺. ☎ *702/946-7000. $.*

An immense bronze lion, the largest statue in the United States, guards the entrance to the equally mammoth MGM Grand hotel.

7 ★ **Ascend the Eiffel Tower for a view of the city.** It's half the size of the original (540 ft. tall/165m, to be specific), and probably has about that same percentage of the romance, but the view from the top of the Bellagio fountains and the Strip in general is pretty swell. Plus the guides here give you all kinds of details about the structure, the kind of re-creation that Vegas used to boast more of, both in the bragging sense and in the possessing sense. Be warned that on windy days, the tower can be shut down for safety reasons. ⏱ *30 min., unless you hang out longer. In Paris Las Vegas; see* **5**. *Admission $10 adults 9:30am–7:30pm, $12 from 7:30pm–close; $7 seniors and kids 6–12 9:30am–7:30pm, $10 from 7:30pm–close; free for kids 5 and under. Daily 9:30am–12:30am, weather permitting.*

8 ★ **CityCenter.** The big question hanging over this futuristic "urban community" of resorts, retail, and entertainment options, which debuted to great fanfare in December 2009, is whether it will ever recoup the zillion-dollar investment it took to open it. Still, that money bought some pretty nifty modern architecture, a sustainable environment (it has the highest casino LEED certification in Vegas), and one of the largest public art installations in the U.S. Stroll past artworks by such notables as Maya Lin and Henry Moore and marvel at the sheer scale of this steel and glass wonder. ⏱ *25 min. Las Vegas Blvd. S. & Harmon Ave. www.citycenter.com. See p 135 for details on CityCenter's hotels; p 69 for details on shopping.*

9 **Bellagio.** The turning point for modern-day Vegas, this elegant cross between hotel as attraction and hotel on steroids set back

The view from the top of Paris Las Vegas's re-creation of the Eiffel Tower is superb.

original owner/visionary Steve Wynn about $1 billion. As you stroll by, admire the ever-so-slightly classy strip mall version of a charming Italian village strung along an 8-acre (3.2-hectare) invocation of Lake Como. ⏱ *20 min. 3600 Las Vegas Blvd. S.* ☎ *888/987-6667 or 702/693-7111. www.bellagio.com.*

10 ★★★ **Bellagio Water Fountains.** The best free show in Vegas. Giant spouts send water shooting (as high as 250 ft./76m in the air), dancing, swaying, and even twirling to music ranging from Sinatra to symphonic. A sophisticated lighting array adds a dash of color to the proceedings. You may think it sounds a bit silly, but catch a show and see if you can stop with just one; for a cinematic preview, check out the fountains' action in the 2001 remake of *Ocean's Eleven.* ⏱ *30 min., to allow for two different shows. In front of the Bellagio; see p 53,* **1**.

The dancing fountains that front the Bellagio are the best free attraction in Las Vegas.

Shows every half-hour starting early afternoon, every 15 min. 8pm–midnight, weather permitting.

The Mirage kicked off the modern hotel era in Las Vegas and still holds its own today.

⑪ ★ Caesars Palace. Vegas' original, simultaneously goofy and romantic hotel—and one of the oldest venues (it opened in 1966) still extant on the Strip. It's expanded so much that the Rat Pack wouldn't recognize it, but you should still enjoy the tacky and over-sized replicas of Greco-Roman statuary that decorate the front. Watch for the four-sided Bhrama shrine, an 8,000-pound (3,629kg) replica of the venerated Thai Buddhist good-luck landmark, on the north lawn. ⏱ *25 min. 3570 Las Vegas Blvd. S. ☎ 877/427-7243 or 702/731-7110. www.caesars.com.*

⑫ ★ Mirage. The hotel that, in 1989, kicked off the "more is more" modern Vegas era. This gleaming gold structure cost $630 million (a record when it was built) and set the pattern for pretty much every hotel that followed, down to its mirrored facade and Y shape, to say nothing of the attention-getting outdoor free attractions. The volcano (revamped in 2008) out front doesn't spew lava, but it does set off an entertaining display of fire, lights, and smoke every 15 minutes after dark. ⏱ *15 min. 3400 Las Vegas Blvd. S.* ☎ *800/627-6667 or 702/791-7111. www.mirage.com.*

⑬ ★★ The Venetian. Arguably the best representative of the be-in-Vegas-but-pretend-you-are-else-where architecture craze (not least because it's still proudly embracing its theme heritage); in this case, a rather admirable (and $1.5-billion) simulation of Venice. There's part of the Doge's palace, there's the Campanile, there's St. Mark's Square, and there are even guys in gondolier outfits. All that is missing is the smell from the canals and those pesky attack pigeons (we forgive them this trespass). And unlike similar storybook lands at New York–New York and Paris, you can actually wander this Italian cityscape. ⏱ *25 min. 3355 Las Vegas Blvd. S.* ☎ *888/2-VENICE (283-6423) or 702/414-1000. www.venetian.com.*

⑭ ★ Wynn Las Vegas. A nearly $3-billion, 60-story effort from Steve Wynn, the man who transformed Las Vegas forever. Disappointingly, you can't see that much from the outside; unlike Wynn's previous efforts, the eye-catching accouterments—in this case, a 150-foot-tall (46m) man-made mountain—can be properly viewed only from inside. Spoilsport! ⏱ *20 min. 3400 Las Vegas Blvd. S.* ☎ *800/627-6667 or 702/791-7111. www.wynnlasvegas. com.*

⑮ Wynn Buffet. For the most part, buffets are no longer the bastion of budget Vegas (itself a thing of the past), but they're still cheaper than dining at one of the city's fabled high-end, celebrity-chef restaurants (and a Vegas tradition, to boot). The buffet at Wynn is a fancy affair, with options running from tandoori chicken to Southern specialties, as well as sublime desserts.

See p 96 for full details on the restaurant.

⑯ ★ Mountain/Lake of Dreams. The 3-acre (1.2-hectare) lake and 70-foot (21m) waterfall at the base of Wynn's 150-foot-tall (46m) man-made mountain are the site of a nightly sound, light, and imagery show that's somewhat psychedelic and really quite weird (and often rather adult). The only free viewing area is the balcony near the Parasol Bar, which gets quite crowded (and there's no sound). But it's worth gawking at, so try to angle your way in there. ⏱ *20 min. In Wynn Las Vegas. See ⑭. Shows run every 20 min., daily 7pm–midnight.*

The jaw-dropping lobby of The Venetian is loaded with marble and exquisitely detailed frescoes.

The Best **in Two Days**

1 Liberace Museum
2 Atomic Testing Museum
3 Bellagio Gallery of Fine Art
4 Jean-Philippe Patisserie
5 Mirage Dolphin Habitat & Secret Garden
6 Madame Tussaud's in the Venetian
7 Bartolotta Ristorante di Mare
8 *Mystère*
9 Stratosphere

Vegas doesn't have a lot of cuhl-cha, but it does have four compelling and wildly different museums, each with its own charms—two are located on casino property! Today, I'll also give you a glimpse of life off the Strip, which might reinforce why most visitors rarely leave Las Vegas Boulevard South; except for a few architectural bright spots, design imagination seems to be have been exhausted and what remain are mostly strip malls. The treasures found inside, however, should more than make up for the bland exteriors. START: **Liberace Museum (1775 E. Tropicana Ave.). It's best to drive here from your hotel; you can park in the free lot outside the museum.**

The Liberace Museum houses its namesake's flamboyant costumes, cars, and other memorabilia.

1 ★★ Liberace Museum. Only outsized personalities can leave their imprint on Vegas, and Wladziu Valentino Liberace (1919–87) certainly did that, bless his jewel-encrusted heart. This campy gem helps define "fabulous," and it does it with sequin-twinkle. Pass through the entrance, dominated by a giant pink piano, and get ready to thrill to the Maestro's dazzling collection of outfits, cars (check your hair in that mirrored Rolls-Royce), pianos (former owners include George Gershwin and Chopin), and jewelry—all lovingly preserved and displayed. Don't miss the 50-pound (23kg) rhinestone—as if you could. ⏱ *1 hr. 1775 E. Tropicana Ave. (at Spencer St.).* ☎ *702/798-5595. www.liberace.org. Admission $15*

adults, $10 seniors over 65 & students with valid school ID, free for kids 10 & under. All kids must be accompanied by adult. Tues–Sat 10am–5pm; Sun noon–4pm. Closed Mon, Thanksgiving, Dec 25, and Jan 1.

2 ★★ Atomic Testing Museum. Nevada, in addition to its other dubious contributions to the cultural history of the world, was the primary location for the testing of atomic weapons from 1951 to 1992. Indeed, aboveground blasts at the nearby Atomic Testing Site were once a tourist attraction in the way hotel implosions are today. This Smithsonian-affiliated museum soberly and carefully explores the development and implications of 40 years of nuclear weapons development. Particularly affecting is a rather intense simulation of an explosion. The docents (some of them former site

Las Vegas once promoted nuclear test explosions as a tourist attraction; check out this part of the city's history at the Atomic Testing Museum.

Few things in the city are more fun than visiting the residents of the Mirage's Dolphin Habitat.

employees) are chock-full of information, so quiz them at will. ⏲ *1 hr. 755 E. Flamingo Rd.* ☎ *702/794-5161. www.atomictestingmuseum. org. $12 adults; $9 seniors, military & students with ID; free for kids 6 & under. Mon–Sat 9am–5pm; Sun 1–5pm. Closed Thanksgiving, Dec 25, and Jan 1.*

❸ Bellagio Gallery of Fine Art. Originally opened as a showcase for former owner Steve Wynn's personal art collection, this small gallery now hosts often critically lauded temporary exhibits, ranging from fine art to Ansel Adams retrospectives. It's pricey, but it's good to rest your eyes on something of true value and quiet impact in a town that's renowned for its loud and busy landscape. ⏲ *45 min. In Bellagio, 3600 Las Vegas Blvd. S.* ☎ *702/693-7871. www.bgfa. biz. Reservations suggested, but walkins taken every 15 min. Admission $17 adults, $14 seniors & Nevada residents, $14 teachers & students with ID. Sun–Thurs 10am–6pm; Fri–Sat 10am–9pm. Last admission half-hour prior to closing.*

Have a sandwich or, best of all, a delectable dessert at the award-winning ⓱ **Jean-Philippe Patisserie,** whose signature attraction is a 27-foot-tall (8.2m) chocolate fountain that Willie Wonka would love. *In Bellagio, 3600 Las Vegas Blvd. S.* ☎ *702/693-8788. $.*

Drive to The Mirage, park your car, and walk until further notice.

❺ ★★★ kids Mirage Dolphin Habitat & Secret Garden. You can get fairly close to some good-looking white tigers and lions at **The Secret Garden,** the daytime quarters for some of Siegfried & Roy's animals (they really live on the duo's ranch). But the best thing here is the **dolphin exhibit,** where a number of the delightful mammals (all born in captivity) live in a state-of-the-art habitat, designed to their specifications. There are no shows per se, but you can watch the dolphins happily cavort with their doting trainers to your heart's content. ⏲ *1 hr. In The Mirage, 3400 Las Vegas Blvd. S.* ☎ *702/791-7111. www.mirage habitat.com. Admission $15 adults, $10 kids 4–10, free for kids 3 & under if accompanied by an adult. Mon–Fri 11am–6:30pm; Sat–Sun & holidays 10am–6:30pm.*

❻ ★ kids Madame Tussaud's in The Venetian. A branch of London's legendary wax museum, here you will find lifelike—or creepy, sometimes it's a fine line—replicas of famous folks. Unlike in other museums, you can actually touch the freestanding exhibits. Go ahead, fondle J. Lo's butt or give Brad Pitt a little smooch. ⏲ *45 min. In The Venetian, 3355 Las Vegas Blvd. S.* ☎ *702/862-7800. www.mtvegas. com. Admission $25 adults, $18* seniors, $18 students, $15 kids 7–12, free for kids 6 & under. Discounts for booking online. Sun–Thurs 10am–10pm; Fri–Sat 10am–9pm; but hours vary seasonally.

7 Have dinner at the super Bartolotta Ristorante di Mare.

To get the full Vegas experience, you need to dine with at least one celebrity chef, and better with James Beard–nominated Paul Bartolotta, who is actually likely to be in his kitchen. Plus, this beauty of a multilevel restaurant, featuring simple yet not simplistic classic Italian seafood cuisine, is a jewel box in its own right. Worth every dime. ⏱ At least 2 hr. In Wynn Las Vegas, 3131 Las Vegas Blvd. S. ☎ 888/352-3463 or 702/248-3463. www.wynnlas vegas.com. See p 86 for details on the restaurant.

8 ★★★ kids Mystère.

The artistically superb productions of the world-famous Cirque du Soleil have largely replaced the old Vegas jiggle top revues. This is the first and most representative of classic Cirque, before it went nuts (happily) with the possibilities afforded by a big budget and elaborate staging. The result is a weird and wonderful mix

Even in a restaurant mecca such as Vegas, Bartolotta Ristorante di Mare stands out thanks to its superb Italian cuisine.

Mystère launched the onslaught of Cirque du Soleil productions in Las Vegas.

of choreography, acrobatics, and music. ⏱ 1½ hr. In TI Las Vegas, 3300 Las Vegas Blvd. S. ☎ 800/963-9634 or 702/796-9999. www.cirque dusoleil.com. Tickets $60–$95 (plus tax). Shows Sat–Wed 7 & 9:30pm. No shows Thurs–Fri.

Take the TI shuttle back to The Mirage (or walk to the parking lot) and drive to the Stratosphere.

9 Stratosphere.

The tallest building west of the Mississippi (1,149 ft./350m) offers eagle's-eye views of the desert, the mountains, and the Strip from its observation deck. Access stays open until 1am, and though lines to get up here can be lengthy, you can stay as long as you like. The panorama up here can't be beat, as the lights of this ridiculous and marvelous city twinkle below and around you. If you want, you can have a drink at the deck's Top of the World bar. Check out the adjacent restaurant (the desserts aren't bad); it revolves, which is a retro hoot. ⏱ 30 min. if you stay for a drink. 2000 Las Vegas Blvd. S. ☎ 702/380-7777. Admission to observation deck: $16 adults; $12 seniors & hotel guests; $10 kids 4–12; free for kids 3 & under. Sun–Thurs 10am–1am; Fri, Sat & holidays 10am–2am. Hours vary seasonally.

The Best **in Three Days**

1 Red Rock Canyon
2 Red Rock Visitor's Center
3 Calico Hills
4 Lost Creek—Children's Discovery Trail
5 Capriotti's
6 Bonnie Springs Ranch
7 Calico Basin
8 Red Rock Resort
9 Fremont Street Experience

Even the most dedicated gambler needs to get outside for some real oxygen, so today I start you off with some of the natural wonders surrounding Vegas before whisking you back to Old Vegas for a look at the city the way it used to be. This tour has a lot of wholesome, child-appropriate activities, but adults need not fear—there's also a stop at a casino hotel, in case you need a fix.

START: **Drive west from the Strip on Charleston Boulevard, which becomes NV 159, until you get to the Red Rock Canyon Visitor's Center.**

① ★★★ kids Red Rock Canyon.

In startling contrast to the sparkling madness of a city that sheds its skin about once every 10 years is this geological wonder, a mere 600 million years in the making. Sandstone monoliths—yes, some of them are quite red, though others are, frankly, sand-colored—rugged canyons, cliffs, and other topographic thrills thrust up from the desert thanks to serious fault action. The **Red Rock Canyon National Conservation Area** consists of 197,000 acres (79,720 hectares), accessible to the public via a 13-mile (21km) scenic driving loop and 19 hiking trails. In addition to even better photo ops and encounters with local flora and fauna, the hikes provide opportunities to view petroglyphs and pictographs. Red Rock is also one of the most popular rock-climbing destinations in the world. ⏱ *30 min., unless you stop to take photos or hike. On NV 159.* ☎ *702/515-5350. www.nv.blm.gov/redrockcanyon.*

The magnificent natural scenery of Red Rock Canyon is only 30 minutes from the Strip.

Admission: $5 for 1-day vehicle pass. Daily 6am–7pm Oct 1–Mar 31, 6am–8pm Apr 1–Sept 30.

② kids Red Rock Visitor's Center.

Stop here for brochures, suggestions for hikes, and other practical advice. The center has a small exhibition hall that helpfully illustrates the natural history of Red Rock. If you time it right—spring and summer—you can also visit with Mojave Max, a 65-plus-year-old desert tortoise, who is the charismatic star of the center. ⏱ *30 min. Just past the park entrance on the scenic loop. Daily 8am–4:30pm.*

③ Calico Hills.

The parking lot at the start of the second trail along the scenic loop provides one of the two best views at the red rocks that give this area its name. ⏱ *20 min. for photographs or 3 hr. to hike, depending on level of fitness. Look for route marker just under a mile (1.6km) from the Visitor's Center.*

④ kids Lost Creek—Children's Discovery Trail.

The easiest of the park's trails, with no more than a 200-foot (61m) gentle elevation, lasts only about an hour round-trip (depending on how fast you go). It's perfect for kids and anyone who doesn't want to commit to a more demanding hike. Vegetation here is a bit more lush, due in part to the year-round stream, and there are some pictographs and an agave (a plant that was once a major source of food for local tribes) roasting pit. ⏱ *1 hr. to hike. Look for route* marker, approx. 7 miles (11km) from Visitor's Center.

Take advantage of the picnic tables at the start of the Lost Creek—Children's Discovery Trail by splitting a sandwich you picked up before entering the park, at **5 Capriotti's,** the justly lauded local submarine sandwich place. Its outlet in the Red Rock Resort is on the drive in from the Strip to the park. *11011 W. Charleston Blvd., Las Vegas, NV 89135. ☎ 702/257-3337. $.*

6 kids Bonnie Springs Ranch. A deliberately hokey re-creation of an old Western town, where it's hard to tell if the weather-beaten look is authentic or the sign of a somewhat aging attraction. The regular satirical dramatic skits provide old-fashioned fun; not slick, but sweet and silly. Play cowboys with your kids as you wander past the saloon, the mill, and the old general store. Next door is a petting zoo, a maze of (scrupulously clean) wire pens with goats, rabbits, snooty llamas, elderly deer living in fat retirement, and a couple of wolves. The aviary provides glimpses of peacocks, while a riding stable offers trail rides into the mountains. *1–2 hr. NV 159, 5 miles (8km) past Red Rock Canyon. ☎ 702/875-4191. www.bonniesprings.com. Admission $20 per car. Daily Nov–Apr 10:30am–5pm, until 6pm the rest of the year.*

7 Calico Basin. About 2 miles (3.2km) west of the turnoff into the Red Rock scenic loop is a half-mile-long (.8km) boardwalk trail, an alternative way for travelers with disabilities or for those with other mobility issues to get out of the car and into the scenery. Look for wildflowers and the foundations of an old cabin. *1 hr. Look for signs*

2 miles (3.2km) west of park entrance, on north side of Charleston Blvd.

8 Red Rock Resort. This fancy resort is the getaway of choice for the famous of face to hide in Vegas. It's a good spot to ease yourself back into a Vegas frame of mind with a drink, and maybe even a little gambling. *30 min. & up, depending on whether you gamble. 11011 W. Charleston Blvd. ☎ 866/767-7773 or 702/797-7777. See p 132 for more information on the resort.*

9 kids ★ Fremont Street Experience. In the heart of Downtown Vegas is a pedestrian-only zone that's covered with a video screen about five football fields in length. The screen's 12.5 million LED modules, and a 500,000-watt sound system, deliver a rotating light-and-sound show. The shows don't necessarily make the best use of the technology, but they are still the best freebie in Vegas after the Bellagio fountains (p 11, **10**). *20 min., unless you see more than one show. Fremont Street, btw. Main St. & Las Vegas Blvd. S. www.vegas experience.com. Shows nightly every hour, dusk to midnight. ●*

Its glory days might be in the past, but Bonnie Springs Ranch still offers lots of old-style fun, especially for families.

Las Vegas for **Sinners**

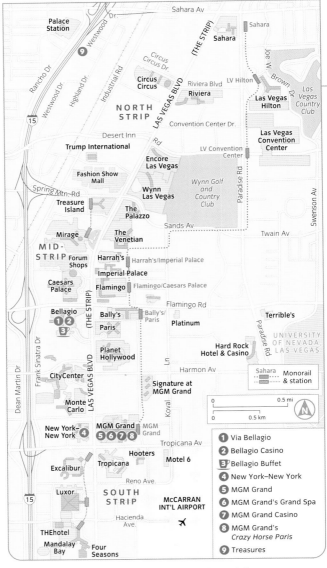

1 Via Bellagio
2 Bellagio Casino
3 Bellagio Buffet
4 New York–New York
5 MGM Grand
6 MGM Grand's Grand Spa
7 MGM Grand Casino
8 MGM Grand's *Crazy Horse Paris*
9 Treasures

Previous page: Las Vegas's nickname as Sin City is well deserved; don't wear your shoes out as you hop from indulgence to indulgence.

Admit it . . . you didn't come here to have a good time. You came here to have a naughty time. More power to you. Vegas is ready to accommodate, having shifted over to a much more, let's say, adult perspective toward rest and relaxation. In fact, let's see if we can fit in all seven deadly sins, shall we? START: **Drive to Bellagio; there is a convenient parking lot by the far entrance to Via Bellagio, so you need not navigate the distance from Bellagio's main parking structure.**

❶ ★★ **Via Bellagio.** Start your day off with a little envy, as you window-shop such high-priced boutiques as Tiffany, Chanel, Hermes, Dior, Prada, and more. There are plenty of shopping malls all over Vegas, and in just about every hotel, but there is something so classy, so high-end about this one that it gives off the impression that you can't even afford the oxygen. And yet, you are surrounded by people who can. ⏱ *45 min. In Bellagio, 3600 Las Vegas Blvd. S. ☎ 702/693-7111. www.bellagio.com. Daily 10am–midnight.*

❷ **Bellagio Casino.** Not jealous enough? Drop by the high rollers section of the Bellagio casino, where well-heeled types drop $500 on one pull of a slot. Notice how even the machines look fancier here, appearing to be encased in marble and wood. Now slink off and go find some penny slots. Bummer. ⏱ *20 min. See p 77.*

New York–New York is loaded with re-created Big Apple landmarks, including this one of the Brooklyn Bridge.

If you have to ask how much it costs, you probably can't afford it at the mucho upscale Via Bellagio.

Nothing says gluttony like a meal at a Vegas buffet. The **3** ★★ **Bellagio Buffet** is particularly large and especially indulgent, with elaborate pastas, duck and game hen, mounds of cold seafood, and more. *In Bellagio.* ☎ *877/234-6358. $$–$$$.*

4 **New York–New York.** Summon up the wrath felt by locals stuck in a NYC gridlock as you wander around this remarkable re-creation of Manhattan. Outside, the famous skyline is squashed down into a multicolored pastiche. Inside, all the famous neighborhoods are similarly crammed together, from Central Park to Times Square to the Village (though the decor inside has been tamed just enough to stir the anger of those who miss the themed architecture). Though the interior is now more sleek and modern, the hotel remains a bit of a nightmare to navigate. Toss in a few thousand (at minimum) other visitors, not to mention the inevitability of getting turned around and heading in the wrong direction, and you'll feel pretty steamed. It won't help if you just lost at blackjack, either. ⏱ *45 min. 3790 Las Vegas Blvd. S.* ☎ *702/740-6969. www.nynyhotel casino.com.*

5 **MGM Grand.** This gleaming mass of green houses the largest casino in town, and even if the hotel itself is no longer quite the biggest in the world, it's still pretty darn big. Realize there is truth to the phrase "size does matter" and why those who created and own this might feel more than a bit of pride. Oddly enough, the powers that be sometimes demur about the vastness of the place, having found that people began to be daunted by the sheer acreage (you'll get lost at least once—I'd make book on it). Consequently, one is now told that this

Take a breather from the buzz of the Strip at the ultra-relaxing Grand Spa.

isn't the largest casino in town, because its 171,500 square feet (15,933 sq. m) have been divided into "four" smaller casinos. Misplaced use of humility, if you ask me. ⏱ *30 min. 3799 Las Vegas Blvd. S.* ☎ *702/891-7777. www.mgm grand.com.*

6 ★★ **MGM Grand's Grand Spa.** Get your sloth on with a pampering treatment at this Asian Zen–themed tranquil spa. It's a minimalist wonder. The Red Lotus Love Ritual, for couples, includes Tibetan ingredients and massage techniques, while the signature Nirvana massage tries to indulge all the senses. ⏱ *1½ hr. In MGM Grand, 3799 Las Vegas Blvd. S.* ☎ *702/891-3077. No kids under 12. Ages 12–18 must be accompanied by an adult. Non-hotel guests may use spa Mon–Thurs. Massages $130– $290. Open Mon–Thurs 6am–7pm; until 8pm Fri–Sun.*

7 **MGM Grand Casino.** Go ahead, play those slots or try a hand or two at the tables. And when you win, play some more . . . you greedy thing. ⏱ *30 min.—or many hours.* See p 79.

Stripping 101

Want to learn to work a pole like a pro, get in touch with your inner vixen, or strut sexily in those stilettos you love? Stripping, when done right (think more tease than strip), is actually hard work, and **Stripper 101,** in the Miracle Mile Mall, 3663 Las Vegas Blvd. S. (☎ 702/260-7200; www.stripper101.com), teaches this very Vegas art form to women (sorry guys, you're strictly *verboten!*) ranging from 50-year-old housewives to 20-something celebrities. The hour-long classes are actually pretty nifty and confidence boosting, showing you the proper way to strut, slide down that pole, and give a lap dance. The shy shouldn't worry; you keep your clothes on for the entire experience. And you'll also burn a couple of hundred calories, so you can go sin without guilt at a buffet afterward. Classes cost $40 (they throw in a drink) and you must be at least 18 years of age.

⑧ MGM Grand's Crazy Horse Paris. A classy way to finish up the list with some lust, this production showcases the "art of the nude." Flawlessly figured girls perform cleverly designed burlesque numbers that tease as they strip down to a wee, letter-if-not-the-spirit strategically placed modesty patch. It really is as artistic as it is sexy. ⏲ *1½ hr. See p 116 for full details on the show.*

⑨ ★★★ Treasures. You can never have too much of a good thing, so continue your lustfest at this fancy strip joint, whose interior looks like it's straight out of a Victorian sporting house. The stage is strictly modern, as gals twirl in some actual routines on light-up poles, action often complete with fog machines and other effects. Be careful about prices and hidden fees, lest you fall victim to someone else's greed! ⏲ *1 hr., or all night. 2801 Westwood Dr. (parking is hard to spot after dark; use Highland Dr. & keep your eyes peeled).* ☎ *702/ 257-3030. www.treasureslasvegas. com. No unescorted women. Topless. Cover $30. Lap dances $30 & up. Daily 4pm–6am.*

Treasures is among the classiest of Sin City's famous strip clubs.

The Best Special-Interest Tours

Las Vegas for Elopers

1 A bachelorette party at *Thunder from Down Under*
2 Gambling with the Pussycat Dolls
3 Bachelor Party at Seamless
4 Qua
5 Agent Provocateur
6 Clark County Marriage License Bureau
7 Little White Wedding Chapel
8 Dinner at Alizé

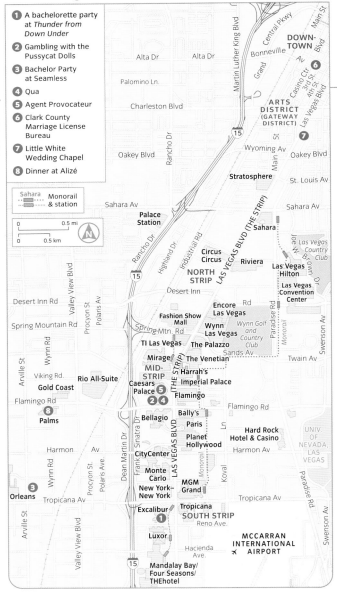

I t's quite easy to get married in Vegas. Too easy. There is little, apart from good sense, to prevent you from getting married to a total stranger, and given those free drinks handed out to anyone playing the slots, after a short time you might not even have much of that. If you want to join the more than 100,000 couples who have walked down the aisle before you, here's a traditional 24-hour tour of Vegas-style wedding action. START: **Brides-to-be should drive or take a taxi to Excalibur; grooms should head for Caesars Palace.**

① A bachelorette party at Thunder from Down Under.

Gals, check out the hunky action at this Aussie male strip revue, featuring some of the cheekiest—and I mean that in all ways—performers you can imagine. Hilarious as well as handsome, they know how to work a room. 🕐 *80 min. In Excalibur, 3850 Las Vegas Blvd. S. ☎ 702/597-7600. www.thunderfromdownunder. com. Must be at least 18 years old. Ages 18–20 must be accompanied by adult. Gentlemen welcome. General admission $40, plus tax. VIP admission $50, plus tax. Shows Sun–Thurs 9pm; Fri–Sat 9 & 11pm.*

② Gambling with the Pussycat Dolls.
An understanding bride-to-be might feel comfortable sending her intended off to gamble at the **Pussycat Dolls Pit** at

The Aussie hunks in Excalibur's Thunder from Down Under are a very popular diversion for women.

Caesars Palace, where the dealers are dressed like America's current favorite burlesque act–turned–band, and go-go dancers suspended in cages above try to make you forget if you should hit or hold at 17. 🕐 *45 min., or until your money runs out. In Caesars Palace, 3570 Las Vegas Blvd. ☎ 702/731-7110. www. caesars.com. Open 24 hr.*

③ Bachelor Party at Seamless.
Really understanding brides-to-be won't mind if their men head for this rocking high-tech strip club, not least because at 4am the clothes go back on the dancers and the place turns into an after-hours club. Women, feel free to join your men—nothing says "Vegas wedding" more than a hangover and a really late night. 🕐 *1 hr., or more. 4740 S. Arville St. ☎ 702/227-5200. www.seamlessclub.com. Cover: $20 if you arrive by taxi, free if you drive yourself. Open 24 hr.*

Gambling is undoubtedly entertaining when the Pussycat Dolls perform in their namesake pit at Caesars Palace.

The luxe Qua spa is the perfect place to relax after a night out on the town.

④ **Qua.** As soon as you can drag yourself out of bed in the morning, head to this lush spa at Caesars Palace. Get a special treatment or just sit in the blissful Roman bath area, moving from ice room (where you can exfoliate with shaved ice), to sauna, to plunge pools of varying temperatures, before finally collapsing in a heated lounge chair. Qua's salon also does hair and makeup to make you picture-perfect. *In Caesars Palace, 3570 Las Vegas Blvd. S. (on the 2nd level of the Augustus Tower).* ☎ *866/782-0655. www.qua bathandspa.com. Full-body massage $140 & up. All treatments must be*

Couples from all over the world come to the very convenient Clark County Marriage License bureau to secure permission to get hitched.

reserved in advance. Daily 6am–8pm.

⑤ **Agent Provocateur.** If you really did come to Vegas in a hurry, and you want to wear something, ahem, special for your wedding night, check out this British import's line of classy but naughty lingerie. ⏱ *30 min. In The Forum Shops at Caesars Palace.* ☎ *702/696-7174. www. agentprovocateur.com. See p 64.*

⑥ **Clark County Marriage License Bureau.** Ready to go? You can't until you've made sure what you are about to do is legal. Get your license here. It's no longer open round-the-clock, which is probably just as well, but the entire process should take no more than an hour—and possibly as little as 10 minutes. Once you have that important piece of paper, you're good to go—there's no set waiting period. ⏱ *10 min.–1 hr. Busiest days are Fri–Sat; slowest period is first thing in the morning on weekdays. 201 Clark Ave.* ☎ *702/671-0600. www. co.clark.nv.us/clerk/marriage_ information.htm. Must be at least 18 years old & have valid proof of age & a Social Security number. Couples must be male–female. License is $60. Open daily 8am–midnight, including holidays.*

For your Honeymoon . . .

It should come as no surprise that a city that holds as many weddings as this one does has plenty of hotel options for that must-have romantic honeymoon. Many hotels offer special packages for newlyweds, so ask when you book. For my favorite properties in Vegas, including some ultraromantic possibilities, see p 120.

Wedding Tip

If you want something a little more traditional . . . or outrageous for your big day, see p 117 for a rundown of my favorite wedding chapels in Las Vegas.

⑦ Little White Wedding Chapel. Hotel chapels tend to be prettier and more traditional, but if you came to Vegas for the kitsch, your search will be best fulfilled by this famous wedding factory. It was good enough for Michael Jordan, Demi Moore and Bruce Willis, and Brittany Spears (though "good" in these cases may be a debatable term). Plus, for those particularly in a hurry, it has a drive-up window. ⏱ *10 min.–1 hr., depending on how busy they are & if you made a*

If you like your weddings kitschy and fast, the Little White Wedding Chapel is the best place to get married in Vegas.

For a romantic dinner in Las Vegas, you can't beat Alizé.

reservation in advance. 1301 Las Vegas Blvd. S. (btw. E. Oakley & Charleston blvds.). ☎ *800/545-8111 or 702/382-5943. www.alittlewhite chapel.com. Base chapel rate $55; add-ons (everything from garters to Elvis) & complete packages are available at extra cost. Open 24 hr.*

⑧ ★★★ Dinner at Alizé. Hold your wedding feast at the city's most romantic restaurant, with nearly floor-to-ceiling windows on three sides, and a virtually unobstructed view of the city and desert. Though surely you won't take your eyes off each other. ⏱ *2 hr. See p 85 for more details on the restaurant.*

Las Vegas with Kids

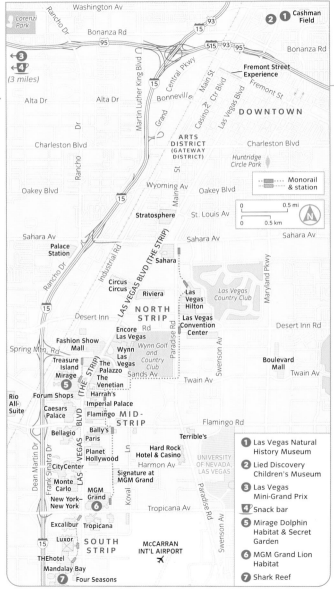

Lorenzi Park

Washington Av

Rancho Dr

Bonanza Rd

93

515 93 95

Cashman Field

2 1

Bonanza Rd

95

3

4

(3 miles)

Martin Luther King Blvd

Central Pkwy

15

Bonneville

Grand

Main St

Casino Ctr Blvd

Las Vegas Blvd

Fremont Street Experience

Fremont St

Alta Dr

Alta Dr

DOWNTOWN

Dr

Rancho

Charleston Blvd

ARTS DISTRICT (GATEWAY DISTRICT)

St

Charleston Blvd

Huntridge Circle Park

Oakey Blvd

15

Wyoming Av

Main St

Oakey Blvd

Monorail & station

Sahara Av

Palace Station

Stratosphere

St. Louis Av

Sahara Av

Sahara Av

0   0.5 mi

0   0.5 km

Rancho Dr

Industrial Rd

Circus Circus

Riviera

LAS VEGAS BLVD (THE STRIP)

Sahara

Las Vegas Hilton

Las Vegas Country Club

Maryland Pkwy

15

Desert Inn

NORTH STRIP

Encore Las Vegas

Rd

Las Vegas Convention Center

Desert Inn Rd

Spring Mtn. Rd

Fashion Show Mall

Treasure Island

Mirage

5

The STRIP

Wynn Las Vegas

Wynn Golf and Country Club

Sands Av

Paradise Rd

Swenson Av

Twain Av

Boulevard Mall

Twain Av

Rio All-Suite

Forum Shops

Caesars Palace

Bellagio

(THE) STRIP

The Palazzo

The Venetian

Harrah's

Imperial Palace

Flamingo

Bally's

Paris

MID-STRIP

Flamingo Rd

Terrible's

Flamingo Rd

Dean Martin Dr

Frank Sinatra Dr

LAS VEGAS BLVD

Planet Hollywood

Hard Rock Hotel & Casino

Harmon Av

UNIVERSITY OF NEVADA, LAS VEGAS

CityCenter

Monte Carlo

Signature at MGM Grand

New York–New York

MGM Grand

6

Koval Ln

Tropicana Av

Paradise Rd

Swenson Av

Excalibur

Tropicana

Luxor

SOUTH STRIP

McCARRAN INT'L AIRPORT

THEhotel

Mandalay Bay

7

Four Seasons

1 Las Vegas Natural History Museum

2 Lied Discovery Children's Museum

3 Las Vegas Mini-Grand Prix

4 Snack bar

5 Mirage Dolphin Habitat & Secret Garden

6 MGM Grand Lion Habitat

7 Shark Reef

Don't kid yourself; Vegas isn't for children. The city markets itself strongly as a haven for distinctly adult pursuits and entertainment. This is obvious when you look at the sides of several of the casino hotels, often featuring multistory adverts for girlie shows in the form of shapely, nearly bare bottoms. But there are some activities appropriate for the younger set, so if you have kids in tow, your vacation won't come up a loser in the short run. START: **Drive to Las Vegas Natural History Museum and park in the museum lot.**

① ★ **Las Vegas Natural History Museum.** Hardly high-tech, this throwback to the era of dioramas of taxidermy animals comes off as small-town when compared to more venerable—and well-funded—institutions found in New York or Los Angeles. But your dinosaur-crazy kid will enjoy it, and you'll enjoy the relaxed pace. Among the hands-on, interactive exhibits is an installation that allows participants to experience life as a nocturnal critter—and not in the Vegas way! ⏱ *1½ hr. 900 Las Vegas Blvd. N. (at Washington Ave.; adjacent to Cashman Center).* ☎ *702/384-3466. www.lvnhm.org. Admission $8 adults; $7 seniors, military & students; $4 kids 3–11; free for kids 2 & under. Daily 9am–4pm.*

The relaxed Las Vegas Natural History museum is loaded with life-size fossils and animal exhibits.

② ★★ **Lied Discovery Children's Museum.** An excellent facility that provides tons of sugar (all kinds of playful, clever, interactive exhibits) to help the medicine—that is, education about physics, nature, the human body, history, and more—go down. Kids are probably savvy enough to realize it's good for

Both kids and parents love the interactive exhibits at the Lied Discovery Children's Museum.

Future Formula One stars can get their speed on at the delightful Las Vegas Mini-Grand Prix.

them, but by the time they are launching tennis balls into the air, they probably won't care they are also learning about air pressure. There is even a special section for the 5-and-under set. ⏱ *2 hr. 833 Las Vegas Blvd. N. (½ block south of Washington Ave., across the street from Cashman Field).* ☎ *702/382-3445. www.ldcm.org. Admission $8 adults; $7 seniors, military & kids 1–17. Open Tues–Fri 9am–4pm, Sat 10am–5pm, Sun noon–5pm. Closed Mon, except school holidays.*

❸ ★★★ **Las Vegas Mini-Grand Prix.** Now that the kids have gotten a little education, let 'em have some fun! This attraction is part arcade, part go-kart racetrack; though the former is well stocked, it's the latter that holds the most appeal. Not only is it a rare outdoor non-water-related activity, but your offspring can work off nervous energy on four different tracks. One is the longest road track in Vegas, full of twists and turns, while another is a high-banked oval where the goal is to make other drivers take a spill on the grass. Well, maybe that's just me . . . and only to the mean kids who deserve it. ⏱ *2 hr. 1401 N. Rainbow Rd., just off U.S. 95 N.* ☎ *702/259-7000. www.lvmgp.com. Ride tickets $6.50 each, $30 for 5. Minimum height requirement for rides is 36 in. (91cm). Sun–Thurs 10am–10pm; Fri–Sat 10am–11pm.*

The pizzas at the ❹ **snack bar** are triple the size and half the price of those you'll find in your hotel or on the Strip. And pretty tasty, too! *In Mini-Grand Prix, 1401 N. Rainbow Rd.* ☎ *702/259-7000. $.*

❺ ★★★ **Mirage Dolphin Habitat & Secret Garden.** There is an actual zoo in Vegas, but I am sending you here because it's more of a highlight, short-attention-span choice. Plus, the inhabitants are just so cool. Siegfried & Roy's show may have come to an abrupt and rather ignominious end, but the furry stars of their show are still on display in this lush setting. It's aesthetically pleasing—more so than a regular zoo—because of its size, which also allows for some fairly up-close encounters with white tigers and the like. (None of the cats lives here, instead putting in regular "shifts" before returning to their expansive digs at their owners' ranch.) The best part is the dolphin habitat, an expensive, carefully constructed and maintained 2.5-million-gallon (9,463,529L) tank where these most delightful mammals frolic. Trainers dote on them, stimulating their charges. If you are really lucky, you might be around for a session of ball. Very little pleases a kid more than trying to catch a wet ball

No Children Allowed!

When I said Vegas doesn't throw out the welcome mat to families, I wasn't kidding. Be advised that many hotels will not allow children who aren't staying on their property through the front door (they'll demand a room key as proof of occupancy). And don't even think about allowing your children to linger anywhere near a casino floor . . . they'll be shooed away pretty quickly. This tour will keep your youngsters happy for a day in the city, but as a long-term family vacation destination, Vegas falls short of ideal. If you have little ones, I strongly advise you to look elsewhere for a long break.

flipped to them by a dolphin snout.
🕐 *1 hr. See p 16,* **5**.

6 ★★ **MGM Grand Lion Habitat.** More cooing at kitties for the kiddies, as visitors to this free exhibit gather around a glassed-in enclosure to watch big cats lounge. Gather under the glass tunnel, the top of which is a favorite napping spot, and check out the underside of a lion. Hold up your kid's paw to the feline above you and marvel at the size and power. Prepare to go "aww" when the trainers, who spent a lot of time becoming accepted as one of the pack, wrestle, play with, and lavish love on their furry companions. The time you spend will depend on how much action the trainers are stirring up. 🕐 *20 min. In MGM Grand, 3799 Las Vegas Blvd. S.* ☎ *702/891-7777. www.mgmgrand.com. Free admission. Daily 11am–10pm.*

7 ★ **Shark Reef.** Guests travel through a tunnel that runs through the middle of this giant aquarium, designed to look like a sunken ancient temple. The sharks (plus other finny friends) glide smoothly and somewhat sinisterly up and around you. It's more active than the MGM lions (see **6**, above), but has less personality and is pricey for what you get. It doesn't take much time to navigate, which is probably just as well, because you—if not the kids—will probably be fairly tuckered out by this point. 🕐 *45 min. The aquarium is in a remote area of Mandalay Bay, a difficult trek for those with mobility problems. In Mandalay Bay, 3950 Las Vegas Blvd. S.* ☎ *702/632-4555. www.mandalaybay.com. Admission $17 adults, $12 kids 5–12, free for kids 4 & under. Daily 10am–11pm. Last admission at 10pm.*

Children love watching the MGM Grand's signature lions carouse in their glass-enclosed habitat.

Las Vegas for **Thrill Seekers**

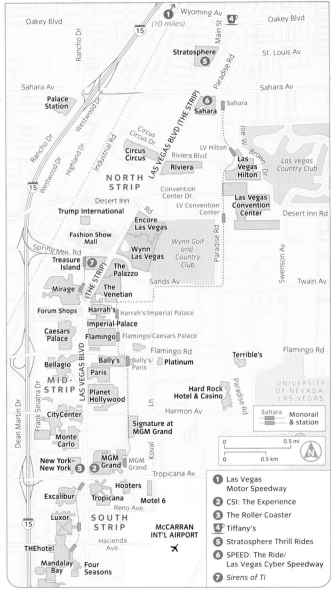

Oakey Blvd

Oakey Blvd

Wyoming Av
(10 miles)

St. Louis Av

Stratosphere

Sahara Av

Sahara Av

Palace Station

Sahara

Circus Circus Dr.

LV Hilton

Circus Circus

Riviera Blvd

Las Vegas Hilton

Riviera

Las Vegas Country Club

NORTH STRIP

Convention Center Dr.

Desert Inn

LV Convention Center

Las Vegas Convention Center

Desert Inn Rd

Trump International

Rd

Encore Las Vegas

Wynn Golf and Country Club

Fashion Show Mall

Spring Mtn. Rd

Swenson Av

Treasure Island

Wynn Las Vegas

Twain Av

The Palazzo

Mirage

The Venetian

Sands Av

Forum Shops

Harrah's

Harrah's/Imperial Palace

Caesars Palace

Imperial Palace

Flamingo

Flamingo/Caesars Palace

Bellagio

Bally's

Flamingo Rd

Terrible's

Flamingo Rd

MID-STRIP

Paris

Bally's/ Paris

Platinum

UNIVERSITY OF NEVADA, LAS VEGAS

CityCenter

Planet Hollywood

Hard Rock Hotel & Casino

Harmon Av

Sahara

Monte Carlo

Signature at MGM Grand

New York–New York

MGM Grand

MGM Grand

Excalibur

Hooters

Tropicana

Motel 6

Luxor

Reno Ave.

SOUTH STRIP

McCARRAN INT'L AIRPORT

THEhotel

Hacienda Ave.

Mandalay Bay

Four Seasons

Tropicana Av

	Monorail & station

| 0 | 0.5 mi |
| 0 | 0.5 km |

1 Las Vegas Motor Speedway

2 CSI: The Experience

3 The Roller Coaster

4 Tiffany's

5 Stratosphere Thrill Rides

6 SPEED: The Ride/ Las Vegas Cyber Speedway

7 Sirens of TI

The thrills in Vegas don't come solely from games of chance. While efforts to sustain full-blown amusement parks have failed, there are still plenty of rides, and other what-a-rush-type activities scattered about the city. Many of the hotels, in an effort to lure business, have some kind of attraction designed to make some of us nauseous and others exhilarated. If you have balance or nerve issues, this ain't the tour for you. START: **Drive to Las Vegas Motor Speedway.**

For speedy thrills, racing fans flock to the Las Vegas Motor Speedway to watch the pros rev their engines.

① ★★ **Las Vegas Motor Speedway.** Just about anything with wheels that goes really, really fast can be found here in one form or another. A $200-million state-of-the-art motor-sports entertainment complex, this 176,000-seat facility serves up drag racing and super-speed courses in the viewing department. If participation is more your thing, get your speed fix at the go-kart tracks, driving schools, and other attractions. ⏱ *At least 2 hr. 7000 Las Vegas Blvd. N., directly across from Nellis Air Force base (take I-15 N to Speedway exit 54).* ☎ *702/644-4443 for ticket information. www.lvms.com. Tickets $10–$75. Race days vary.*

② ★★ kids **CSI: The Experience.** This good exercise in forensics will give your brain a workout—think mental thrill (uncommon in Vegas) more than a physical one. The 3-D whodunit (best for age 12 and up)

puts you in the middle of a crime scene investigation studying DNA, fingerprints, and more as you make your way through an interactive lab and get to the bottom of one of three crimes. Think Colonel Mustard in the library with the candlestick, times 1,000. *At MGM Grand, 3799 Las Vegas Blvd. S. (at Tropicana Ave.).* ☎ *877/660-0660 or 702/891-7006. www.mgm grand.com. Reservations suggested. Admission $30 adults, $23 kids 4–11. Daily 9am–8:30pm. Map p 34.*

③ kids **The Roller Coaster.** I consider this "classic" Las Vegas, not because it harkens back to the Rat Pack days, but because it's a remnant of a "quickly becoming similarly remote" era—that of the Family Friendly promotions. More than a decade ago, the attitude was "why *not* put the Coney Island–themed

Zip around the Sahara hotel on SPEED: The Ride, one the city's best coasters.

roller coaster (originally known as the Manhattan Express) right through the lobby and around the outside of the hotel?" Why not, indeed? In any case, it's indisputable that the coaster (which pours on the adrenaline with a 144-ft./44m drop, plus various inversions and twists) does replicate a ride in the New York City cabs its cars resemble—with all that entails. ⏱ *10 min., depending on the lines. In New York–New York, 3790 Las Vegas Blvd. S.* ☎ *800/689-1797. www. nynyhotelcasino.com. Must be at least 54 in. (137cm) to ride. Single-ride pass $14, day pass $25. Daily 10:30am–midnight.*

There's no better place in town for good ole American comfort food of the old school variety (think burgers, shakes, and breakfast) than **Tiffany's.** Open around the clock, it's a cheap but great diner in a city where such things are vanishing entirely too quickly. *1700 Las Vegas Blvd. S. (at East Oakey Blvd.).* ☎ *702/444-4459. $.*

Soar high above the Strip on the Stratosphere's very appropriately named Insanity.

Follow the evidence at simulated crime scenes at CSI: The Experience.

5 ★★ **Stratosphere Thrill Rides.** The Stratosphere tower is the tallest building west of the Mississippi. That's 1,149 feet (350m) up, for those keeping track. So naturally, one puts thrill rides on the top of it. The **Big Shot** takes you up the final 160 feet (49m) or so of the spire before letting you free-fall back down again. Once your heart is back where it belongs, you can then try the **X-Scream,** a giant teeter-totter that teeters and totters over the edge of the 100-story tower. Try not to throw up on the smart people who stayed safely below on the Strip, okay? Finally, there is **Insanity**—an appropriate moniker, given that the very thought of this ride elicits an "are you nuts?" from me—which whirls you around 1,000 feet (305m) in the air. ⏱ *45 min., depending on how long the lines are. In Stratosphere Las Vegas, 2000 Las Vegas Blvd. S.* ☎ *702/380-7777. www.stratospherehotel.com. Admission $13, plus fee to ascend Tower ($14 adults; $10 seniors & hotel guests; $8 kids 4–12; free for kids 3 & under & those dining in the buffet room or Top of the World. Discount* multiride & all-day packages available. Sun–Thurs 10am–1am; Fri, Sat & holidays 10am–2am. Hours vary seasonally. Minimum height requirement for all rides is 48 in. (122cm).

6 ★★ kids **SPEED: The Ride/ Las Vegas Cyber Speedway.** This two-parter capitalizes on the increasing popularity of auto racing in America. Part one is a virtual reality–ride allowing you to effectively take the wheel of a NASCAR race car and drive it around the Las Vegas Motor Speedway, or through the streets of Vegas. Watch out for that pyramid! Racing fans ought to be in virtual heaven. Part two is a roller coaster that whips around the NASCAR Cafe and the Sahara Hotel, zooms straight up a 250-foot-tall (76m) tower, and then propels you through the whole thing all over again—this time, backward. ⏱ *At least 45 min. In the Sahara, 2535 Las Vegas Blvd. S.* ☎ *702/734-RACE (7223). www.nascarcafelasvegas. com. Cyber Speedway simulator $10 (you must be at least 54 in./137cm*

From its cab-themed cars to its adrenaline-inducing drops, The Roller Coaster perfectly captures New York's breakneck speed.

The Sirens of TI walk the planks outside TI Las Vegas every night.

tall to ride); SPEED: The Ride roller coaster $10 for single ride. $23 for all-day pass on both rides. Daily noon–10pm.

7 **Sirens of TI.** Pirates and strippers (okay . . . not exactly the latter, but it's close)—and it won't cost you a cent! How much more thrilling can you get? A free live-action show on the Strip is pretty irresistible, and the production values on Treasure Island's racy nighttime entry are high enough that I'm mostly willing to overlook the cringe-inducing plot as buccaneers battle the lingerie-clad lovelies who are now the "villains" of this show. ⏱ *20 min. In front of TI Las Vegas, 3300 Las Vegas Blvd. S.* ☎ *702/894-7111. www.treasureisland.com. Shows nightly at 7, 8:30, 10 & 11:30pm.*

A Deadly Bet

Some thrill-seekers, when faced with a seriously long walk to that next crosswalk on the Strip, might be tempted to try the pedestrian version of Russian Roulette in Vegas: darting across Las Vegas Boulevard without benefit of a traffic signal. Don't! That bet is a guaranteed loser.

Las Vegas for **Culture Lovers**

1. Clark County Heritage Museum
2. Liberace Museum
3. Freed's Bakery
4. Marjorie Barrack Museum
5. Atomic Testing Museum
6. Neil Leifer Gallery
7. Madame Tussaud's in the Venetian
8. Wynn Las Vegas Atrium

A cultural capital Vegas is not. When things fall out of favor here, the city tends to blow them up rather than preserve them for posterity. But there are a number of museums and galleries (most housed in unpromising strip malls or within hotels) that enshrine everything from the sublime to the ridiculous. And there are even some oases in this desert city of sin, where you can stop and (literally) smell the roses. START: **Drive to Clark County Heritage Museum, and park in lot.**

An old-fashioned train depot is just one of the many historic buildings preserved at the Clark County Heritage Museum.

1 ★★ **Clark County Heritage Museum.** Charming and cheap, this surprisingly large facility is a collection of restored historic buildings from significant points in Vegas history. There are a train depot, a print shop, a mine, a ghost town, and much more to remind us that up until the days of Bugsy Siegel, Vegas was just another Wild West town, trying to make it in the desert. An exhibit center features changing displays on different eras in local

The best museum in Las Vegas, the Liberace Museum preserves the memory (and belongings) of one of the city's most beloved (and bejeweled) residents.

history. On the downside, it's not particularly close to anything, and because most of it is outside, summer is not an optimum time for a visit unless you go early in the day. 🕐 *1 hr. 1830 S. Boulder Hwy., East Las Vegas.* ☎ *702/455-7955. www. accessclarkcounty.com. Admission $1.50 adults, $1 seniors & kids 3–15, free for kids 2 & under. Daily 9am–4:30pm.*

② ★★★ **Liberace Museum.** You can keep your Celine Dions and Manilows. Liberace, now, *there* was a showman, a walking bundle of unashamed, over-the-top glitz and absurdity, all backed up by a classically trained pianist who really knew how to tickle the ivories—and the audience's funny bone. No wonder he was a top Vegas box office attraction during the sequin-drenched 1970s. Here is a shrine to the legend more than the man (you will view plenty of the costumes, jewels, and other excess that made him famous, but you won't learn much about the guy underneath it all). Still, not only is it an only-in-Vegas kind of place, but it also serves as a reminder that this

city needs to stop taking itself so seriously. 🕐 *1 hr. See p 15,* **①**.

③ **Freed's Bakery,** with its gooey, sugary delights, provides a sort of caloric counterpart to the Liberace way of life. The physical shop itself is nothing special, but the frosting sure is. *4780 S. Eastern Ave. (at Tropicana Blvd.).* ☎ *702/ 456-7762. www.freedsbakery.com. $.*

④ ★ **Marjorie Barrick Museum.** Somewhat on the musty side, but worth a stop for those interested in local Native American and Mojave desert natural history. Permanent exhibits include crafts from Hopi, Navajo, and Southern Paiute tribes, plus glass-enclosed displays of local reptiles. Temporary exhibits tend to be a bit spiffier, with the focus on photography and Native American topics. 🕐 *45 min. On the UNLV campus, 4505 S. Maryland Pkwy.* ☎ *702/ 895-3381. http://barrick museum.unlv. edu. Suggested donation $5; $2 for ages 62 and over. Mon–Fri 8am– 4:45pm; Sat 10am–2pm.*

A statue of a shaman dancer from the Native American collection at the Marjorie Barrick Museum.

⑤ ★★★ **Atomic Testing Museum.** Sixty miles (97km) from Vegas is a large swath of desolate desert, the perfect place for the testing of nuclear weapons—which is exactly what the government did on that spot for 40 years. Once upon a time, aboveground blasts were a tourist attraction. Such naiveté is part of the complicated

The free atrium inside the Wynn Las Vegas sports lovely floral arrangements and a gorgeous mosaic floor.

political, historical, scientific, and moral legacy of the nuclear testing program, and this excellent museum is as much dedicated to trying to sort it all out as it is to preserving this troubled part of Vegas heritage. Look among the excellent displays for the motion-simulator theater that attempts to demonstrate what it feels like to ride out a test blast in a bunker. 🕐 *1½ hr. See p 15, ②.*

⑥ ★★ Neil Leifer Gallery.

Award-winning photographer Neil Leifer shot over 150 covers for *Sports Illustrated* and dozens more for *Time* and *People*. He is best known for his iconic shot of Muhammad Ali standing over a defeated Sonny Liston in 1966; that photo and many others are on display at this gem of a gallery. And if you fall in love with one of the fabulous pics and have cash to burn, they'll sell it to you! 🕐 *20 min. In Caesars Palace (casino level of Augustus Tower), 3570 Las Vegas Blvd. S.* ☎ *702/731-7110. www.caesars.com. Free admission. Daily 1–9pm.*

⑦ ★ kids Madame Tussaud's in The Venetian.

A branch of London's legendary wax museum, here you will find lifelike—or creepy, sometimes it's a fine line—replicas of famous folks. Unlike in other museums, you can actually touch the freestanding exhibits. Go ahead, fondle J. Lo's butt or give Brad Pitt a little smooch. 🕐 *45 min. In The Venetian, 3355 Las Vegas Blvd. S.* ☎ *702/862-7800. www.mtvegas. com. Admission $25 adults, $18 seniors and students, $15 kids 7–12, free for kids 6 & under. Discounts for booking online. Daily 10am–10pm, but hours vary seasonally.*

⑧ ★ Wynn Las Vegas Atrium.

A blessed breath of fresh air in the midst of the casino hubbub. It's designed along similar lines as the Bellagio Conservatory (p 53, ③), though it has a long strolling layout rather than a square one, and its location is more accessible. The botanicals and other ornamentation are less fancy than Bellagio's, but it's still nice to wander through, and the floral mosaic tiles underneath are a pretty touch. 🕐 *15 min. 3400 Las Vegas Blvd. S.* ☎ *800/627-6667 or 702/791-7111. www.wynnlasvegas. com. Free admission. Open 24 hr.* ●

Elvis (okay... his wax replica) hasn't left the building at Madame Tussaud's, and there are lots of other famous people keeping him company.

South Strip

1 Mandalay Bay
2 Shark Reef
3 Luxor
4 Excalibur
5 Tribute to Heroes
6 New York–New York
7 Coney Island Emporium
8 The Roller Coaster
9 Jody Maroni's Sausage Kingdom
10 Monte Carlo
11 MGM Grand Lion Habitat
12 Cirque du Soleil's *KÀ*

O f the three major sections of the Strip, this is probably the one with the most variety and the greatest concentration of over-the-top Vegas hotels. Wacky theme hotels are sadly giving way to good-taste resort hotels, which, though grand, are starting to seem a bit cookie-cutter. Not these babies. START: **Mandalay Bay's main lobby.**

1 **Mandalay Bay.** This is the point, chronologically, when designers began to pull back, if ever so slightly, from full Design Madness. Consequently, the Southeast Asia theme (think Kipling's poem "Mandalay," and the era of British Colonialism) is more subdued than I might like. There are still statues, foliage, and a large round aquarium in the lobby, but this hotel's appeal lies more in the whole package. Check out the 11-acre (4.5-hectare)

Mandalay Beach pool area from the casino windows; it's the best in town. And do wander down the hotel's restaurant row, where design has truly run amok. There's a **statue of Lenin** (covered in fake pigeon droppings, and beheaded) outside **Red Square** (p 93), whose interior is covered with the ephemeral trappings of Bolshevik and Stalinist highs and lows. **Aureole** (p 86) has a four-story glass wine tower, accessed by cat-suited wine gals hoisted up on pulleys. And on it

Previous page: Dale Chihuly's Fioro di Como glass sculpture adorns the ceiling of the Bellagio's lobby.

A headless statue of Lenin marks the entrance to Mandalay Bay's stylish Red Square restaurant.

goes, each establishment demonstrating its own level of interior design cleverness. ⏲ *45 min., if you don't stop to eat. 3950 Las Vegas Blvd. S. (at Hacienda Ave.).* ☎ *702/632-7000. www.mandalaybay.com.*

② ★ **kids Shark Reef.** Don't think this is Animal Planet's "Shark Week" come to life. This is really just a beautifully designed (and expensive) aquarium, though not a particularly large one. But because you travel via a glass tunnel that passes right through the exhibits, it does give you the illusion of joining the fish. It's more peaceful than stimulating, but it's decidedly cool to get that up close and personal with a shark or to see a piranha feed. ⏲ *45 min., unless you are hypnotized by fish-watching. See p 33,* **⑦**.

③ **Luxor.** This Egyptian repro has sadly been downgraded in the theme department (the *Titanic*'s here instead of King Tut!), but

enough of the old scheme remains to warrant a trip inside. Do tip your hat to the 30-foot (9.1m) sphinx that guards the entrance. *See p 46 for a walking tour of this hotel.*

④ **kids Excalibur.** Named for the mythical sword of King Arthur, this cute and colorful hotel was the largest in the world when it opened in 1990. Its medieval theme is no longer the outsized wonder that it once was, but this hotel retains some of the more kid-friendly options in Vegas (including some multi-sensory simulator rides, one of them featuring SpongeBob SquarePants), though, in keeping with the city's more adult tone, many of them have been relegated to the dungeon (literally, in the case of the hotel's arcade in the basement). For a picture-perfect view of the castle, take the faux drawbridge passage out of the hotel, use the overhead walkway to New York–New York, and turn around. ⏲ *20 min. 3850 Las Vegas Blvd. S.* ☎ *800/937-7777 or 702/597-7700. www.excalibur.com.*

⑤ **Tribute to Heroes.** At the base of New York–New York's 150-foot-tall (46m) Statue of Liberty, this granite structure holds a permanent collection of notes, pins, and

This lionfish is one of the many denizens of the deep you'll find at Shark Reef.

Excalibur is the city's tacky but entertaining take on the Arthurian legend.

other mementos left outside the hotel post-9/11 to honor the victims and those who so valiantly worked at the tragic site. It's a rare somber note amid the Strip's carefully orchestrated irreverence. *Outside New York–New York, see p 43,* **6**.

6 New York–New York. The audacious Manhattan exterior—12 skyscrapers (one-third the size of the originals), including a 47-story Empire State Building, the New York Public Library, Ellis Island, and more—is riveting. It makes me sorry that Vegas hotels now trend toward good taste. Be sure to cross over the ⅛th-size (300-ft.-tall/91m) replica of the Brooklyn Bridge to stroll the hotel's interior, which is sadly less theme intensive than it used to be. Nevertheless, you'll still find a re-creation of Central Park (complete with trees, streams, and bridges) and detailed mock-ups (check out the graffiti on the walls and cobblestone floors) of Park Avenue, Times Square, and Greenwich Village. It's also still one of the most confusing and crowded properties, but surely that's only one more faithful re-creation, this time of midtown during rush hour. *3790 Las Vegas Blvd. S.* ☎ *702/740-6969.* *www.nynyhotel casino.com.*

7 kids Coney Island Emporium. Most Vegas hotels have arcades, partly as a distraction for non-gamblers, especially children, and partly as a way to start indoctrinating said younger set into the ways of gambling. This is the city's most inspired example, because instead of concentrating on video machines, here you have genuine arcade-style money traps—er, games. C'mon, win a stuffed teddy! S'easy! Just above the casino level, in New York–NewYork. *www.coney islandemporium.com.* See **6**.

8 kids The Roller Coaster. This 203-foot-tall (62m) roller coaster has classic cars designed to look like old-fashioned checker cabs and swoops not only around the outside of the New York–New York complex (at speeds hovering around 67 mph/108kmph), but right through the interior. Enthusiasts will note that it was the first coaster to feature a 180-degree "heartline" twist and turn. 🕐 *up to 1 hr., depending on lines; ride is only 5 min. Go early in the morning to avoid crowds.* See **6**. Must be at

New York–New York's famous whimsical exterior is dominated by a replica of Lady Liberty.

Modeled on its namesake's famous casino, the Monte Carlo is elegant, but a little bland when compared to its Strip neighbors.

least 54 in. (137cm) to ride. Single-ride pass $13, day pass $25. Open Sun–Thurs 11am–11pm, Fri–Sat 10:30am–midnight.

You won't find as many exotic combinations at the Vegas branch of L.A. fixture **9** ★★★ **Jody Maroni's Sausage Kingdom,** but the quality of the Italian sausage, and even the basic hot dog, makes this gourmet fast food. *In New York–New York, 2nd floor; see* **6**. ☎ *702/740-6969. www.jodymaroni.com. $.*

10 Monte Carlo. The $344-million project was supposed to be named the Grand Victoria, but MGM Grand objected, so instead, this 44-acre (18-hectare) resort was named after the city in which the Place du Casino (on which this hotel was modeled) resides. It ostensibly captures European elegance (and the grand entranceway on the Strip, loaded with classy statuary and arches, is a great place for a snapshot), but it's not as theme intensive or detailed as its Strip brethren, which sort of makes it the Vegas equivalent of a wallflower. Though a nice wallflower, to be sure. *3770 Las Vegas Blvd. S. (btw. Flamingo Rd. & Tropicana Ave.).* ☎ *800/311-8999 or 702/730-7777. www.montecarlo.com.*

11 ★★ **kids MGM Grand Lion Habitat.** A glass enclosure allows for some up-close-and-personal encounters with the MGM's mascot lions. A rotating cast of lions (no cat does more than a few hours' duty before returning to larger digs) lounge around just like Fluffy at home, or play gently with their trainers. The lions you see today are, in fact, descendants of the legendary Leo, whose famous roar started off every picture released by MGM Studios back in its heyday; it's his giant bronze likeness that now guards the hotel. The gift shop has some cute options (including a great T-shirt that perversely purrs "Here . . . human, human.") ⏲ *20 min. See p 33,* **6**.

12 ★★★ **kids Cirque du Soleil's KÀ.** This stellar Cirque creation is a superb mix of production values, stage, showmanship, storytelling, and derring-do. And unlike the other Cirque shows in town, this one has a story line (a simple tale about separated royal siblings trying to reunite with one another). The incredible moving stage puts other mechanical theatrical gee-whiz gimmicks to shame, while simultaneously providing just the right literal and figurative platform for Cirque artistry. ⏲ *1½ hr. In MGM Grand, 3799 Las Vegas Blvd. S.* ☎ *866/774-7117 or 702/531-2000. www.cirque dusoleil.com. Shows scheduled Tues–Sat at 7 & 9:30pm. No shows Sun–Mon. See p 112 for more details.*

Luxor Las Vegas

ATRIUM LEVEL

- Wedding Chapel
- The Atrium Showroom
- Food Court
- finish here ★ 5
- Tickets
- 3

CASINO LEVEL

- Pool
- Inclinator 3
- Inclinator 4
- Sports Book
- Luxor Theater
- Inclinator 2
- Inclinator 1
- start here 1
- 2
- Sphinx
- Luxor Station
- Tram to Excalibur
- Tram to Mandalay Bay

1 Lobby
2 Inclinators
3 Luxor Atrium
4 Bodies...The Exhibition
5 Titanic: The Exhibit

Elevators
Restrooms
Escalators

Attractions
Gaming
Dining
Shopping
Nightlife
Entertainment
Customer Service

A perfect example of the city's move to scale down themes that should be embraced. In this case, it's a 30-story black glass pyramid—a three-quarter-scale kinda-replica of the famous one at Giza—but then again, Luxor's Sphinx has its nose intact. This South Strip stalwart (it opened in 1993 and was named for the ancient city of Thebes, aka Luxor) is one of the best examples of late-20th-century postmodern architecture—unfortunately, the 21st century hasn't been as kind as hotel execs are doing their darnedest to strip the interior of its fun Egyptian theme. START: **Valet park your car (it's free) at the hotel, at 3900 Las Vegas Blvd. S. (btw. Reno and Hacienda aves.).**

Touring Tip

For more information on The Luxor, check out my hotel review on p 128.

1 Lobby. This Art Deco/Egyptian Revival space is dominated by two giant Ramses statues (ostensibly guarding the entrance to that Holy of Holies, the casino). Part of the point of the original Egyptian architecture was to remind mere mortals of their insignificance; it works just as well for the difference between monolithic casino hotels and the average slot player.

2 Inclinators. Sneak on the best free ride in town, the hotel's "inclinators"—the high-speed elevators that slant up at a 39-degree angle to deliver guests to their rooms. (In theory they're for guests only, but you can often jump on.)

3 Luxor Atrium. One of the largest atriums in the world, occupying almost 29 million cubic feet (821,189m cubic). From here you can gaze at the vast inner space of the pyramid and recite "Ozymandias" to yourself ("look on my works, ye mighty, and despair!").

4 ★★ Bodies… The Exhibition. Instead of the old Luxor mummies you now get this strangely fascinating and controversial collection of dissected body parts and stripped down cadavers demonstrating the human body's mechanics. It's

The Grand Staircase is just one of many perfect re-creations at Titanic: The Exhibit.

pretty educational, if not for the faint of stomach. 🕐 **45 min. Admission $31 adults, $29 seniors, $23 kids 4–12, free ages 3 and under. Daily 10am–10pm; last admission 9pm.**

5 ★ Titanic: The Exhibit. A can't-miss for buffs of the 1912 disaster thanks to its relics and atmospheric re-creations of the ship's ill-fated voyage. 🕐 **45 min. Admission $27 adults, $25 seniors, $20 kids 4–12, free ages 3 and under. Daily 10am–10pm (last admission 9pm).**

Mid-Strip

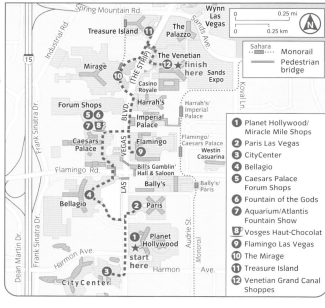

1. Planet Hollywood/Miracle Mile Shops
2. Paris Las Vegas
3. CityCenter
4. Bellagio
5. Caesars Palace Forum Shops
6. Fountain of the Gods
7. Aquarium/Atlantis Fountain Show
8. Vosges Haut-Chocolat
9. Flamingo Las Vegas
10. The Mirage
11. Treasure Island
12. Venetian Grand Canal Shoppes

Here's the most crowded part of the Strip, though some of the larger casino hotels take up a great deal more space than may first appear. That's because this is, for the most part, the luxury-resort-hotel-on-steroids portion of Vegas. In between are leftovers from Vegas's tacky era. With a few exceptions, most items of interest will be inside, where there are all kinds of distractions designed to keep visitors within the property rather than straying to competitors. START: **Sidewalk in front of the Paris Las Vegas.**

---

1 Planet Hollywood/Miracle Mile Shops. On April 17, 2007, the historic but fiscally troubled Aladdin (the original incarnation of which hosted Elvis and Priscilla's wedding) officially became the Planet Hollywood Resort & Casino, and work began on obliterating its *Arabian Nights* theme in favor of L.A. sophistication (or what passes for it). And its famed Desert Passage mall has become the Miracle Mile Shops, which has mostly rid itself of

its Middle East Kasbah in favor of something that is sort of high-tech and a lot generic (though there is a touch of glitz there, too). Too bad; I like my themes along with my retail therapy. ⏱ *1 hr., depending on how dedicated a shopper you are. 3667 Las Vegas Blvd. S.* ☎ *702/785-5555. www.planethollywoodresort.com or www.miraclemileshopslv.com. Hotel is open 24 hr.; mall is open Sun–Thurs 10am–11pm, Fri–Sat 10am–midnight.*

Planet Hollywood's Miracle Mile Shops is one of the best hotel shopping arcades on the Strip.

② Paris Las Vegas. After admiring the mashup of the landmarks of Paris outside, take a stroll within, where the feet of the Eiffel Tower replica rest on the casino floor, itself watched over by a ceiling painted to resemble a Parisian spring day. Revolutionary-era facades ring the casino area, and lead to **Le Boulevard,** the hotel's cobblestone shopping area. The original plan was for the smell of fresh bread to waft through here, complete with the occasional dash of a bike rider ferrying fresh baguettes to the eateries. That attention to detail has been lost, but the Disneyland version of Paris is still in place. It's not so much romantic as it is amusing—but heavily themed is the way Vegas ought to be; and this $785-million fantasyland certainly fits the bill. *See p 10,* **⑤**.

③ ★ CityCenter. Vegas entered the 21st century with the opening of this mammoth "community" of hotels, condo residences, and retail—a joint venture of MGM Mirage and Dubai World that cost almost $11 billion! Did they get their money's worth? It definitely has the bling factor (the retail complex earns its name, Crystals); the green factor (it earned Gold LEED certification for all its components—a big

deal in a city not known for its environmental savvy); the culture factor (almost $40 million in public art), the luxe factor (those hotels, including a Mandarin Oriental, aren't for the budget set), and it's actually good for strolling. Just be sure to wear your shades as you wander the well-landscaped walkways—that glass and steel is sort of blindingly brilliant. See p 11, **⑧**.

④ Bellagio. The opening of this lightly themed behemoth in the fall of 1998 marked the beginning of the end for the Vegas theme trend and the start of the march toward hotel elegance. *See p 52 for a walking tour of the hotel.*

⑤ Caesars Palace Forum Shops. The first great absurd hotel shopping mall in Vegas, and still The One to See. Walk down corridors designed to look like the streets of ancient Rome—if new and gleaming—with a sky-painted ceiling overhead that tricks you into thinking it's broad daylight when it's really approaching midnight. The 160-store sprawling complex includes a more modern-looking (though just as liberally adorned with Roman

The Treehouse inside CityCenter's Crystals retail complex.

statues) expansion featuring a three-story atrium accessed by a spiral-shaped escalator. It's a hoot even if you don't care about shopping. *Daily 10am–11pm. See p 69.*

⑥ kids Fountain of the Gods. This fountain appears to sport the same faux marble statue copies that pop up all over Caesars—until Bacchus, in his drunken glory, comes to creaky animatronic life and delivers a somewhat muffled speech about the wonders of decadence and living it up. The other statues concur. There are some laser effects to try to make it more up-to-date, but it remains cheesy and hokey. It's what passed for a marvel in old Vegas. It's amazing it's still there. ⏱ *8 min. In The Forum Shops, section D on the casino level; see ❸. Free shows on the hour from 10am–11pm.*

⑦ kids Aquarium/Atlantis Fountain Show. More elaborate and ambitious than the fountain show listed above, this one tells the "story" of the fall of Atlantis. Look for an actual story line, bigger special effects, and correspondingly bigger crowds. For the low-tech and less demanding, behind the

It's not what it was back in Bugsy's day, but the Flamingo is still a Strip mainstay worth seeing.

The Fountain of the Gods inside the Forum Shops may not be divine, but it is quite the kitschy diversion.

fountains is a nifty (and free) 50,000-gallon (189,271L) saltwater aquarium. With luck, you'll arrive during one of the regular (and entertaining) fish feedings. *In The Forum Shops, section F on the casino level; see ❸. Free 8-min. fountain shows on the hour from 10am–11pm. Aquarium daily feedings at 1:15 & 5:15pm.*

Get a shot of energy at **⑧ Vosges Haut-Chocolat,** which, in addition to exotic chocolate-based candy confections, offers a cocoa bar (my favorite: the white chocolate with lavender and lemon myrtle) and fancy ice cream. *In Caesars Palace Forum Shops, section H on the street level.* ☎ *702/836-9866. www.vosges chocolate.com. $.*

⑨ Flamingo Las Vegas. When mobster Bugsy Siegel's $6-million Art Deco–ish baby was born in 1946, all the staff (even the janitors!) wore tuxedos. Siegel met an infamous end in 1947, and little of his original structure remains. The Flamingo no longer rules the Strip roost, but its free wildlife sanctuary

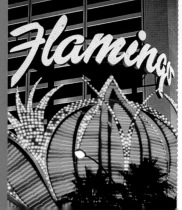

(yes, there are flamingos) and gardens are still beautiful and worth a gander. *3555 Las Vegas Blvd. S. (btw. Sands Ave. & Flamingo Rd.).* ☎ *800/732-2111 or 702/733-3111. www.harrahs.com.*

⑩ The Mirage. Built on the site of the old Castaways hotel, The Mirage made Steve Wynn's rep as the king of Las Vegas hoteliers when it opened in 1989. Say "hi" to the scary-looking statues in front of the resort commemorating magicians Siegfried & Roy, who performed almost 6,000 shows here before Roy Horn was seriously injured onstage in 2003 after a disastrous encounter with one of the famous duo's beloved white tigers. *See p 12,* ⑫.

⑪ Treasure Island. When it opened in 1993, this $450-million property was designed to attract families with a Disneyesque Caribbean pirates theme. That idea walked the plank in 2003 and the property was turned into an

The atmosphere at Treasure Island nowadays is more tropical than pirate, though there's still booty to be won here.

adult-oriented resort with nary a trace of theme. And its once kid-friendly free pirate battle now features sexed-up sirens. Yo Ho Hum. *See p 37,* ⑦.

⑫ Venetian Grand Canal Shoppes. Every bit as over-the-top as The Forum Shops, but less cheesy, provided you don't automatically sneer at architectural reproductions (which are wonderfully rendered). Given how well executed the place is—including a rather cunning scaled-down replica of St. Mark's Square and canals with actual gondoliers—and that there are even period costumed performers who actually sing and otherwise interact with customers, it qualifies as a mall-as-theme-park experience, and I mean that in a good way. ⏱ *45 min.; more if you actually shop. 3355 Las Vegas Blvd. S.* ☎ *702/414-4500. www.thegrandcanalshoppes. com. Sun–Thurs 10am–11pm; Fri–Sat 10am–midnight.*

Let a gondolier serenade you beneath a fake blue sky as you sail past the stores and restaurants of the Venetian's Grand Canal Shoppes.

Bellagio

CAESARS PALACE

FLAMINGO ROAD

Walkway to Caesars Palace

Walkway to Bally's

North Entrance

Via Bellagio

Race and Sports Book

Terrazza di Sogno

O Theater

Buffet

Bellagio Gallery of Fine Art

Arcade

CASINO

Pool Promenade

Fountains at Bellagio **1**

LAS VEGAS BOULEVARD (THE STRIP)

Pool

finish here ★ **3**

Lobby **2**

Main Entrance

Via Fiore

start here ★

Spa/Salon/ Fitness Center

South Parking Garage

Moving Walkway

JOCKEY CLUB HOTEL

COSMOPOLITAN HOTEL & CASINO
(under construction; opening 2010)

| 0 | 100 yds |
| 0 | 100 m |

N

HARMON AVENUE

CITYCENTER

↑↓ Elevators	Public thoroughfare	**1** Lake Como Fountains
♦♦ Restrooms	Dining, bars and lounges	**2** *Fiori di Como*
	Shops and boutiques	**3** Bellagio Conservatory

When it opened in 1998 on the site of the old Dunes hotel, this $1.6-billion brainchild of casino magnate Steve Wynn (who's since moved on to properties named for himself) was the most expensive ever built. This is the luxury resort that ushered in the new adults-only elegance epoch in Vegas. It's not quite the relaxing oasis that ads for the hotel make it out to be, but it is probably the closest thing Vegas has to a European casino hotel. And this expensive resort is, ironically, home to some of the best freebies in the city. START: **Valet-park your car (it's free) at the hotel, at 3600 Las Vegas Blvd. S. (at the corner of Flamingo Rd.), then walk to the sidewalk in front of the hotel.**

Touring Tip

For more information on Bellagio, check out my hotel review on p 124; for dining opportunities in the hotel, check out chapter 6.

❶ Lake Como/Fountains. It's too bad that, after having gone to so much trouble to create this beautiful 8-acre (3.2-hectare) reproduction of Lake Como, the scenic provincial Italian village strung along the lake's banks is not accessible to visitors. Still, it remains a top spot for shutterbugs. If you haven't seen one of the fountain shows that take place on the lake yet and it's past noon, wait for one—you won't regret it. See p 11, ❿, for more on the fountain shows.

❷ Fiori di Como. This $10-million Dale Chihuly glass sculpture adorns the ceiling of the reception area. When it was commissioned in 1998, this extravagant floral creation, measuring 30 by 70 feet (9.1 by 20m) and containing 2,000 handblown flowers, was the largest glass sculpture in the world. Nearly 5 tons (4,536kg) of steel affix the sculpture to the ceiling.

❸ ★★★ Bellagio Conservatory. The botanical theme is continued in the hotel's 14,000-square-foot (1,300-sq.-m) indoor garden, basking beneath a 55-foot-tall (17m) glass ceiling. As the plants and flowers are freshened daily, and decorations regularly changed in their entirety to correspond to seasons and holidays (Easter and Chinese New Year bring particularly spectacular displays), and given that access to this oasis of life and color is entirely free, this is surely one of the great follies in a town otherwise totally dedicated to commerce. The hotel's yearly bill for all this floral goodness? Close to $8 million. Note that the fountain that stands just outside the conservatory entrance is over 100 years old. *3600 Las Vegas Blvd. S. (at the corner of Flamingo Rd.).* ☎ *702/693-7111. www.bellagio.com.*

The rotating floral displays inside the Bellagio Conservatory are among the city's best free attractions.

Downtown

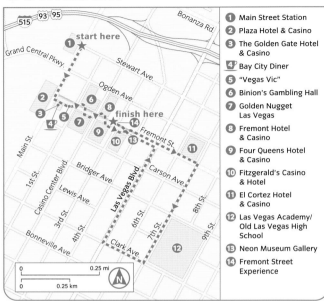

1. Main Street Station
2. Plaza Hotel & Casino
3. The Golden Gate Hotel & Casino
4. Bay City Diner
5. "Vegas Vic"
6. Binion's Gambling Hall
7. Golden Nugget Las Vegas
8. Fremont Hotel & Casino
9. Four Queens Hotel & Casino
10. Fitzgerald's Casino & Hotel
11. El Cortez Hotel & Casino
12. Las Vegas Academy/ Old Las Vegas High School
13. Neon Museum Gallery
14. Fremont Street Experience

The former "Glitter Gulch" and glamour spot of Las Vegas, this smaller stretch of correspondingly decreased-in-size hotels and casinos is overlooked in favor of the flashy deal down south. Too bad— you can cover the whole thing so easily, thanks to pedestrian-only Fremont Street; the crowds are usually friendlier; and the minimum bets are cheaper. START: **Entrance to the Main Street Station; if you're driving, park in one of the many lots off Fremont Street and walk to the hotel.**

1 Main Street Station. Start your tour off in early-20th-century San Francisco . . . Vegas style, at this lovely property. As you stroll through, note the many Victorian decor elements, from the wrought-iron railings to the antique brass casino cages. Ask at the lobby for the casino's worthwhile self-guided tour of its lovely antiques collection. The males in your party should check out the men's room on the main casino floor—that slab of rock holding up the urinals is a genuine

piece of the Berlin wall. *200 N. Main St.* ☎ *800/713-8993 or 702/387-1896. www.mainstreetcasino.com.*

2 Plaza Hotel & Casino. It opened in 1971 as the Union Plaza, its name an homage to the Union Pacific Railroad station that originally occupied this site. Though by no means the oldest hotel in the area, the Plaza's facade is so typically "Vegas" that it tends to pop up often in movies (*Back to the Future II, Cool World,* and *The Mexican,* among others) as a generic casino. *1 Main St.* ☎ *702/386-2110. www. plazahotelcasino.com.*

③ The Golden Gate Hotel & Casino. This four-story building is Sin City's oldest hotel, dating back to 1906 (it opened as the Hotel Nevada), when room and board cost $1 a day. In one incarnation, it was the Sal Sagev (spell each word backward for the inside joke) hotel. Today, the exterior facade reflects the original building's roots. *1 Fremont St.* ☎ *702/385-1906. www.goldengate casino.com.*

The Plaza Hotel & Casino's ultra-Vegas exterior has been featured in many a cinematic production.

Vegas Vic, arguably the most famous neon sign in Las Vegas.

The Golden Gate Hotel & Casino's 99¢ shrimp cocktail, the symbol of bargain Las Vegas, originated back in 1959 (it cost only 50[ce] then); in the ensuing decades, they've served over 30 million of them. The price jumped to $1.99 in 2008 and the shrimp served today in the hotel's **④ Bay City Diner** is just bay shrimp, but it's actually a pretty good snack, and a Vegas must. *In the Golden Gate Hotel & Casino, 1 Fremont St.* ☎ *702/385-1906. www. goldengatecasino.com. $.*

⑤ "Vegas Vic." This 40-foot-tall (12m) neon cowboy, one of the city's most recognized icons, went up for the first time in 1951 and has suffered many an indignity since. He lost his voice (he once offered up a "howdy partner" to visitors) when actor Lee Marvin (in town, to shoot *The Professionals*) complained in 1966 that he was too loud and had him silenced. His arm used to wave, and that doesn't work anymore either. Then his hat was partially cut off to make way for the canopy for the Fremont Street Experience in 1994. And that ever-present cigarette ain't too popular nowadays either. But he (and across-the-street neighbor "Sassy Sally"—you can't miss her) is one of the last bastions of Old Vegas, and you should tip your hat to him. *25 Fremont St.*

⑥ Binion's Gambling Hall. The former Horseshoe Casino dates back to 1951, when it was built on the site of the old Apache Hotel by legendary casino operator Benny Binion (1904–89). One of the most venerable gambling establishments in Vegas, and up until a couple of years ago the home of the World Series of Poker (which began life in 1970), Binion's is pretty desiccated, but is still where hard-line gamblers go to play. The place isn't nearly as dazzling as its lurid history (former owner Ted Binion's stripper girl-friend was tried for his murder in 1998, a story that includes a vault filled with treasure buried in the desert), but 2008 did see the return of its famed "$1 Million Dollar Display." *128 Fremont St.* ☎ *702/382-1600. www.binions.com.*

⑦ Golden Nugget Las Vegas. Its 1946 construction date makes this one of Vegas's oldest extant hotels; but renovations have kept it looking fresh, and it's the indisputable star of Downtown. It's had moments of fame, notably when it became casino magnate Steve Wynn's first local purchase in 1973, and then during its brief run in 2004 as the setting of a short-lived reality series called *The Casino,* which

Stop in at the Golden Nugget Las Vegas to rub the solid gold Hand of Faith for luck.

Hard-core gamblers still flock to Binion's, though the World Series of Poker is no longer played here.

documented the antics of later owners. But its biggest claim to fame nowadays resides in its lobby: The **Hand of Faith,** the world's largest gold nugget, was found in Australia and weighs in at nearly 62 pounds (28kg). *129 Fremont St.* ☎ *702/385-7111. www.goldennugget.com.*

⑧ Fremont Hotel & Casino. This 15-story hotel debuted in 1956 as Nevada's tallest building. It's also where Mr. Las Vegas, Wayne Newton, got his start in Sin City. For that alone it gets a *Danke schoen. 200 Fremont St.* ☎ *702/385-3232. www. fremontcasino.com.*

⑨ Four Queens Hotel & Casino. Opened in 1966, this venerable property was named in homage to the original builder's four daughters. Today the 3.2-acre (1.3-hectare) giant property occupies an entire city block right in the heart of Downtown, and is notable in that it's home to Downtown's only major club, The Canyon Club, and a usually crowd-free discount ticket booth for all the major shows. *202 Fremont St.* ☎ *702/385-4011. www.fourqueens.com.*

⑩ Fitzgerald's Casino & Hotel. A relative newcomer to Downtown (it first opened as the Sundance Hotel in 1979), this 34-story property is most noteworthy for its somewhat fading Irish theme, and its ownership—it's the only African-American–owned casino in Las Vegas. *301 Fremont St.* ☎ *702/388-2400. www.fitzgeralds. com.*

⑪ El Cortez Hotel & Casino. When it opened in 1941 (at a then whopping cost of $245,000—gotta love inflation), this small hotel was Downtown's largest and most luxurious resort. So good was it that Bugsy Siegel bought it in 1946, but he later dumped it in order to finance his dream of the Strip. It's been renovated and gutted over the years, but you'll still spot some of the original's Spanish-flavored details. And wave to the top of the hotel tower while you're here; former owner Jackie Gaughan, a local legend, lives at the tippy top! *600 Fremont St.* ☎ *702/385-5200. www. elcortezhotelcasino.com.*

⑫ Las Vegas Academy/ Old Las Vegas High School. And now for a rare bit of culture in Downtown. This beauty of a school building, built in 1930 and on the National Register of Historic Places, was the first high school built in Las

Vegas and is the best Art Deco building in the city. Note the elaborate concrete and stucco friezes on the facade; they depict a number of species of animal, plants, and other figures of interest. It's now home to the city's school of performing arts. *315 E. 7th St.*

⑬ Neon Museum Gallery. Though Vegas is still all about the bright lights, the introduction of computer-generated signage has meant the slow death of a great art form, the city's iconic neon signs. These have been gradually phased out, condemned as hokey and old-fashioned, and would have been consigned to trash heaps had this nonprofit not stepped in. There are plans in the works for a permanent facility to display many of its recovered treasures, but in the meantime some have been erected around Fremont Street and other parts of Downtown. The **Hacienda's horse and rider** stands above the intersection of Fremont Street and Las Vegas Boulevard South, while the **Aladdin's glittery lamp** is at the northwest corner. *On Fremont St. (btw. Main St. & Las Vegas Blvd.). www.neonmuseum.org. Free admission. Open 24 hr. Best viewed after dark.*

The old Hacienda's horse and rider is one of the most famous signs in the Neon Museum.

⑭ ★★ kids Fremont Street Experience. Sauntering down Fremont Street is the closest you can get these days to the archetypal Vegas (because buildings and corresponding lighted signs are set so much closer together). Nowadays, most visitors come for the giant 90-foot-high (27m) canopy erected over the pedestrian mall, which displays a genuinely impressive light-and-sound show (the whole thing appropriately named "Viva Vision"). Several different shows play in rotation, including ones based on Area 51, KISS, and Queen. Good views are available just about anywhere on the mall, as all it requires is neck-craning, but if you want to get a little closer to the action, stand on a balcony at Fitzgerald's or in that hotel's branch of McDonald's. *Fremont St., btw. Main St. & Las Vegas Blvd. www.vegasexperience.com. Free admission. Shows nightly every hour, dusk to midnight.* ●

Fremont Street during the day: The canopy over the pedestrian zone helps protect shoppers and gamblers from the hot Nevada sun.

Fremont Street is best toured at night, when it's lit up in all of its neon- and laser-enhanced glory.

Shopping Best Bets

Best Place for **Tacky Vegas Souvenirs**
Bonanza Gift and Souvenir Shop, *2460 Las Vegas Blvd. S. (p 68)*

Best **Classy but Naughty Underthings**
Agent Provocateur, *The Forum Shops at Caesars Palace, 3500 Las Vegas Blvd. S. (p 64)*

Best **Sweets & Pastries**
Jean-Philippe, *Bellagio, 3600 Las Vegas Blvd. S. (p 67)*

Best **Jewelry**
Tiffany & Co., *Via Bellagio, 3600 Las Vegas Blvd. S. (p 71)*

Best **Place for a Showgirl Wig**
Serge's Showgirls Wigs, *953 E. Sahara Ave. (p 64)*

Best **Place for Wizard Paraphernalia**
Dragon's Lair, *The Realm Shops at Excalibur, 3850 Las Vegas Blvd. S. (p 68)*

Best **Place for Books on Gambling**
Gambler's Book Shop, *630 S. 11th St. (p 64)*

Best **Place to Buy the Makings for Your Own Casino**
Gambler's General Store, *800 S. Main St. (p 68)*

Best **Outlets**
Fashion Outlets Las Vegas, *32100 Las Vegas Blvd. S. (p 66)*

Best **Vintage Clothes**
The Attic, *1018 S. Main St. (p 64)*

Best **Toys**
FAO Schwarz, *The Forum Shops at Caesars Palace, 3500 Las Vegas Blvd. S. (p 72)*

Best **Pret a Porter**
Prada, *Via Bellagio, 3600 Las Vegas Blvd. S. (p 66)*

Best **Museum Shop**
Atomic Testing Museum, *755 E. Flamingo Rd. (p 68)*

Best **High-Fashion Casual**
Juicy Couture, *The Forum Shops at Caesars Palace, 3500 Las Vegas Blvd. S. (p 65)*

Best **Place for Antiques**
Antique Square, *2014–2034 E. Charleston Blvd. (p 63)*

For designer duds and accessories, it's hard to beat Prada.

Previous Page: A window display at Agent Provocateur, the city's best lingerie shop.

Shopping **on the Strip & Downtown**

Shopping **off the Strip**

Charleston Blvd

ARTS DISTRICT (GATEWAY DISTRICT) ❶

Las Vegas Blvd

Main St

Lake Mead Blvd.

Washington Ave.

Charleston Blvd.

Sahara

Sahara Monorail & station

0   0.25 mi
0   0.25 km

Area of detail

Rancho Dr

Rainbow Blvd

Jones Blvd

Valley View Blvd.

Decatur Blvd.

Desert Inn Rd.

Flamingo Rd.

Tropicana Ave.

Las Vegas Blvd (The Strip)

Paradise Rd.

Maryland Pkwy

Eastern Ave

0   2 mi
0   2 km

McCARRAN INT'L AIRPORT ❻

Sunset Rd.

Stratosphere

St. Louis Av

Sahara Av

State St

Kendale St

Joe W.

Brown

Dr

❷

Sahara

LV Hilton

Las Vegas Hilton

Las Vegas Convention Center

LV Convention Center

Paradise Rd

Las Vegas Country Club (private)

Desert Inn Rd

La Canada St

Vegas Valley Dr.

Eastern Av

Desert Inn Rd

Sierra Vista Dr.

Swenson Av

Cambridge St.

Twain Av

Boulevard Mall ❼

Twain Av

Las Vegas National Golf Club

Flamingo Rd

❽

Terrible's

Hard Rock Hotel & Casino

Paradise Rd

UNIVERSITY OF NEVADA, LAS VEGAS

Maryland Pkwy

Rochelle Ave.

University Ave.

Harmon Av

Thomas & Mack Center ❾

Swenson Av

Tropicana Av

Spencer St

❿ ⓫

Tropicana Av

Eastern Av

McCARRAN INT'L AIRPORT

Alternate Reality Comics 9
Antiques at the Market 6
The Boulevard 7
British Foods, Inc. 4
Buffalo Exchange 8
Dead Poet Books 3
Gambler's Book Shop 10
Liberace Museum Gift Store 11
Meadows Mall 5
Serge's Showgirls Wigs 2
Valentino's Zoot Suit Connection 1

Las Vegas Shopping A to Z

Antiques

★ Antiques at the Market

EAST OF STRIP Sixty stalls of antiques, memorabilia, collectibles, vintage clothes, jewelry, and accessories. The selection and a close-to-the-airport location make this a convenient stop for voracious antiques shoppers on their way home with weekend winnings burning a hole in their pockets. *6665 S. Eastern Ave. (btw. Sunset & Warm Springs rds.).* ☎ *702/307-3960. AE, MC, V. Map p 62.*

★ Antique Square DOWNTOWN

It's the smallest of the city's three antiques malls, but careful shoppers can uncover a plethora of treasures, including comics, vintage Las Vegas matchbooks, postcards, ashtrays, and other souvenirs of bygone casinos. *2014–2034 E. Charleston Blvd.* ☎ *702/ 471-6500. AE, MC, V. Map p 61.*

★ Red Rooster Antique Mall

DOWNTOWN Think lots of stuff stuffed into 25,000 square feet (2,323 sq. m): Vegas memorabilia,

Red Rooster Antique Mall is one of the largest in Las Vegas.

Kiehl's is not as exclusive as it once was, but is still an excellent place to pick up cosmetics.

vintage jewelry, clothes, furnishings, and such collectibles as carnival glass. Plus the dealers are on hand to answer questions (not always a given elsewhere). *1109 Western Ave. (at Charleston Blvd. & I-15).* ☎ *702/382-5253. AE, MC, V. Map p 61.*

Beauty Products & Accessories

★★ Jo Malone NORTH STRIP

This London-based perfumer combines aromas such as pomegranate and pepper, and verbena and basil in her scents and candles for the home. Her fresh non-fussy personal care items include refreshingly light orange blossom and signature grapefruit eau de colognes. *Wynn Esplanade, 3131 Las Vegas Blvd. S.* ☎ *702/770-3485. www.wynnlas vegas.com. AE, DISC, MC, V. Map p 61.*

★★★ Kiehl's MID-STRIP This

150-year-old cosmetics line isn't quite as limited in access as it used to be, thanks to a buy-out from a much larger cosmetics company. But the line's skin and hair products, particularly the popular Lip Balm #2, still make any store visit a treat. *In*

The Forum Shops at Caesars Palace, 3500 Las Vegas Blvd. S. ☎ *702/784-0025. www.kiehls.com. AE, DC, MC, V. Map p 61.*

★ **Sephora** MID-STRIP False eyelashes! Nail polish! Perfume! Lipstick! Toenail clippers! If you need a beauty item, you'll find it here. And if you want to wow them at the tables or get ready for a night of club hopping, have your face made up for free by a staff member. *In The Venetian Grand Canal Shoppes, 3355 Las Vegas Blvd. S.* ☎ *702/735-3896. www.sephora.com. AE, DISC, MC, V. Map p 61.*

★★★ **Serge's Showgirls Wigs** EAST OF STRIP The name says it all. What, you thought those long falls of luscious locks were real? Less of a commitment than extensions, but loaded with fantasy, wigs run the gamut from expensive to disposable. *953 E. Sahara Ave.* ☎ *702/732-1015. www.showgirlwigs.com. AE, DISC, MC, V. Map p 62.*

Books & Stationery
★ **Alternate Reality Comics** EAST OF STRIP As the name suggests, the emphasis here is on underground comics, but the stock is comprehensive enough to include mainstream titles. *4800 S. Maryland Pkwy., Ste. D.* ☎ *702/736-3673. www. alternaterealitycomics.net. AE, DISC, MC, V. Map p 62.*

★★ **Dead Poet Books** WEST OF STRIP Even in Vegas, I love a musty old bookstore, and the owners here are particularly literary types. *3874 W. Sahara Ave.* ☎ *702/227-4070. MC, V. Map p 62.*

★ **Gambler's Book Shop** DOWNTOWN I keep telling you, you can't beat the system. And yet, this shop swears that you can. Or at least that one of their thousands of titles knows how and will tell all. *1550 E. Tropicana Ave., #4.*

☎ *702/382-7555. www.gamblers book.com. AE, MC, V. Map p 62.*

Clothing & Shoes
★★★ **Agent Provocateur** MID-STRIP This British lingerie line, favored by Kate Moss and other slinky celebs, is for those who want some art and style in their seduction wear. The black silk satin Nikita line and the lacy Love styles definitely fit the bill; some of their stuff has to be seen to be believed. *The Forum Shops at Caesars Palace, 3500 Las Vegas Blvd. S.* ☎ *702/696-7174. www.agentprovocateur.com. AE, MC, V. Map p 61.*

★ **The Attic** DOWNTOWN It's lost a little of its hipster luster, but in addition to funky used clothing of varying vintages, this shop makes its own poodle skirts. *1018 S. Main St.* ☎ *702/388-4088. www.theatticlas vegas.com. AE, MC, V. Map p 61.*

Betsey Johnson MID-STRIP Playful, sexy, strong, and boldly

Literary lovers will find lots of good buys at Dead Poet Books.

The Attic is one of the best vintage shops in Las Vegas.

feminine fashions—flouncy dresses with bright-floral prints, lacy tops, vibrant knits and velvet skirts, and curve-displaying garments—have been Betsey Johnson's signature styles since the mid-1980s. *In Planet Hollywood's Miracle Mile, 3663 Las Vegas Blvd. S.* ☎ *702/731-0286. www.betseyjohnson.com. AE, MC, V. Map p 61.*

★★ Bettie Page Boutique MID-STRIP

Can you leave Sin City without paying homage to the pin-up? No, you can't. And this shop—done up in leopard, no less—sells a rather cute line of Page-inspired '50s-style dresses, corsets, hosiery, and more. It's a hoot. *In Planet Hollywood's Miracle Mile, 3663 Las Vegas Blvd. S.* ☎ *702/636-1100. www.bettiepageclothing.com. AE, MC, V. Map p 61.*

★ Buffalo Exchange EAST OF STRIP

This vintage chain store relies a lot on consignment, so selection will vary. The hip staff has good taste, though the stock edges more toward recent decades rather than rare finds from the '40s. *4110 S. Maryland Pkwy. (at Flamingo Rd.).* ☎ *702/791-3960. www.buffalo exchange.com. MC, V. Map p 62.*

★★★ Gianni Versace MID-STRIP

This designer line, synonymous with opulent celebrity-endorsed high fashion, manages to be both cutting edge and classic, with attention paid to detail and fabric. *The Forum Shops at Caesars Palace, 3500 Las Vegas Blvd. S.* ☎ *702/796-7222. www.versace.com. AE, MC, V. Map p 61.*

★ Juicy Couture MID-STRIP

Single-handedly responsible for the ubiquity of velour sweat suits, not to mention the word "Juicy" along backsides. To be fair, the designers tapped into the casual wear zeitgeist by making some genuinely cute clothes. *In The Forum Shops at Caesars Palace, 3500 Las Vegas Blvd. S.* ☎ *702/365-5600. www. juicycouture.com. AE, MC, V. Map p 61.*

★★★ Kate Spade MID-STRIP

Bright colors and sleek styles with a modern vibe have made this line of handbags, luggage, stationery, and accessories hip from the Hamptons to Hollywood. *In The Fashion Show Mall, 3200 Las Vegas Blvd. S.* ☎ *702/691-9968. www.katespade.com. AE, DISC, MC, V. Map p 61.*

At the Playboy Store, you'll find everything you need to bring out your inner Bunny.

★★★ **Manolo Blahnik** NORTH STRIP Revealing just the right amount of "toe cleavage," this store's expensive, sexy, and strappy sandals and stiletto-heeled shoes were enshrined in pop culture by *Sex and the City. Wynn Esplanade, 3131 Las Vegas Blvd. S.* ☎ *702/770-3477. www.manoloblahnik.com. AE, DC, DISC, MC, V. Map p 61.*

Playboy Store MIDSTRIP Because you'll want to wear something slinky from Playboy's fashion line on a visit to the only Playboy Club in existence. *In The Forum Shops at Caesars Palace, 3500 Las Vegas Blvd. S.* ☎ *702/851-7470. AE, DISC, MC, V. Map p 61.*

★★★ **Prada** MID-STRIP Its clothes are the opposite of Vegas: timeless, classy, and simple. Equally elegant are the shoes and accessories. *Via Bellagio, 3600 Las Vegas Blvd. S.* ☎ *702/866-6886. www. prada.com. AE, DC, DISC, MC, V. Map p 61.*

★ **Two Lips Shoes** MID-STRIP Cute flats and satin Mary Janes share space with hip, high-heeled

sandals and leather pumps—all fashion forward and reasonably priced. Some are even well padded enough to add comfort to your style. *In Planet Hollywood's Miracle Mile, 3663 Las Vegas Blvd. S.* ☎ *702/737-0369. www.twolips shoes.com. AE, DISC, MC, V. Map p 61.*

★ **Valentino's Zoot Suit Connection** WEST OF STRIP This savvy shop caters to Kool cats with quality vintage holdings that include zoot suits, evening gowns, coats, a large variety of hats, and jewelry. *107 E. Charleston Blvd., Ste. 135.* ☎ *702/383-9555. www.valentinos zootsuitconnection.com. AE, DISC, MC, V. Map p 62.*

Factory Outlets
★★★ **Fashion Outlets Las Vegas** PRIMM A 40-minute schlep from the city, but worth it for dedicated bargain hunters: you get inside shopping (air-conditioning!), plus Versace, Tommy Hilfiger, Williams Sonoma, and Banana Republic outlets, among others. *32100 Las Vegas Blvd. S.* ☎ *702/874-1400.*

Two Lips Shoes is a great place to pick up fashion-forward footwear on the cheap.

The whimsical Shoppes at the Palazzo is a primo mall for the serious (and wealthy) fashionista.

www.fashionoutletlasvegas.com. AE, DISC, MC, V. Map p 61.

Las Vegas Premium Outlets DOWNTOWN The high-end names here—Armani, Dolce & Gabbana, Calvin Klein—make this most conveniently located outlet center enticing for dedicated bargain hunters, but amateurs may not have the stamina to endure the open-air facility on hot days. *875 S. Grand Central Pkwy. (at I-15).* ☎ *702/474-7500. www.premiumoutlets.com. AE, DISC, MC, V. Map p 61.*

Food & Chocolate
★★ **British Foods, Inc.** WEST OF STRIP Britannia rules at this import grocer, which stocks more than 750 types of edibles (and a couple of trinkets) from all over Her Majesty's Commonwealth. Come here for a Cadbury fix (you can get options that you'll rarely find anywhere else in the U.S.), or to stock up on teas, biscuits, sausage rolls, jams, puddings, British bacon, pasties, and even haggis. *375 S. Decatur Blvd., #11. 702/579-7777. www.british grocer.com. Map p 62.*

★ **Ethel's Chocolate Lounge** NORTH STRIP This fun store/

lounge/cafe—run by famed local confectioner Ethel M—is a top spot for a blood-sugar pick-me-up. Flavors for the fancy chocolates run the gamut from pomegranate to cinnamon to cheesecake! *In Fashion Show Mall, 3200 Las Vegas Blvd. S.* ☎ *702/796-6662. www.ethels chocolate.com. AE, DC, DISC, MC, V. Map p 61.*

★★★ **Jean-Philippe Patisserie** MID-STRIP Come for the chocolate fountain, stay for the award-winning pastries (including a brioche-oozing *dulce de leche*) and maybe some authentic gelato, and then leave with a box full of expensive truffles. Repeat as necessary. *Bellagio, 3600 Las Vegas Blvd. S.* ☎ *702/693-8788. www.jpchocolates.com. AE, DC, DISC, MC, V. Map p 61.*

★ kids **M&M's World** SOUTH STRIP Walls filled with tubes of unusually colored M&Ms and themed merchandise. It's totally gimmicky until you realize what an awesome assortment you can make by mixing hot pink with black. *In the Showcase Mall, 3785 Las Vegas Blvd. S. (just north of MGM Grand).* ☎ *702/736-7611. AE, DISC, MC, V. Map p 61.*

Want to taste a gray M&M? Hot pink? Both? M&M's World is the place to do it.

Gift Shops

★★ Arts Factory Complex

DOWNTOWN You'll find more than neon cityscapes and desert scenes on display and for sale in this two-story complex (once a crematorium), where a number of painters, photographers, and sculptors maintain studios and galleries. *107 E. Charleston Blvd.* ☎ *702/383-3113. www.theartsfactory.com. AE, MC, V. Map p 61.*

★★★ Atomic Testing Museum Store

MID-STRIP The museum is as serious as its subject matter, but its shop is where absurdity—atomic tests used to be tourist attractions—is allowed to sneak in, in the form of Albert Einstein action figures, fallout shelter signs, and other bomb-and-blast–themed trinkets. *755 E. Flamingo Rd.* ☎ *702/794-5161. www.atomictestingmuseum. org. AE, DISC, MC, V. Map p 61.*

★★ Bonanza Gift & Souvenir Shop

NORTH STRIP The self-proclaimed "world's largest gift shop." All I can say for sure is that it is indeed big, contains everything from dice earrings to pseudo "Indian" goods, and has never let me down when I'm looking for the perfect tacky souvenir. *2460 Las Vegas Blvd. S.* ☎ *702/385-7539. www.worldslargestgiftshop.com. AE, DISC, MC, V. Map p 61.*

kids Dragon's Lair

SOUTH STRIP Crystal balls, magic wands, dragon figurines, and magically themed knickknacks to help bring out your inner wizard. *In the Castle Walk at Excalibur, 3850 Las Vegas Blvd. S.* ☎ *702/597-7850. AE, DISC, MC, V. Map p 61.*

★ Gambler's General Store

DOWNTOWN Eight thousand square feet (743 sq. m) filled with all manner of gambling-related merchandise. It's *the* place to purchase that most splendid of Vegas souvenirs, your very own antique (or current) slot machine. Or you could settle for a book on blackjack. *800 S. Main St.* ☎ *702/382-9903. www. gamblersgeneralstore.com. AE, DISC, MC, V. Map p 61.*

★ Il Prato

Need a mask for Mardi Gras? A gown fit for Carnivale? This Venetian-themed gift shop stocks

For the perfect tacky Vegas souvenir, look no further than the immense Bonanza Gift & Souvenir Shop.

Want a cool pair of fuzzy dice? Your own slot machine? If it's gambling related, then the Gambler's General Store has it.

items ranging from beautiful masks and marionettes to detailed miniatures and fine stationery. The prices will make you wince, but the quality is there. *In The Grand Canal Shoppes, 3355 Las Vegas Blvd. S.* ☎ *702/733-1201. www.ilpratousa.com. AE, DC, DISC, MC, V. Map p 61.*

★★ Liberace Museum Gift Store SOUTH STRIP   Not enough bedazzled and bejeweled objects to suit my tastes, but if you need a refrigerator magnet with the honoree's mug on it—or even a mug with his face—here's the place. *1775 E. Tropicana Ave.* ☎ *702/798-5595. www.liberace.org. AE, MC, V. Map p 62.*

★ Swarovski MID-STRIP   Crystals (made by a company that has specialized in the finest of same for generations) adorn everything from purses to picture frames in this glittering shop. Costly? Yes. But it's high-quality bling. *In Planet Hollywood's Miracle Mile, 3663 Las Vegas Blvd. S.* ☎ *702/732-7302. www. swarovski.com. AE, DISC, MC, V. Map p 61.*

Hotel Shopping Arcades
★★ Bellagio: Via Bellagio MID-STRIP   I can't even afford the small bit of oxygen it takes to walk this short, but high-priced, luxury shopping promenade, marked by such names as Armani, Hermes, and

Chanel. But I sure do like pretending I can. *3600 Las Vegas Blvd. S. (at the corner of Flamingo Rd.).* ☎ *702/693-7111. AE, DC, DISC, MC, V. Map p 61.*

★★★ Caesars Palace: Appian Way & The Forum Shops MID-STRIP   Every bit as much an attraction as it is a shopping destination. Think Rodeo Drive—Christian Dior, Louis Vuitton, and so on—reimagined as the Via Veneto and other Italian cityscapes, plus some ridiculous talking statues. *3500 Las Vegas Blvd. S.* ☎ *702/731-7110. www. caesars.com. AE, DISC, MC, V. Map p 61.*

★★ CityCenter: Crystals MID-STRIP   Break out your platinum card. Vegas's newest house of retail worship glitters with such high-end names as Zegna, Louis Vuitton, Cavalli, Tom Ford, and H. Stern. If your budget doesn't extend into the stratosphere, check out the three-story "tree house" and the art installations between Crystals and ARIA (p 123). *3720 Las Vegas Blvd. S.* ☎ *702/590-9299. www.crystalsat citycenter.com. AE, DISC, MC, V. Map p 61.*

Encore: Encore Esplanade NORTH STRIP   Eleven boutiques selling high-priced merchandise to the wealthy (or suddenly wealthy). Aside from major luxe brands (Chanel, Hermès, and the like), you'll find

Rock & Republic (hip clothes) and the Homestore (furnishings, bath items, and such from the hotel in case you must take them home with you). *3121 Las Vegas Blvd. S.* ☎ *702/770-8000. www.encore lasvegas.com. AE, DISC, MC, V. Map p 61.*

Harrah's: Carnaval Court MID-STRIP Notable for being the only outdoor hotel shopping mall on the Strip itself, this collection of stalls sells purses, hippie-style clothes, jewelry, and other inexpensive trinkets. *3475 Las Vegas Blvd. S.* ☎ *702/369-5000. www.harrahs. com. AE, DC, DISC, MC, V. Map p 61.*

Mandalay Bay: Mandalay Place SOUTH OF STRIP In appearance, more like an actual indoor mall than a hotel shopping arcade, but in content it has neither the rarified atmosphere of Via Bellagio or the Wynn Promenade, nor the variety of The Forum Shops. But there is a men's shop called The Art of Shaving, and a LUSH. That may be just enough. *3930 Las Vegas Blvd. S. (btw. Luxor & Mandalay Bay).* ☎ *702/632-9333. AE, DC, DISC, MC, V. Map p 61.*

★★ **The Palazzo: Shoppes at The Palazzo** MID-STRIP It's less fun than its sister Grand Canal Shoppes, but if you're a fashionista with money to burn go ahead and empty your wallet at Christian Louboutin, Michael Kors, Chloe, and the other luxe boutiques here. Anna Wintour would approve. *3327 Las Vegas Blvd. S.* ☎ *702/414-4525. www.theshoppesatthepalazzo.com. AE, DC, DISC, MC, V. Map p 61.*

Paris Las Vegas: Le Boulevard SOUTH STRIP Ooo-la-la! It's *le petit Paree,* complete with cobblestone streets, quaint lampposts, replicas of the Pont Alexandre III and the Eiffel Tower, shops carrying chic sunglasses and watches, French imports such as Yves Saint-Laurent and Christian Lacroix, and a host of premium foods and wines. *3655 Las Vegas Blvd. S.* ☎ *702/739-4111. www.parislv.com. AE, DC, DISC, MC, V. Map p 61.*

★★ **Planet Hollywood: Miracle Mile Shops** SOUTH STRIP The once sumptuous, exotically themed Desert Passage has been remodeled into a gizmo-equipped whiz-bang generic version of an upper-end American mall. The

Combine top-notch shopping and an Ancient Roman–theme with some tacky elements, and you get The Forum Shops, the quintessential Vegas shopping destination.

stores themselves stand out, but the experience ain't what it used to be. *3667 Las Vegas Blvd. S.* ☎ *702/866-0703. www.miracle milesshopslv.com. AE, DC, DISC, MC, V. Map p 61.*

★★ The Venetian: The Grand Canal Shoppes MID-STRIP   Stroll through St. Mark's Square and wander along a faux Grand Canal replete with serenading gondoliers. *Trompe l'oeil* clouds float past the "roofs" of the 15th-century-style "houses" that are home to stores fit for the Doge, including Jimmy Choo, Mikimoto, Valentino, and Kenneth Cole. Performers who interact with shoppers while in period costume complete the experience. *3355 Las Vegas Blvd. S.* ☎ *702/414-4525. www. thegrandcanalshoppes.com. AE, DC, DISC, MC, V. Map p 61.*

Wynn Las Vegas: Wynn Esplanade NORTH STRIP   Not as large as Via Bellagio, this marble-walled stroll features such dream-and-drool-inducing retailers as Cartier, Judith Leiber, and Oscar de la Renta. *In Wynn Las Vegas, 3131 Las Vegas Blvd. S.* ☎ *702/770-7000. www. wynnlasvegas.com. AE, DC, DISC, MC, V. Map p 61.*

Jewelry

★★★ Fred Leighton MID-STRIP   Specializing in period estate jewelry—including expensive turn-of-the-20th-century and Art Deco baubles dripping with emeralds, sapphires, rubies, and other precious and semi-precious stones—this boutique showcases one-of-a-kind works of envy- and swoon-inducing art. This is where I would blow all my jackpots. *In Via Bellagio, 3600 Las Vegas Blvd. S.* ☎ *702/693-7050. AE, DC, MC, V. Map p 61.*

★★ Harry Winston MID-STRIP   *The* diamond dealer for haute couture consumers. Winston's stones

Won a slot jackpot and want some bling to celebrate the victory? Harry Winston is the place . . . but it better have been a big jackpot.

shine as brightly as the stars who wear them on red carpets. *In The Forum Shops at Caesars Palace, 3500 Las Vegas Blvd. S.* ☎ *702/933-7370. www.harrywinston.com. AE, DC, MC, V. Map p 61.*

★ Mikimoto Pearls MID-STRIP   The originator of cultured pearls, Mikimoto has been creating the famous smooth white Akoyo pearl since 1893. The store also carries cultured South Sea pearls in shades of gray, pink, and cream. *In The Venetian Grand Canal Shoppes, 3355 Las Vegas Blvd. S.* ☎ *702/414-3900. www.mikimotoamerica.com. AE, DC, DISC, MC, V. Map p 61.*

★★ Tiffany & Co. MID-STRIP   There may be some who are unmoved by the power of Tiffany, even after Truman Capote and Miss Hepburn explained it to all, but I am not one of them. Even just a simple diamond seems to sparkle more brightly in a Tiffany setting. *In Via Bellagio, 3600 Las Vegas Blvd. S.* ☎ *702/697-5400. AE, DC, DISC, MC, V. Map p 61.*

Malls

The Boulevard EAST OF THE STRIP Dillard's, Macy's, Sears, and JCPenney are the anchors at this mall, which has 140 retail stores, including Old Navy, The Body Shop, and Radio Shack. Out-of-state visitors can visit the Customer Service Center for special offers. *3528 S. Maryland Pkwy. (btw. Twain Ave. & Desert Inn Rd.).* ☎ *702/735-8268. www.blvdmall. com. AE, DISC, MC, V. Map p 62.*

★★ Fashion Show MID-STRIP One of the strangest design elements ever seen in a shopping center—or anywhere else for that matter—is the giant twisted steel sculpture called *The Cloud,* which hovers above the entrance as part of a multimedia display featuring LED screens, flashing lights, and music. During the winter, fake snow drifts down on shoppers visiting the 240 shops, including Neiman Marcus, Macy's, Saks Fifth Avenue, and Nevada's only branch of Nordstrom. It's so very Vegas. *3200 Las Vegas Blvd. S.* ☎ *702/784-7000. www.thefashionshow.com. AE, DISC, MC, V. Map p 61.*

★ The Galleria at Sunset WEST OF STRIP Along with Macy's, Dillard's, and JCPenney, this immense and well-stocked suburban mall is home to a Sanrio store (home of Hello Kitty and friends), Lane Bryant, and a slew of other mall standards. *1300 W. Sunset Rd. (at Stephanie St., just off I-15), Henderson.* ☎ *702/434-0202. www.galleriaatsunset.com. AE, DISC, MC, V. Map p 61.*

★ Meadows Mall WEST OF STRIP This ultramodern mall combines a wide range of traditional mall shops, such as Victoria's Secret, Kay Jewelers, Sunglass Hut, and Foot Locker, with an anchor lineup of Macy's, Dillard's, Sears, and JCPenney. *4300 Meadows Lane.* ☎ *702/878-3331. www.meadowsmall.com. AE, DISC, MC, V. Map p 62.*

★ Town Square Las Vegas SOUTH OF STRIP Each of this attractive outdoor mall's 22 buildings is designed in a different international style, luring shoppers and architecture buffs alike. The eclectic collection of retailers and restaurants includes Whole Foods, H&M, Guess, and a giant movieplex. *6605 Las Vegas Blvd. S. (south of Mandalay Bay).* ☎ *702/269-5000. www. townsquarelasvegas.com. AE, DISC, MC, V. Map p 61.*

Toys

★ kids FAO Schwarz MID-STRIP An animatronic two-story Trojan horse will bid you welcome and a warm farewell as you leave bearing gifts from this landmark toy store, which sells its own line of stuffed animals, plus trains, dolls, action figures, and so forth. *In The Forum Shops at Caesars Palace, 3500 Las Vegas Blvd. S.* ☎ *702/796-6500. www.fao.com. AE, DISC, MC, V. Map p 61.* ●

Guarded by an animatronic Trojan horse that wows shoppers, FAO Schwarz is Vegas's top toy store.

5 The Best **Casinos**

Casino Best Bets

The casino at the MGM Grand is arguably the largest in the world—you'll get lost at least once.

Most **Glamorous**
Bellagio, *3600 Las Vegas Blvd. S. (p 77)*

Most **Visually Stimulating**
New York–New York, *3790 Las Vegas Blvd. S. (p 79)*

Best **Casino for Budget Gamblers**
Main Street Station, *200. N. Main St. (p 78)*

Best **Layout**
Red Rock Resort, *10973 W. Charleston Rd. (p 80)*

Least **Smoky**
Mandalay Bay, *3930 Las Vegas Blvd. S. (p 79)*

Most **Comfortable Chairs**
Wynn Las Vegas, *3131 Las Vegas Blvd. S. (p 80)*

Most **Airy**
Luxor, *3900 Las Vegas Blvd. S. (p 78)*

Most **Likely to Become Lost In**
MGM Grand, *3799 Las Vegas Blvd. S. (p 79)*

Best **Smoke-Free Poker Rooms**
Bellagio, *3600 Las Vegas Blvd. S. (p 77);* or Mirage, *3400 Las Vegas Blvd. S. (p 79)*

Best **Fake Sky**
Paris, *3655 Las Vegas Blvd. S. (p 79)*

Most **Confusing to Navigate**
Caesars Palace, *3500 Las Vegas Blvd. S. (p 77)*

Most **Rock 'n' Roll**
Hard Rock, *4455 Paradise Rd. (p 78)*

Best **Classic Casino**
Binion's Horseshoe, *128 E. Fremont St. (p 77)*

Friendliest **Poker Tables**
MGM Grand, *3799 Las Vegas Blvd. S. (p 79)*

Most **Distracting**
Circus Circus, *2880 Las Vegas Blvd. S. (p 77)*

Best **Lit**
Gold Coast, *4000 W. Flamingo Rd. (p 78)*

Previous Page: The casino floor at the Rio All-Suite Hotel & Casino.

Casinos **on the Strip**

Downtown Casinos

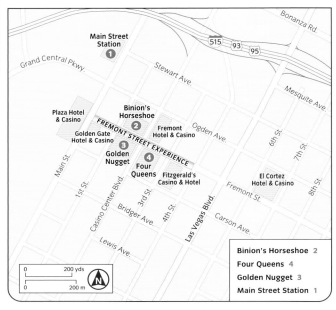

Binion's Horseshoe 2
Four Queens 4
Golden Nugget 3
Main Street Station 1

Casinos A to Z

Rating Alert

When it comes to casinos, the general rule is "you love where you win, you hate where you lose." A casino could be stunning and you'll still loathe it if you lose a bundle there. Because luck is so annoyingly unpredictable and casino choice so personal a selection, you won't find star ratings in this chapter. I hope you end up loving all of them.

Bally's MID-STRIP Something of an afterthought on the Strip, there's still a lot to like about this casino. Ceilings are high and machines are well spaced, so it doesn't feel

crowded. Because it has less of a profile, the casino seems to try harder, and that results in a pleasant place to gamble. *3645 Las Vegas Blvd. S.* ☎ *702/739-4111. www. ballyslv.com. Map p 75.*

For a big thrill—if not the largest jackpot—visit one of the casinos and play a giant slot machine like this one in Bally's.

Bellagio MID-STRIP The fancy-pants casino in town. It's just a tiny bit intimidating for some, sophisticated and grown-up for others, and a little bit bland for me. It does get points for the high ceilings and the grid layout, which make navigating this place less of a chaotic experience. *3600 Las Vegas Blvd. S.* ☎ *702/693-7111. www.bellagio.com. Map p 75.*

Binion's Horseshoe DOWN-TOWN The former home of the World Series of Poker (now moved to the Rio), Binion's is still the place serious gamblers are about their business, which isn't to say it's not fun, but rather a particular kind of fun. Thanks to the newest in a long string of owners, the place looks a little less dingy. Lower table limits and good craps odds are big attractions. *128 E. Fremont St.* ☎ *702/382-1600. www. binions.com. Map p 76.*

Caesars Palace MID-STRIP It's a great big rambling mess of a casino (getting lost is a Vegas rite of passage), but despite the sprawl this is still an oh-so-Vegas place to gamble, with glitzy chandeliers, toga-clad waitresses, and ginormous "Roman" statues. Some parts of the casino are lighter and more airy than others. The huge sports book and city's largest poker room are pluses. Weekend nights bring the Pussycat Dolls Pit, where go-go girls gyrate above burlesque-clad dealer girls at pink-colored tables with very high limits. *3570 Las Vegas Blvd. S.* ☎ *702/731-7110. www.caesars.com. Map p 75.*

Circus Circus NORTH STRIP Surely the most gimmick-laden casino in town, where the main action is covered by a Big Top in which various highflying circus performers do their thing virtually around the clock. Obviously, this is meant as a way to entertain the kids—many of whom pass through the area, making it exceedingly noisy and crowded—while

adults spend their college tuition funds. *2880 Las Vegas Blvd. S.* ☎ *702/734-0410. www.circuscircus. com. Map p 75.*

Encore Las Vegas NORTH STRIP This pretty and unique space is small enough that it's easy to navigate and it's loaded with natural light, unlike the vampire-friendly confines of most casinos. Low rollers and those who like umpteen options for wagering their cash, however, should look elsewhere. *3121 Las Vegas Blvd. S.* ☎ *800/320-7125. www.encorelasvegas.com. Map p 75.*

Excalibur SOUTH STRIP It's adorned with suits of armor, stained-glass panels, heraldic banners, impressively massive iron chandeliers, and other castle-ready accouterments. Unfortunately, the atmosphere is more cluttered than cool, and the theming appeared less intensive on my last visit, making it even less fun. *3850 Las Vegas Blvd. S.* ☎ *702/597-7777. www.excalibur. com. Map p 75.*

Flamingo Las Vegas MID-STRIP It's been updated here and there over the years, but still reads old school, so though it lacks the pretension of the newer joints on the Strip (a plus), it has a high claustrophobia rating and is a trifle gaudy. Its central location and retro feel make it a good choice for basic play. *3555 Las Vegas Blvd. S.* ☎ *702/733-3111. www.flamingolv.com. Map p 75.*

Four Queens DOWNTOWN Sweetly anachronistic, the Four Queens is just the sort of Downtown casino—low limits and unintimidating crowds—that makes you wonder why you bothered with the behemoths on the Strip in the first place. *202 Fremont St.* ☎ *702/385-4011. www.fourqueens.com. Map p 76.*

Gold Coast WEST OF STRIP   I like this locals' favorite because it's one of the few in Vegas that has windows! It also has high ceilings, and a relatively high number of video-poker machines (and some of those may actually have odds favorable to you . . . the wonders never cease). *4000 W. Flamingo Rd.* ☎ *702/367-7111. www.goldcoastcasino.com. Map p 75.*

Golden Nugget DOWNTOWN   A classy Downtown casino made even better thanks to renovations by its latest owner. In looks and feel, it's the closest thing in the area to a Strip casino, though its table minimums thankfully don't ascend that far. *129 E. Fremont St.* ☎ *702/385-7111. www.goldennugget.com. Map p 76.*

Hard Rock Hotel & Casino EAST OF STRIP   An admirable work of Boomer marketing, where rock music blares, and gamers play on tables designed like piano keyboards with chips emblazoned with musicians' faces. You drop change into Jimi Hendrix–brand slots or kick back in the sports book's reclining leather chairs. Too loud for some, it's the only place to gamble for others. *4455 Paradise Rd.* ☎ *702/693-5000. www.hardrockhotel.com. Map p 75.*

Harrah's MID-STRIP   It's too crowded, smoky, claustrophobic, and dated to make it a first-choice casino, but the Party Pits—where rock music blares and dealers cavort—are a draw. *3475 Las Vegas Blvd. S.* ☎ *702/369-5000. www.harrahs.com. Map p 75.*

Las Vegas Hilton EAST OF STRIP   This classy casino is polished (check out those crystal chandeliers), but the main draw here is the enormous sports book—it's the world's largest and has a video wall that's second in size only to NASA's. *3000 Paradise Rd.* ☎ *702/732-7111. www.lvhilton.com. Map p 75.*

Some of the best bets in town are available inside casino sports books, where you can usually sit down and watch the race you've wagered on.

Learning the Ropes

Hitting up a one-armed bandit (that's a slot machine in gaming lingo) isn't exactly brain surgery, but ignorance won't likely result in bliss if you sit at a poker or craps table when you don't know what you're doing. For a rundown of the major games in town, complete with basic strategy tips, check out "The Savvy Gambler," p 146.

Luxor Las Vegas SOUTH STRIP The tallest casino ceiling on the Strip makes for a low-claustrophobia gambling situation, though I can't forgive them for de-Egyptifying it and making gambling here way less fun. *3900 Las Vegas Blvd. S.* ☎ *702/262-4000. www.luxor.com. Map p 75.*

Main Street Station DOWNTOWN   It's got high ceilings and a delightfully realized theme (turn-of-the-last-century San Francisco, with old-fashioned fans dropping down from a Victorian tin ceiling). The atmosphere, combined with lower-than-Strip limits, makes it a winner. *200 N. Main St.* ☎ *702/387-1896. www.mainstreetcasino.com. Map p 76.*

Mandalay Bay SOUTH STRIP
Thanks to the higher-than-average ceiling, spacious layout, and an attempt to create an elegant atmosphere, this is an appealing place to play. Its southern location means it's often not overwhelmingly crowded, but if there is an event at the hotel's arena or the House of Blues, expect a massive influx of additional players. *3950 Las Vegas Blvd. S.* ☎ *702/632-7777. www. mandalaybay.com. Map p 75.*

MGM Grand SOUTH STRIP   The biggest of the big—171,500 square feet (15,933 sq. m) of gaming space—is divided into four areas in an attempt to reduce it to a manageable size. It doesn't help (getting lost here is a badge of honor). But big doesn't mean impersonal, and some of the friendliest poker tables are found here. *3799 Las Vegas Blvd. S.* ☎ *702/891-7777. www. mgmgrand.com. Map p 75.*

The Mirage MID-STRIP   The old-school tortuous layout makes navigating here a little difficult (as do

The steady ring of a slot machine is one of the signature sounds of a casino.

the crowds), but the vibe is good and the Asian-sleek decor is almost relaxing. *3400 Las Vegas Blvd. S.* ☎ *702/791-7111. www.mirage.com. Map p 75.*

Monte Carlo Resort & Casino SOUTH STRIP   This place tries to evoke gambling in Monaco, and though the decor shows lots of attention, it's a little bit busy. That said, the ceilings are high, it's easy to navigate, and it's definitely one of the best-smelling casinos in town. *3770 Las Vegas Blvd. S.* ☎ *702/730-7777. www.montecarlo. com. Map p 75.*

New York–New York SOUTH STRIP   The N.Y. theming here has been toned down (drat!) to a more generic look, which means that this massive gaming place now doesn't have as much of a fun factor to offset its too hectic, crowded, and distracting atmosphere. *3790 Las Vegas Blvd. S.* ☎ *702/740-6969. www.nynyhotelcasino.com. Map p 75.*

The Orleans WEST OF STRIP
A low claustrophobia level, good video-poker options, and cheaper table minimums lure locals and tourists seeking better odds than those available on the Strip. The Cajun and zydeco music they occasionally play on the sound system makes it that much more fun. *4500 W. Tropicana Ave.* ☎ *702/365-7111. www. orleanscasino.com. Map p 75.*

Paris Las Vegas MID-STRIP
One of the few casinos that's still reveling in its theme (a fact I applaud): It's set beneath a ceiling painted like an April day in Paris and is partly under the feet of the hotel's Eiffel Tower re-creation. The 83,000-square-foot (7,710-sq.-m) gaming area is ringed by Disney-esque European facades. *3655 Las Vegas Blvd. S.* ☎ *702/946-7000. www.parislv.com. Map p 75.*

The Best Casinos

Planet Hollywood SOUTH STRIP An impressive interior showcases classic Hollywood glamour, and all the usual gambling suspects have been rounded up for your betting pleasure. It's not exactly serene (and a little hard to navigate), but it's way calmer—and more fun—than it used to be. *3667 Las Vegas Blvd. S. ☎ 702/736-0111. www. aladdincasino.com. Map p 75.*

Red Rock Resort WEST OF STRIP For sheer, non-theme design, this is the best-looking casino in town, utilizing natural woods, glass ornaments, and stone. Like the rest of the resort, it's a stunner. It's also a convivial place to play. *10973 W. Charleston Blvd. ☎ 702/797-7773. www.redrockstation.com. Map p 75.*

Rio All-Suite Hotel & Casino MID-STRIP The 85,000-square-foot (7,900-sq.-m) main casino is dark and claustrophobic; stick to the section in the Masquerade Village area,

Paris Las Vegas is one the few casinos to still feature a theme—gamble in the shadow of the Eiffel Tower.

which has much higher ceilings and is way more pleasant. And don't get distracted by those scantily costumed waitresses . . . who might break into song and dance every now and then. *3700 W. Flamingo Rd. ☎ 702/252-7777. www.harrahs. com. Map p 75.*

Stratosphere Casino Hotel & Tower NORTH STRIP You'll get more bang for your buck at this low-limit haven, which is often less crowded than many of its Strip cohorts. It's especially good for video poker aficionados. *2000 Las Vegas Blvd. S. ☎ 702/380-7777. www.stratospherehotel.com. Map p 75.*

Treasure Island MID-STRIP They've completely obliterated the dripping-with-plunder pirate theme that used to make this place fun, and all that remains is a nice casino. For most of you, that will be enough. *3300 Las Vegas Blvd. S. ☎ 702/894-7111. www.treasure island.com. Map p 75.*

The Venetian MID-STRIP A theme-happy casino—check out the Venetian art on the ceilings!—that still exudes class. It's hard to navigate, but because the smoke factor is very low and I hit it big here once, I love it. *3355 Las Vegas Blvd. S. ☎ 702/414-1000. www.venetian. com. Map p 75.*

Wynn Las Vegas NORTH STRIP A large but simple layout and the overall classy gestalt are pluses, but on the minus side, table limits are expensive and it's not all that exciting either. No matter; the machines (tight as they may be) run from nickels on up, so park yourself in the most comfortable slot seats in town and save the tables for Downtown. *3131 Las Vegas Blvd. S. ☎ 702/770-7100. www.wynnlasvegas.com. Map p 75.* ●

Dining Best Bets

Best **Coffee Shop**
★★ Peppermill $ *2985 Las Vegas Blvd. S. (p 92)*

Best **Burger**
★★ Burger Bar $ *Mandalay Place, 3930 Las Vegas Blvd. S. (p 87)*

Best **Bakery**
★★ Freed's $ *4780 S. Eastern Ave. (p 90)*

Best **Sushi**
★★★ Shibuya $$$ *MGM Grand, 3799 Las Vegas Blvd. S. (p 94)*

Best **Place to Blow All Your Jackpot Winnings**
★★★ Joël Robuchon $$$$$ *MGM Grand, 3799 Las Vegas Blvd. S. (p 90)*

Best **Thai**
★★★ Lotus of Siam $ *The Commercial Center, 953 E. Sahara Ave. (p 91)*

Best **In-House Celebrity-Chef Meal**
★★★ Alex $$$$ *Wynn Las Vegas, 3131 Las Vegas Blvd. S. (p 85)*

Best **View**
★★ Mix $$$ *Mandalay Place, 3950 Las Vegas Blvd. S. (p 92)*

Best **Breakfast**
★★ Hash House a Go Go $ *6800 W. Sahara Ave. (p 90)*

Best **Off-Strip Dining**
★★★ Raku $ *5030 W. Spring Mountain Rd. (p 93)*

Best **Italian**
★★★ Bartolotta Ristorante di Mare $$$ *Wynn Las Vegas, 3131 Las Vegas Blvd. S. (p 86)*

Best **Steak**
★★★ SW $$$ *Wynn Las Vegas, 3131 Las Vegas Blvd. S. (p 95)*

Previous Page: A gourmet dish from the highly regarded kitchen of L'Atelier Joël Robuchon.

Most **Romantic**
★★★ Alizé $$$ *Palms Casino Resort, 4321 W. Flamingo Rd. (p 85)*

Best **Buffet**
★★★ Wynn Las Vegas Buffet $$ *Wynn Las Vegas, 3131 Las Vegas Blvd. S. (p 96)*

Best **Bistro**
★★★ Bouchon $$ *The Venetian, 3355 Las Vegas Blvd. S. (p 87)*

Best **Inexpensive Meal**
★★★ Capriotti's $ *322 W. Sahara Ave. (p 88)*

Best **Mexican**
★★ Tacos & Tequila $$ *Luxor, 3900 Las Vegas Blvd. S. (p 95)*

Best **Place to Eat Like Liberace**
★★ Carluccio's Tivoli Gardens $$ *1775 E. Tropicana Blvd. (p 88)*

Best **Food Court**
★★ Cypress Street Marketplace $ *Caesars Palace, 3570 Las Vegas Blvd. S. (p 88)*

A peppercorn burger is just one of the tasty offerings served at Burger Bar.

South Strip Restaurants

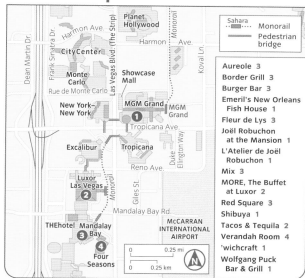

Aureole 3
Border Grill 3
Burger Bar 3
Emeril's New Orleans
  Fish House 1
Fleur de Lys 3
Joël Robuchon
  at the Mansion 1
L'Atelier de Joël
  Robuchon 1
Mix 3
MORE, The Buffet
  at Luxor 2
Red Square 3
Shibuya 1
Tacos & Tequila 2
Verandah Room 4
'wichcraft 1
Wolfgang Puck
  Bar & Grill 1

Mid-Strip Restaurants

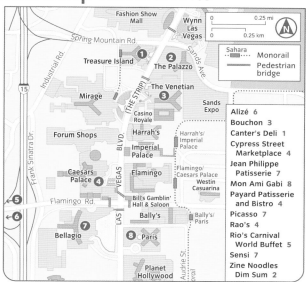

Alizé 6
Bouchon 3
Canter's Deli 1
Cypress Street
  Marketplace 4
Jean Philippe
  Patisserie 7
Mon Ami Gabi 8
Payard Patisserie
  and Bistro 4
Picasso 7
Rao's 4
Rio's Carnival
  World Buffet 5
Sensi 7
Zine Noodles
  Dim Sum 2

Las Vegas Restaurants

Alex **10**
Bartolotta Ristorante
  di Mare **10**
Capriotti's **5**
Carluccio's Tivoli
  Gardens **13**
Dona Maria Tamales **1**
Florida Café **2**
Freed's **12**
Hash House a Go Go **4**
Lotus of Siam **6**
Peppermill **8**
Raku **11**
Society Café Encore **9**
The Steak House **7**
SW **10**
Tiffany's **3**
Wynn Las Vegas
  Buffet **10**

Downtown Restaurants

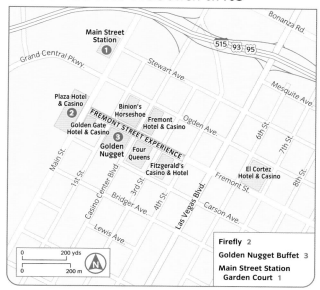

Firefly **2**

Golden Nugget Buffet **3**

Main Street Station
Garden Court **1**

Las Vegas Restaurants A to Z

★★★ **Alex** NORTH STRIP *CONTI-NENTAL* Chef-owner Alex Stratta did a stint on *Iron Chef America*, and though his prix-fixe menus don't come cheap, the complex dishes are thoughtfully put together and don't ignore delicate touches, such as tiny vegetables cooked to the right crunch. The service is equally superb. *In Wynn Las Vegas, 3131 Las Vegas Blvd. S.* ☎ *888/352-DINE [3463] or 702/248-DINE [3463]. Reservations required. Jacket recommended. 3-course prix-fixe menu $165; 7-course tasting menu $210, $350 with wine pairings. AE, DC, DISC, MC, V. Wed–Sat dinner. Map p 84.*

★★★ **Alizé** MID-STRIP *FRENCH* Perhaps the most dazzling space in Vegas, in that the space itself is

simple, but the setting—floating above Vegas and the desert at the top of the Palms—is not. Sit next to one of the floor-to-ceiling windows, and bask. The food is just as ethereal, though the fish is sometimes dry; stick to meat and you'll be happy. *In Palms Casino Resort, 4321 W. Flamingo Rd.* ☎ *702/951-7000. www.alizelv.com. Reservations strongly recommended. Food*

The French cuisine at Alizé is more than a match for its superb views.

minimum $45 per person. Main courses $36–$75; 5-course tasting menu $105; 7-course tasting menu $125. AE, MC, V. Dinner nightly. Map p 83.

★★ **Aureole** SOUTH STRIP *NOUVELLE AMERICAN* The food here is American regional haute, but many also come for the height—the four-story glass wine tower, where bottles are fetched by enticing cat-suited "wine angels" in harnesses. It's a Vegas-style gimmick, but the cuisine is strong enough to stand on its own. *In Mandalay Bay, 3950 Las Vegas Blvd. S.* ☎ *877/632-1766 or 702/632-7401. www.aureolelv.com. Reservations suggested. Prix-fixe dinner $75; tasting menu $95. AE, MC, V. Dinner daily. Map p 83.*

★★★ **Bartolotta Ristorante di Mare** NORTH STRIP *ITALIAN* Award-winning chef Paul Bartolotta gets his fish flown in daily from the Mediterranean, and then cooks it simply, classically, and divinely. You can choose from a variety that may well include species hitherto

The magnificent decor at Bartolotta Ristorante di Mare serves as a proper backdrop to its equally delectable Italian cuisine.

unfamiliar to you, or have an excellent pasta dish instead. The restaurant also has a rare outdoor dining area, complete with modern art. *In Wynn Las Vegas, 3131 Las Vegas*

Dining Tips

Vegas is not the bastion of low-priced dining that many travelers imagine it is. You can eat well or you can eat cheap, but it's not often that you can do both (though I do give you a number of options in this chapter that fit the bill). Even the vaunted buffet doesn't offer as much bang for the buck as it used to if you want food that is more than forgettable. So if you want to please your palate without emptying your wallet, here are a couple of options:

1. **Hit the primo restaurants at lunch.** Prices in this chapter, unless otherwise specified, are for main courses at dinner. Prices at lunch are often discounted 20% to 50%.
2. **Get off the Strip.** Restaurants that don't have to shell out big bucks for the real estate they sit on tend to have lower prices. Plus, restaurants that depend on locals are more invested in keeping their quality up and their prices from reaching the height of the stratosphere.

Blvd. S. ☎ 888/352-DINE (3463) or 702/248-DINE [3463]. Reservations recommended. Main courses dinner $24–$55; family-style tasting $140 per person; Grand Seafood Feast $155 per person. AE, DC, DISC, MC, V. Lunch & dinner daily. Map p 84.

★★ **Border Grill** SOUTH STRIP MEXICAN The Food Network's Two Hot Tamales, Mary Sue and Susan, learned Mexican home-style cooking south of the border, and put their own twist on traditional dishes. It's not the place to go for plain old tacos—though you can, if you like—and you should skip the often bland fish dishes. In Mandalay Bay, 3950 Las Vegas Blvd. S. ☎ 702/632-7403. www.bordergrill.com. Reservations recommended. Main courses $15–$30. AE, DC, DISC, MC, V. Lunch & dinner daily. Map p 83.

★★★ **Bouchon** MID-STRIP BISTRO You won't find famed owner-chef Thomas Keller in the kitchen, but you also won't be disappointed. There's a deep satisfaction that comes from consuming this superlative bistro's regional French cooking in all its deserved glory. In The Venetian, 3355 Las Vegas Blvd. S.

Border Grill is renowned for its twists on traditional Mexican cuisine.

You can't do much better for bistro cooking in Vegas than Thomas Keller's Bouchon.

☎ 702/414-6200. www.bouchon bistro.com. Reservations strongly recommended. Main courses $8–$48. Oyster bar $15–$99. AE, DC, MC, V. Breakfast & dinner daily. Sat–Sun brunch. Map p 83.

★★ **Burger Bar** SOUTH STRIP DINER A little costly for "just" a burger; but diners get to build their own custom creation from a menu containing dozens of topping options, so the markup is nearly worth it. It can be fun and creative (though I think there is no good reason to have truffles and lobster on your burger). Skip the Kobe beef—it's too much money for a meat that doesn't make a good patty anyway. In Mandalay Place, 3930 Las Vegas Blvd. S. ☎ 702/632-9364. www.fleurdelyssf.com. Main courses $8–$60. AE, DISC, MC, V. Lunch & dinner daily. Map p 83.

★★ **Canter's Deli** MID-STRIP DELI A semireplica of a Los Angeles institution, though minus the ageless waitstaff and with a menu only one-fifth the size of the original's. Still, the pastrami is authentic and so is the brisket, and it smells like a real deli. Plus, black-and-white cookies! In TI, 3300 Las Vegas Blvd. S. ☎ 702/894-7111. AE, DISC, MC, V. Main courses $10–$20. Lunch & dinner daily. Map p 83.

★★★ Capriotti's NORTH STRIP

DELI A rare combination for Vegas: something affordable and delicious. Capriotti's makes enormous submarine sandwiches that inspire such loyalty that many an out-of-town customer has planned their entrance and exit from Vegas around a stop here. Try the Slaw B. Joe, the Bobby, or design your own; opt for the "large" of anything and you can easily feed two. *322 W. Sahara Ave.* ☎ *702/474-0229. www.capriottis. com. All sandwiches under $13. AE, DISC, MC, V. Lunch daily. Map p 84.*

★★ Carluccio's Tivoli Gardens

EAST OF STRIP *ITALIAN* Liberace owned and designed this place, and the interior still look likes it. Need I say more? Okay, it's classic (and very satisfying) American-Italian comfort food: heavy pastas, heavy red sauce, and lots of butter. It's hard to go wrong with a menu where everything is so right. *1775 E. Tropicana Blvd. (next to Liberace Museum).* ☎ *702/795-3236. www. carlucciosvegas.com. Main courses $8–$18. AE, DC, DISC, MC, V. Dinner Tues–Sun. Map p 84.*

Dine on first-class French cuisine in sophisticated surroundings at Fleur de Lys.

★★ 🄺🄸🄳🅂 Cypress Street Marketplace MID-STRIP *FOOD COURT*

A better-than-average food court, with an array of unexpected dishes, including North Carolina pulled pork, Vietnamese noodles, and more. Customers are given cards on which their purchases are swiped at each booth, and the total is billed at the cash register. It's an excellent choice for families with a wide array of dietary desires. *In Caesars Palace, 3570 Las Vegas Blvd. S.* ☎ *702/731-7110. Most items under $15. AE, DC, DISC, MC, V. Breakfast, lunch & dinner daily. Map p 83.*

★★ Dona Maria Tamales NORTH STRIP *MEXICAN*

Classic Mexican food that's heavy on the lard, heavy on the sauces, heavy on the crowds (especially at lunch), and light on the wallet. You definitely want to try the tamales, but the enchiladas and chiles rellenos are excellent, too. *910 Las Vegas Blvd. S.* ☎ *702/382-6538. www.donamariatamales.com. Main courses $8–$17. AE, DC, DISC, MC, V. Breakfast, lunch & dinner daily. Map p 84.*

★ Emeril's New Orleans Fish House SOUTH STRIP *CREOLE*

Not as reliable as the original in New Orleans, and the fish dishes are often the least impressive. But a Creole-spiced rib-eye has Emeril's infamous kick, and the decadent lobster cheesecake is like nothing you've ever tried before. *In MGM Grand, 3799 Las Vegas Blvd. S.* ☎ *702/891-7374. www.emerils.com. Reservations recommended. Main courses $28–$46 (more for lobster). AE, DC, DISC, MC, V. Lunch & dinner daily. Map p 83.*

★★ Firefly DOWNTOWN *TAPAS*

Late hours, flashy Downtown views and tantalizing Spanish tapas account for Firefly's popularity. The

The classic Mexican cuisine at Dona Maria Tamales is beloved by young and old alike.

glass-dome location looks directly out on the Fremont Street Experience, so you can watch both the light show and the leering tourists drinking beer out of giant plastic football-shaped mugs as you savor white sangria and bacon-wrapped dates from your sexy red circular booth. *In The Plaza, 1 Main St. ☎ 702/380-1352. www.fireflylv.com. All items under $10. AE, DISC, MC, V. Dinner and late-night. Map p 85.*

★★★ **Fleur de Lys** SOUTH STRIP *FRENCH* From celebrity chef Hubert Keller you get a sexy, sophisticated setting where you dine on cunningly designed seasonal creations in multicourse tasting menus priced better than many peers in town. From the scallops served with smoked salmon and sour cream ravioli to the artfully constructed desserts to the wonderful service, you won't go wrong here. *In Mandalay Bay, 3950 Las Vegas Blvd. S. ☎ 702/632-9400. www.fleurdelyssf.com. Reservations recommended. Jacket recommended. A la carte $19–$125, tasting menu $130. AE, DC, DISC, MC, V. Dinner daily. Map p 83.*

★ **Florida Café** DOWNTOWN *CUBAN* Located in a HoJo's surrounded by wedding chapels, this

Getting a Table

The growing reputation of Vegas as a foodie haven means that getting a table at the best spots is a lot harder than it used to be. If you can, make reservations in advance or you may find that spot you had your hearts set on totally booked throughout your stay. And note that at places that don't take reservations (especially in the casino hotels), you may find yourself standing in line for a while to get inside (unless you gamble enough to get a pass that will get you in faster—see p 146 for details on comps).

downtown spot is a pretty random place for a Cuban restaurant, but one taste of the authentic yucca with mojo, and I forget all about Howard Johnson. The tropical decor sets the mood and the inexpensive *ropa vieja* and *croquetas de jamon* seal the deal. Come for the tasty food, not the service, which can be fairly apathetic. *In Howard Johnson, 1401 Las Vegas Blvd. S.* ☎ *702/385-3013. www.floridacubancafe.com. Main courses $7–$12. MC, V. Breakfast, lunch & dinner daily. Map p 84.*

★★ **Freed's** EAST OF STRIP *BAKERY* An old-fashioned bakery in a new-fashioned town. It sells creamy cakes, buttery cookies, and sugary and gooey everything. Much of it is made with incredibly fresh ingredients; all of it works for those of us with a sweet tooth. *4780 S. Eastern Ave.* ☎ *866/933-5253. www.freeds bakery.com. Most pastries under $6. AE, DISC, MC, V. Open daily. Map p 84.*

★★ **Golden Nugget Buffet** DOWNTOWN *BUFFET* Downtown is one of the last holdouts for bargains; you'd pay least $2 to $3 more for a buffet of this quality on the Strip. Most of the seating is in plush

The best Strip-side dining in Vegas is at Mon Ami Gabi; the bistro fare is great too.

booths, and the tables are laden with an extensive salad bar, delicious fruit, fresh seafood, and marvelous desserts. Most lavish is the Friday-through-Sunday Seafood and More buffet. *In the Golden Nugget, 129 E. Fremont St.* ☎ *702/385-7111. Breakfast $10; lunch $11; dinner $18, Sat–Sun brunch $17; Fri–Sun Seafood & More buffet $21. AE, DC, DISC, MC, V. Breakfast, lunch & dinner daily. Map p 85.*

★★★ **Hash House a Go Go** WEST OF STRIP *BREAKFAST* A suitably goofy concept restaurant, where breakfast is taken to the limit as salmon and cream cheese are worked into the hash, the pancakes are the size of a large pizza, and the waffles have bacon baked right into them. Dinner brings other excellent options, but you want to make the drive here for breakfast. Prices aren't dirt-cheap, but everything is meant to be shared. *6800 W. Sahara Ave.* ☎ *702/804-4646. www.hash houseagogo.com. Main courses $9–$20. AE, MC, V. Breakfast & lunch daily, dinner Mon–Sat. Map p 84.*

★★★ **Jean Philippe Patisserie** MID-STRIP *CAFE/BAKERY* The product of an award-winning pastry chef, the Patisserie first attracted notice for its immense chocolate fountain, and then inspired deep devotion with such fare as a *dulce de leche*–stuffed brioche, serious gourmet chocolates, authentic gelato, and much more. It also serves sandwiches and crepes both savory and sweet, making this a perfect spot for a light meal. *In Bellagio, 3600 Las Vegas Blvd. S.* ☎ *702/693-8788. All items $3.50–$12. AE, DC, DISC, MC, V. Open daily. Map p 83.*

★★★ **Joël Robuchon at the Mansion** SOUTH STRIP *FRENCH* Knowledgeable foodies worldwide were all atwitter when much-lauded master chef Robuchon was coaxed

In the battle for best buffet in Vegas, the Wynn wins.

out of early retirement and into this lush fine-dining venture. It will be a pricey experience, but you shouldn't expect to pay less for great art—and that's what Robuchon offers, masterpieces on a plate, all served with multi-Michelin-starred attention and care. *In MGM Grand, 3799 Las Vegas Blvd. S.* ☎ *702/891-7925. www.joel-robuchon.com. Reservations strongly recommended. 6-course tasting menu $250, 16-course tasting menu $385. AE, DC, DISC, MC, V. Dinner daily. Map p 83.*

★★★ **L'Atlier de Joël Robuchon** SOUTH STRIP *FRENCH* This is the casual, counter-seating version of the formal restaurant run by legendary chef Joël Robuchon. Prices here are lower, the vibe is lively rather than reverent, and the food not only is just as good as over at the main facility, but is some of the finest French food in the world. Plan enough time and appetite to sample as many of the delicate, playful, fanciful creations as you can. *In MGM Grand, 3799 Las Vegas*

One of the divine pastries sold at Jean Phillipe Patisserie: Each is worth every calorie.

Blvd. S. ☎ *702/891-7358. www.joel-robuchon.com. Reservations strongly recommended. Average check $60–$70 per person. AE, DC, DISC, MC, V. Dinner daily. Map p 83.*

★★★ **Lotus of Siam** EAST OF STRIP *THAI* Its legend rests on its coronation, some years ago, by *Gourmet* magazine as the best Thai food in North America. Really? I haven't tried them all, but I have journeyed to this strip mall hole-in-the-wall restaurant, and was glad. Be sure to ask for the special-items menu to get the full effect of the authenticity. *In the Commercial Center, 953 E. Sahara Ave.* ☎ *702/735-3033. www.saipin chutima.com. Reservations strongly recommended for dinner. Lunch buffet $9; main courses $9–$24. AE, DISC, MC, V. Lunch Mon–Fri; dinner daily. Map p 84.*

★★★ kids **Main Street Station Garden Court** DOWNTOWN *BUFFET* Like pretty much everything else in Vegas, the classic buffet—and by that I mean mounds of food for budget prices—is gradually getting edged out in favor of flashy-looking high-cost places. This place has found the sweet spot of value, serving really quite good buffet staples for value prices. *In the Main Street Station, 200 N. Main St.* ☎ *702/387-1896. Breakfast $7; lunch $8; dinner $11–$16; weekend champagne brunch $11. Free for children 3 & under.*

AE, DC, DISC, MC, V. Breakfast, lunch & dinner daily. Map p 85.

★★ **Mix** SOUTH STRIP *FRENCH AMERICAN* With its white decor and 15,000-bulb chandelier (cost: $500,000), the interior of Chef Alain Ducasse's ultra mod restaurant feels bubbly like champagne. But it's the 360-degree views from the 64th floor of Mandalay Bay that will really make you dizzy. The menu is a balanced mix of meat, game, and seafood, each with its own subtle French twist. Though the food's decadent, you'll leave feeling satisfied but not uncomfortable. *In Mandalay Bay, 3950 Las Vegas Blvd. S.* ☎ *877/632-1766 or 702/632-9500. www.chinagrillmgt.com/mixlv. Reservations suggested. Average check $90/person. AE, MC, V. Dinner daily. Map p 83.*

★★ **Mon Ami Gabi** MID-STRIP *BISTRO* Along with a delicious steak and pommes frites, Mon Ami Gabi delivers some of the best first-floor views in Las Vegas. The French bistro is located at the foot of the fake Eiffel Tower and across from Bellagio's fountain show. Despite a minor identity crisis (Am I in Paris? Italy? A drug-addled *Fear and Loathing* dream?), this is prime territory to enjoy Las Vegas' frenetic beauty, as well as a good, affordable meal). *In Paris Las Vegas, 3655 Las Vegas Blvd. S.* ☎ *702/944-4224. www. monamigabi.com/vegas. Main courses $12–$40. AE, DC, DISC, MC, V. Breakfast, lunch & dinner daily. Map p 83.*

★★ **kids** **MORE, The Buffet at Luxor** SOUTH STRIP *BUFFET* In a move to de-Egypt a hotel set in a pyramid (as if!), what used to be a fun, themed buffet is now neato modern classy. I want my mummies back! That said, the food is the best in its price range and the offerings are satisfyingly diverse. The

For masterful French cuisine in an equally inspired setting, look no further than Joël Robuchon at the Mansion.

desserts are notable only for the pretty large selection of diabetic-friendly options. *In Luxor, 3900 Las Vegas Blvd. S.* ☎ *702/262-4000. Breakfast $15; lunch $16; dinner $20; Champagne brunch $20. AE, DC, DISC, MC, V. Breakfast, lunch & dinner daily. Map p 83.*

★★★ **Payard Patisserie and Bistro** MID-STRIP *BISTRO/BAKERY* The invisible chocolate-scented come-hither finger will guide you through Caesars to Payard, owned by renowned Pastry Chef Francois Payard. Though famous for its sweets, this is actually the go-to spot for a power breakfast. The eggs Florentine are hearty, the chocolate croissants decadent, and the crepes are calling your name. *In Caesars Palace, 3570 Las Vegas Blvd. S.* ☎ *877/ 346-4642. Main courses $14–$27. AE, DC, DISC, MC, V. Breakfast & lunch daily. Map p 83.*

★★ **Peppermill** NORTH STRIP *COFFEE SHOP* When a high-end coffee shop collides with a swanky '70s lounge, the Peppermill happens. Fake cherry trees and servers in floor-length regalia add to the strangely colorful spot—think Denny's on LSD—that's open 24 hours a day. The food is overpriced but reliable, from the 24-hour breakfast and burgers to the hearty steaks. *2985 Las Vegas Blvd. S.* ☎ *702/735-4177. www.peppermillasvegas.com. Entrees $9–$27. AE, D, MC, V. Open 24 hours. Map p 84.*

★★★ **Picasso** MID-STRIP *FRENCH* Julian Serrano is one of the few celebrity chefs in town who actually works in his own kitchen. Meals are multicourse tasting menus, which rotate regularly, but for your sake, I hope it includes the Maine lobster with corn trio, including a corn flan that is like consuming sunshine. It's hard to compete with the many Picassos hanging on the walls, but Serrano manages it. *In Bellagio, 3600 Las Vegas Blvd. S.* ☎ *877/234-6358 or 702/693-8105. Reservations recommended. 4-course menu, $113; 5-course degustation $123. AE, DC, DISC, MC, V. Dinner Wed–Mon. Map p 83.*

★★★ **Raku** WEST OF STRIP *JAPANESE* Curious where celebrity chefs such as Joël Robuchon eat? The answer is Raku, a tiny restaurant serving some of the most innovative food in town. The Japanese small plates range from soups and skewers to Kobe beef liver and Kurobuta pork cheek and are made even more delicious when seasoned with the house-made salt (seaweed-, shitake mushroom–, and green tea–flavored) and soy sauce. *5030 W. Spring Mountain Rd. #2* ☎ *702/367-3511. www.raku-grill.com. Small plates $1.50–$16. AE, MC, V. Dinner Mon–Sat. Map p 84.*

★★ **Rao's** MID-STRIP *ITALIAN* The legendary New York eatery is notorious for the impossibility of actually eating there because of its small size. So thank Caesars for increasing the odds of getting a seat

at this Vegas branch by re-creating the interior twice over, plus adding a new patio area. They've also imported the menu untouched, so you can try the famous lemon chicken, baseball-sized meatballs, or any of the other Italian home-cooked items that have made Rao's name. *In Caesars Palace, 3570 Las Vegas Blvd. S.* ☎ *877/346-4642. www.raos.com. Reservations recommended. Main courses $23–$45. AE, DC, DISC, MC, V. Lunch Wed–Sun, dinner daily. Map p 83.*

★★ **Red Square** SOUTH STRIP *CONTINENTAL/RUSSIAN* When I think of this restaurant, it's usually because of the hilarity of its over-the-top interior—a post-Communist party riot of Bolshevik and Soviet-era gewgaws. Then I think of the ice bar and the impressive vodka selection, one of the largest in the world. Then I remember that the food, especially the Roquefort-crusted filet mignon, is really quite good. And I wonder why I don't think of that first. Then I remember the headless statue of Lenin out front and get distracted all over again. *In Mandalay Bay, 3950 Las Vegas Blvd.*

Dine on excellent French cuisine while surrounded by millions of dollars worth of art at Picasso.

The Soviet theme at Red Square may cause a double take, but nobody complains about the Russian cuisine—or the world-class collection of vodkas.

S. ☎ 702/632-7407. www.chinagrill mgt.com. *Reservations recommended. Main courses $26–$39. AE, DC, MC, V. Dinner daily. Map p 83.*

★★ **Rio's Carnival World Buffet** MID-STRIP *BUFFET* Locals have long voted this the best in Vegas; I say that, qualitywise, it's probably better than ever, if not the best. The cuisines offered are pretty global (Mexican, Chinese, Brazilian, Italian, and more), and there's even a diner setup for burgers, fries, and milkshakes. Best of all, the desserts (usually disappointing at Vegas buffets) are worth blowing your diet on. *In Rio All-Suite Hotel & Casino, 3700 W. Flamingo Rd. ☎ 702/252-7777. Breakfast $15; lunch $17; dinner $24; Sat–Sun champagne brunch $24. AE, DC, MC, V. Breakfast, lunch & dinner daily. Map p 83.*

★★ **Sensi** MID-STRIP *ECLECTIC* Usually a place with "a little of this, a little of that" is an example of the adage "jack of all trades and master of none." But despite featuring Italian, American, grilled, and Asian-influenced dishes, Sensi is successful across the entirety of its eclectic menu. The lunchtime bento box is a popular item. *In Bellagio, 3600 Las Vegas Blvd. S. ☎ 702/693-7223. Main courses $14–$22 lunch; $22–$42 dinner. AE, MC, V. Lunch & dinner daily. Map p 83.*

★★★ **Shibuya** SOUTH STRIP *ASIAN/ SUSHI* A must for sushi fans and sake connoisseurs alike. Rejoice over such signature dishes as *toro tartare* and wild miso salmon, or order the divine tasting menu. The sommelier will gladly pair each course with sake by the glass (the list is the largest in the U.S., and much of it is exclusive to Shibuya) to complete the experience. *In MGM Grand, 3799 Las Vegas Blvd. S. ☎ 702/891-3100. Reservations highly recommended. Average dinner $75 per person. AE, DC, DISC, MC, V. Map p 83.*

★★ **Society Café Encore** NORTH STRIP *AMERICAN* The Belle Epoch–meets–South Beach aesthetic matches the old-meets-new twist on food at Society, with its sliders (filet mignon, charred tuna, and sloppy joe), lobster rolls, and mac and cheese bites with truffle dipping sauce. At first glance, Society appears to be Encore's coffee shop; at first bite, it's clear why it was just named one of "The Best New Restaurants in America" by *Esquire*. *In Encore Las Vegas, 3131 Las Vegas Blvd.* ☎ *702/248-3463. www. encorelasvegas.com. Main courses $19–$40. AE, DISC, MC, V. Breakfast, lunch & dinner daily. Map p 84.*

★ **The Steak House** NORTH STRIP *STEAK* Stifle your cynicism and hear me out: The Steak House at Circus Circus *is* good. It's one of the last true vintage steakhouses in town, with cushy booths, dark wood, and dry-aging beef hanging on display as you enter. The no-nonsense, affordable steak house fare—steaks, prime rib, crab legs, chicken—is more delicious than you would ever expect from an age-stained clown-filled casino. *In Circus Circus, 2880 Las Vegas Blvd. S.* ☎ *702/794-3767. Main courses $23–$70. AE, DISC, MC, V. Dinner daily. Map p 84.*

★★★ **SW** NORTH STRIP *STEAK* When Steve Wynn puts his initials on something, you can expect it to be a cut above, and SW fits the bill.

Sensi's bento box is a popular and tasty lunch option.

Chef David Walzog excels at the steak-house classics, such as Caesar salad and a perfectly marbled bone-in rib-eye. It's pricey but worth it. Dine outside by the Lake of Dreams if you can. *In Wynn Las Vegas, 3131 Las Vegas Blvd. S.* ☎ *888/352-3463 or 702/248-3463. www.wynnlasvegas. com. Main courses $28–$60. AE, DISC, MC, V. Dinner daily. Map p 84.*

★ **Tacos & Tequila** SOUTH STRIP *MEXICAN* Vegas might be the only city where you can reasonably expect to find great Mexican food inside of a giant pyramid. Tacos and Tequila goes beyond the goopy enchilada stand-bys, offering light and fresh ceviches (tuna, mahi mahi, and shrimp), memorable *carnitas,* and eclectic tacos (falafel, spicy Mexican pork, and so forth). With more than 100 tequilas to choose from, expect a spirited crowd. *In Luxor, 3900 Las Vegas Blvd. S.* ☎ *702/262-5225. www.tacosandtequilalv.com. Main courses $13–$24. AE, DISC, MC, V. Lunch & dinner daily. Map p 83.*

★ **Tiffany's** NORTH STRIP *DINER* This unflashy, 60-year-old coffee shop was Las Vegas's first 24-hour restaurant. Plunk down at the counter and gorge yourself on basic American comfort food; the best bet is the ⅓-pound burger and "thick, creamy shake"—both for around $6! Note, however, that the surrounding neighborhood can be rough. *1700 Las Vegas Blvd. S. (at East Oakey Blvd.).* ☎ *702/444-4459. Most items under $8. No credit cards. Daily 24 hr. Map p 84.*

★ **Verandah Room** SOUTH STRIP *BREAKFAST/BRUNCH* Dine outdoors if you can at this elegant Mediterranean-style restaurant at Four Seasons. The breakfast/brunch buffet offered on weekends is so deliciously eye-opening—think fresh squeezed juices, homemade donuts, addictive scones, and innovative egg creations—it manages to stand above competition. In Vegas buffetland, that's saying a lot. *In Four Seasons, 3960 Las Vegas Blvd. S. ☎ 702/632-5000. www. fourseasons.com/lasvegas. Weekend breakfast buffet adults $35, children 4–12 $16. AE, DC, DISC, MC, V. Sat & Sun 8am–1pm. Map p 83.*

★ **'wichcraft** SOUTH STRIP *SAND-WICHES* Too often "sandwich" is synonymous with "boring." Not so at Tom Colicchio's 'wichcraft, where the *Top Chef* judge layers intrigue between slices of bread, along with soups, salads, and panini. It's pricier than your typical chain sub shop, but sink your teeth into the Sicilian tuna with fennel, black olives, and lemon on baguette, and you'll understand why. *In MGM Grand, 3799 Las Vegas Blvd. S. ☎ 702/891-1111. Average check $10–$15. AE, DC, DISC, MC, V. Lunch daily. Map p 83.*

★★ **Wolfgang Puck Bar & Grill** SOUTH STRIP *CALIFORNIA* Get your Puck fix at this moderately priced establishment, where there is nothing surprising on the menu (except maybe the potato chips drizzled with truffle oil and blue cheese) and the wine list is quite solid. *In MGM Grand, 3799 Las Vegas Blvd. S. ☎ 702/891-3000. www.wolfgangpuck.com. Reservations recommended. Main*

courses $18–$35. AE, DC, DISC, MC, V. Lunch, dinner & late-night daily. Map p 83.

★★★ **Wynn Las Vegas Buffet** NORTH STRIP *BUFFET* It may be the most expensive buffet in town, but it's also the best. Hands down. After all, there is Indian food, Kansas City–style barbecue, Southern specialties, ceviche, jerk chicken, and a dessert station that for once isn't a waste of calories. *In Wynn Las Vegas, 3131 Las Vegas Blvd. S. ☎ 702/770-3463. Breakfast $18; lunch $22; dinner Sun–Thurs $34, Fri–Sat $38; Sat–Sun brunch $30–$37. AE, DC, DISC, MC, V. Breakfast, lunch & dinner Mon–Fri; brunch & dinner Sat–Sun. Map p 84.*

★★ **Zine Noodles Dim Sum** MID-STRIP *CHINESE* Chinatown flavors collide with Strip luxury. The tastes here are so authentic that *Chinese News* named Zine 1 of the top 100 Chinese restaurants in the U.S. You won't find Americanized classics such as General Tso's chicken, but when you try the soy-flavored beef chow fun, Peking duck, and *siu mai* (steamed shrimp and pork dumpling) you certainly won't be missing it. *In Palazzo, 3325 Las Vegas Blvd. S. ☎ 877/883-6423 or 702/607-2220. Main courses $16–$29. AE, DISC, MC, V. Lunch & dinner daily. Map p 83.* ●

Sushi fans and sake lovers are catered to at Shibuya, where the general Asian cuisine is nothing to sneeze at.

Nightlife Best Bets

Best Cocktail Lounge
★★ Petrossian, *Bellagio, 3600 Las Vegas Blvd. S. (p 102)*

Best Retro Scene
★ Peppermill's Fireside Lounge, *2985 Las Vegas Blvd. S. (p 102)*

Best Place to Celebrity Watch
★★★ Tao, *The Venetian, 3355 Las Vegas Blvd. S. (p 106)* or ★★★ PURE, *Caesars Palace, 3570 Las Vegas Blvd. S. (p 105)*

Best Gay Bar
★★ Krave, *Planet Hollywood Hotel & Casino, 3667 Las Vegas Blvd. S. (p 107)*

Best Place to Make a Fool of Yourself
★ Coyote Ugly, *New York–New York, 3790 Las Vegas Blvd. S. (p 101)*

Best Downtown Nightlife
★ Hogs & Heifers, *201 N. 3rd St. (p 102)*

Best View
★★ ghostbar, *Palms Resort & Casino, 4321 W. Flamingo Rd. (p 102)*

Best Blues
Sand Dollar Blues Lounge, *3355 Spring Mountain Rd. (p 103)*

Best Microbrews
★ Triple 7 Brew Pub, *Main Street Station, 200 N. Main St. (p 103)*

Best Grown-Up Nightclub
★★ PURE, *Caesars Palace, 3570 Las Vegas Blvd. S. (p 105)*

Best Neighborhood Punk Rock Hangout
★★★ Double Down Saloon, *4640 Paradise Rd. (p 101)*

Friendliest Club on the Strip
★ Tabu, *MGM Grand, 3799 Las Vegas Blvd. S. (p 106)*

Best Piano Bar
★★ The Bar at Times Square, *New York–New York, 3790 Las Vegas Blvd. S. (p 101)*

Best Strip Club
★★★ Treasures, *2801 Westwood Dr. (p 108)*

It's a tourist trap, but Coyote Ugly is packed every night by visitors eager to see its bar-dancing waitresses. Previous page: The bars in Las Vegas are renowned for mixing a wide array of fabulous cocktails.

Las Vegas Nightlife

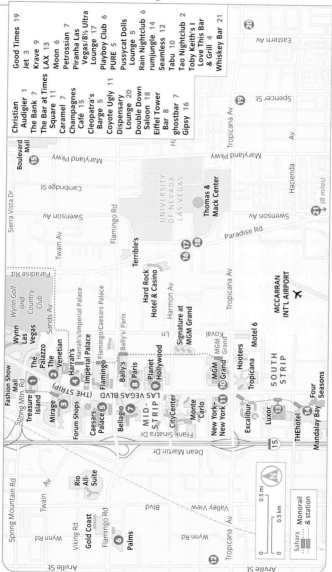

Christian Audigier 1
The Bank 7
The Bar at Times Square 11
Caramel 7
Champagnes Café 15
Cleopatra's Barge 5
Coyote Ugly 11
Dispensary Lounge 20
Double Down Saloon 18
Eiffel Tower Bar 8
ghostbar 7
Gipsy 16

Good Times 19
Jet 3
Krave 9
LAX 13
Moon 6
Petrossian 7
Piranha Las Vegas/8½ Ultra Lounge 17
Playboy Club 6
PURE 5
Pussycat Dolls Lounge 5
Rain Nightclub 6
rumjungle 14
Seamless 12
Tabu 10
Tao Nightclub 2
Toby Keith's I Love This Bar & Grill 4
Whiskey Bar 21

Nightlife North & West of the Strip

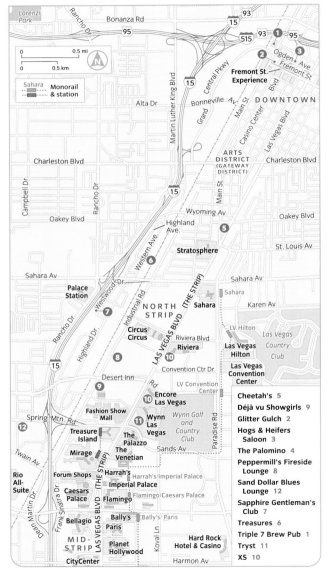

Cheetah's **5**

Déjà vu Showgirls **9**

Glitter Gulch **2**

Hogs & Heifers Saloon **3**

The Palomino **4**

Peppermill's Fireside Lounge **8**

Sand Dollar Blues Lounge **12**

Sapphire Gentleman's Club **7**

Treasures **6**

Triple 7 Brew Pub **1**

Tryst **11**

XS **10**

Las Vegas Nightlife A to Z

Bars

★★ The Bar at Times Square
SOUTH STRIP   If one piano is good, two must be better. Dueling pianos rule this lively lounge, smack in the middle of Vegas's homage to the Big Apple. If you make requests, try to give the poor performers more to do than just play Billy Joel. *New York–New York, 3790 Las Vegas Blvd. S. ☎ 702/740-6969. $10 cover after 8pm Fri–Sat. Map p 99.*

★★ Caramel MID-STRIP   Warm, comfortable, and classy but not stodgy, thanks to a mix of contemporary music and novelty drinks. True cocktail aficionados will sniff at any place that mixes alcohol and dessert (in the same drink!) as recklessly as they do here, but for the rest of us, it's all part of the fun. *Bellagio, 3600 Las Vegas Blvd. S. ☎ 702/693-7111. Map p 99.*

★★ Champagnes Café EAST OF STRIP   Every time I despair the loss of old Vegas—and I mean sleazy Vegas, not finger-snapping Rat Pack Vegas—I find a little corner of it still holding on. A little dark, a little seedy, and completely ossified—except for the karaoke nights on weekends. *3557 S. Maryland Pkwy. (btw. Twain Ave. & Desert Inn Rd.). ☎ 702/737-1699. Map p 99.*

★ Coyote Ugly SOUTH STRIP
Part tourist trap, part genuinely good fun (as if that combo doesn't describe the whole city). You know the gimmick: The waitresses get up on the bar and dance around. A little frat boy, or even pedestrian-guy-trying-for-naughty-thrills, sure, but no less fun for all that. *New York–New York, 3790 Las Vegas Blvd. S. (at Tropicana Ave.). ☎ 702/740-6969. www.coyote uglysaloon.com. Cover varies, but it's usually $10 after 9pm. Map p 99.*

★ Dispensary Lounge EAST OF STRIP   The 1970s idea of cool, but not a retro re-creation—this is the real thing, complete with ferns and a water wheel. You just know Quentin Tarantino hangs out here when he's in town. *2451 E. Tropicana Ave. (at Eastern Ave.). ☎ 702/458-6343. Map p 99.*

★★★ Double Down Saloon
EAST OF STRIP   Local iconoclasts (from Manic Panic punks to strippers to even some famous faces) love this perfect dump, where the jukebox has selections ranging from Zappa to Rev. Horton Heat, the bartenders push something called Ass Juice, and signs remind patrons that "you puke, you pay." *4640 Paradise Rd. (at Naples Dr.). ☎ 702/791-5775. www.doubledownsaloon.com. Map p 99.*

The Double Down Saloon is the best dive bar in Vegas.

If you're feeling daring, add your own bra to the collection that hangs above the bar at the boisterous Hogs & Heifers.

★ **Eiffel Tower Bar** SOUTH STRIP Look down on everyone (just like a real Parisian—I'm kidding . . . mostly) from this chic and elegant room on the 11th floor of the Eiffel Tower. Drop by this date-impressing bar for a sophisticated and relatively affordable drink if your attire meets the business-casual dress code. *In Paris Las Vegas, 3655 Las Vegas Blvd. S.* ☎ 702/948-6937. *Map p 99.*

★★ **ghostbar** WEST OF STRIP Hovering over the city, this beautifully designed space age bar boasts a stunning setting and some of the most superb views around. It's usually crammed with beautiful people paying absurd prices for drinks. If you've had one shot too many or generally suffer from vertigo, avoid the glass floor that's set over the pool area many stories below. *Palms Resort & Casino, 4321 W. Flamingo Rd. (just west of the Strip).* ☎ 702/942-7778. *Cover varies, usually $10 & up. Map p 99.*

★ **Hogs & Heifers Saloon** DOWNTOWN That's "hogs" as in bikes. The movie *Coyote Ugly* was actually based on the original NYC Hogs & Heifers, and for a copy, this works pretty well. The most boisterous and partying place in

Downtown. *201 N. 3rd St. (btw. Ogden & Stewart aves.).* ☎ 702/676-1457. *Map p 100.*

★ **Peppermill's Fireside Lounge** NORTH STRIP Hilariously wrong and wonderful, this bar is a mélange of '80s fuchsia fluorescent lights, a '70s fire pit (the star attraction), and fake bougainvillea. Cozy up in the cushy pit or get a snack at the adjoining coffee shop. The enormous-sized drinks just add to the fun. *2985 Las Vegas Blvd. S.* ☎ 702/735-7635. *Map p 100.*

★★ **Petrossian** MID-STRIP Located right off the Bellagio lobby, and thus taking advantage of that space's impressive beauty, Petrossian is visually one of the prettiest places to drink in the city. Its cocktails don't come cheap, but they come with much knowledge— bartenders are required to attend continuing education classes—and are made with the finest ingredients; and thus true cocktailians will tell you it's better to pay somewhat more for something so very right. *Bellagio, 3600 Las Vegas Blvd. S.* ☎ 702/693-7111. *Map p 99.*

Cozy up to a fire-pit at Peppermill's Fireside Lounge, where the interior wows, as do the large drinks.

★ **Playboy Club** WEST OF STRIP
It was a sad day for an entire generation when the last Playboy Club shuttered its doors. It was a happy day for swingers, ironically retro and deadly serious alike, when a new one opened. There's expensive gambling, there are vintage magazine covers rotating on video screens, there's not nearly the bastion of cool that it once so proudly bore, and it's still kind of swell to see the Bunnies again. Even if they do make lousy dealers. *In the Palms, 4321 W. Flamingo Rd.* ☎ *702/942-7777. Cover varies & includes admission to Moon nightclub. Map p 99.*

★★ **Pussycat Dolls Lounge**
MID-STRIP Don't expect to see the international recording stars perform in this multimillion-dollar lounge just off the PURE nightclub. Still, the local gals (and the occasional celeb guest) strut their stuff (a couple of times an hour) well enough that you probably won't mind. *In Caesars Palace, 3570 Las Vegas Blvd. S.* ☎ *702/731-7873. www.pcdlounge.com. Cover varies. Map p 99.*

Sand Dollar Blues Lounge
WEST OF STRIP Locals and tourists flock to this old-time but (only slightly) cleaned up dive bar, where the blues (and jazz) are still as down and dirty as ever. In a town full of prefab places (House of Blues, anyone?), something genuine is to be celebrated. As are the affordable drinks. *3355 Spring Mountain Rd. (at Polaris Ave.).* ☎ *702/871-6651. www.sanddollarblues.com. Cover Mon–Fri $5; Sat–Sun $7. Map p 100.*

★ **Triple 7 Brew Pub** DOWNTOWN Its first demographic appeal is to microbrew buffs, though anyone longing to drink somewhere in Downtown that isn't smoky and noisy (except for the dueling piano acts) will find this

something of a haven; glass walls separate it from the casino, cutting out much of that chaos. They also serve solid bar food. *In Main Street Station, 200 N. Main St.* ☎ *702/387-1896. Map p 100.*

★★ **Whiskey Bar** EAST OF STRIP
A bit of a trek, but a great place to play, given all its perfect elements: Rande Gerber (Mr. Cindy Crawford, to you) interior design, check; go-go dancers, check; pounding beats, check; sultry outdoor area complete with mattress and cabanas for lounging and canoodling, check; the Strip in the distance for an excellent view, check. *In the Green Valley Resort, 2300 Paseo Verde Pkwy., Henderson.* ☎ *702/617-7560. Cover varies, usually $10 & up. Map p 99.*

Dance Clubs
★★ **The Bank** MID-STRIP It's for a "discerning audience with higher sensibilities." That translates as rich, exclusive, and uppity—though its top-of-the-line everything nearly justifies the stratospheric prices. You can bank on it being packed every

Hit Downtown's Triple 7 Brewpub for a microbrew and a chance to drink in relatively peaceful surroundings.

The Bank is a popular nighttime refuge for the rich, famous, and trendy.

night, but we think this trend is a bust. *In Bellagio, 3600 Las Vegas Blvd. S.* ☎ *702/693-8300. www. lightgroup.com. Cover varies, usually $30. Map p 99.*

★ **Christian Audigier** MID-STRIP This typical party spot is dark, loud, crowded, overpriced, and the designer name means you need to unleash your inner fashionista . . . in other words, all the ingredients that seem to add up to a hugely successful Vegas nightclub. The Strip-view patio is a highlight. *In Treasure Island, 3300 Las Vegas Blvd. S.* ☎ *702/894-7580. www.treasure island.com. Cover varies. Map p 99.*

★ **Cleopatra's Barge** MID-STRIP It was such a big deal when this bar/club opened because the boat setting—yes, it looks like an Egyptian barge and actually floats on water—was just a novelty and wonder. Oh, more innocent times indeed, but the place is still a landmark and it's still kind of a kick. *In Caesars Palace, 3570 Las Vegas Blvd. S.* ☎ *702/731-7110. 2-drink minimum. Map p 99.*

★★ **Jet** MID-STRIP A technical wonder of a vast nightclub, it's composed of three different rooms, each with its own distinct vibe (and usually different music). The main room features a dance floor that is usually steaming. It's wildly successful, but can be a bit exhausting. *In The Mirage, 3400 Las Vegas Blvd. S.* ☎ *702/632-7600. Cover varies, usually $30. Map p 99.*

★ **LAX** SOUTH STRIP You might need a flashlight to properly see the swank supper club decor at this hugely popular if dim nightclub. It caters to an aggressively young and hip clientele (including plenty of celebs—Christina Aguilera is an investor) with multiple bars and ultra-high-tech dance floor. *In Luxor Las Vegas, 3900 Las Vegas Blvd. S.* ☎ *702/242-4529. www.laxthenight club.com. Cover varies. Map p 99.*

★ **Moon** WEST OF STRIP Another basic trendy nightclub—dance floor, smoke machines, house music—but not nearly as inviting as Jet or Rain. It can be hot one night,

The very hot Jet caters to a hip crowd with three separate dance floors and a state-of-the-art sound system.

cold the next. On the plus side, your pricey cover will get you in here and into the Playboy Club (p 103) just above it. *In Palms Resort & Casino, 4321 W. Flamingo Rd.* ☎ *702/492-3960. Cover varies. Map p 99.*

★★★ **PURE** MID-STRIP   At this writing, the hottest club in town. It's two stories and 36,000 square feet (3,345 sq. m) of white/ivory/silver design, intense crowding, hot sounds, and pure madness. Lines to get in are long; tales of A-list celebrity embarrassment within are even longer. *In Caesars Palace, 3570 Las Vegas Blvd. S.* ☎ *702/731-7110. Cover varies. Map p 99.*

★★ **Rain Nightclub** MID-STRIP   Though the beat is eardrum shatteringly loud, one has to admit they sure know how to do a nightclub right. Assuming you can get inside (the lines start early and stay long), you should maneuver the multilevels, check out all the electronic gee-whiz gizmos (a serious lighting system, for starters) that add even more to the experience, and wonder at how little body fat is on the 20-somethings inside. *In Palms Resort & Casino, 4321 W. Flamingo Rd.* ☎ *702/940-7246. $25 cover. Map p 99.*

If you can stomach the lines to get in, PURE is the hottest club in Vegas and a major celeb hangout.

★ **rumjungle** SOUTH STRIP   Too many of the clubs in Vegas are interchangeable, so rumjungle's distinctive elements are refreshing. From the fire-lined wall of water to the bottles illuminated with laser beams to the largest collection of rum in Vegas to the food on skewers, it's a scene not like any other. *In Mandalay Bay, 3950 Las Vegas Blvd. S.* ☎ *702/632-7408. $20–$25 cover Fri–Sat for men & free for women. Map p 99.*

★★ **Seamless After Hours** WEST OF STRIP   By day—and most of the night—this is a strip club, but around 4am the girls leave the stage, and tables and chairs are cleared for a dance floor that is the

Getting in the Door

Club hopping in Vegas isn't a very practical affair, given the number of hours you may spend in line to get past the velvet rope guarding the entrance to the top nightspots. You're best off picking a club and then sticking around for the evening. To help increase the amount of time you spend on the dance floor, be sure to dress appropriately (see "You are what you wear," on p 108), be on time if you've made a reservation, and try to have at least one woman (preferably showing some cleavage) in your party (ladies rule on club lines). Ask your hotel concierge if he can get you onto the club's guest list, or call the club yourself. If all else fails, you can try a discreet tip ($20 or more) to the doorman.

Don't let the Zen decor fool you—the hip don't wait to get into Tao Nightclub for peace and quiet, but for its pounding dance music.

site of the most intense after-hours action in Vegas. The party goes on until everyone gives up, which can be as late as noon the next day, whereupon the girls reappear and their clothes again disappear. *4740 S. Arville St.* ☎ *702/227-5200. $20 cover if you come in a cab, free if you drive yourself. Map p 99.*

★ **Tabu** SOUTH STRIP You'll hear the phrase "ultra lounge" a lot in Vegas. All it means is "fancier than a bar, smaller than a nightclub." This is probably the best of an admittedly choice (if often interchangeable) lot. Which might sound like I'm damning it with faint praise, but it really is smooth. *In MGM Grand, 3799 Las Vegas Blvd. S.* ☎ *702/891-7183. www.tabulv.com. Cover*

Seamless is half dance club, half strip club, and the best club for after-hours partying in Vegas.

$10–$20 for men & free for women. Map p 99.

★★★ **Tao Nightclub** MID-STRIP A gorgeously designed space that seems to span forever, encompassing an ultra lounge, restaurant, and nightclub—all of which covers a couple of floors. The decor is Zen-Asian, which is absurd, because thanks to the anxious crowds hoping to gain entrance, the flashing lights, and the pounding music, this celeb fave is anything but peaceful. *In The Venetian, 3355 Las Vegas Blvd. S.* ☎ *702/388-8588. Cover varies. Map p 99.*

★ **Toby Keith's I Love This Bar & Grill** MID-STRIP Country, convivial, and crowded, especially when its music-star owner turns up to play a set or two. No, really, he does. Try the deep-fried Twinkies. *In Harrah's, 3475 Las Vegas Blvd. S.* ☎ *702/369-5084. Map p 99.*

★★ **Tryst** NORTH STRIP It's a bit more sophisticated and mellow than its club brethren . . . but this is Vegas, so that's all relative. It is a pretty sexy space, notable also for the 90-foot (27m) waterfall and the patio that opens over a lagoon; it's rare to have a shot at fresh air in a Vegas club. *In Wynn Las Vegas, 3131 Las Vegas Blvd. S.* ☎ *702/770-3375. Cover varies. Map p 100.*

★★ **XS** NORTH STRIP The "encore" of Tryst (see above) is aptly named in that it definitely ups the wow and energy factor over its sister club. It's notable for being more grown-up and sophisticated than the club norm—thanks to decent lighting, you can see the crowds you'll be bumping into on the dance floor and immense outdoor patio. *In Encore Las Vegas, 3121 Las Vegas Blvd. S.* ☎ *702/770-0097. www.xslasvegas.com. Cover varies. Map p 100.*

Gay Bars

★★ **Gipsy** EAST OF STRIP The Grande Dame of the local gay scene, and still a very popular one. The sunken dance floor, the excellent location, and renovations help keep it fresh. Look for gimmicks, including the occasional stripper, and a pretty young crowd. *4605 Paradise Rd. (at Naples Dr.).* ☎ *702/731-1919. www. gipsylv.net. Cover varies but is usually $5 & up on weekends, less or even free on weekdays. Map p 99.*

★★ **Krave** MID-STRIP The first gay club on the Strip, but open enough to attract a mixed

Technically, Krave is the first gay club on the Strip, but it's a popular party place with people of all orientations.

Tryst is popular with celebs, who like to hang out beneath the sexy club's waterfall.

crowd—unlike most other joints, its go-go dancers come in both genders. That's probably the key; the club wants to promote itself more as "alternative" than anything sexuality specific, but the result is a fine place to party regardless of your goals. *In Planet Hollywood Hotel & Casino, 3667 Las Vegas Blvd. S. (entrance on Harmon).* ☎ *702/836-0830. www.kravelasvegas.com. Cover varies. Map p 99.*

★ **Piranha Las Vegas/8½ Ultra Lounge** EAST OF STRIP One building, two distinct gay hot spots. Piranha is a celeb-favorite dance club (Britney and Janet have been spotted here) with a walk-through aquarium filled with, yes, piranhas. The 8½ side is cool and groovy, with lots of space to relax. Lines for both are long, prices are high, and you need to dress to impress. *4633 Paradise Rd. (at Naples Dr.).* ☎ *702/791-0100. www.piranhavegas.com. Cover varies, usually $20. Map p 99.*

Strip Clubs

★ **Cheetah's** WEST OF STRIP Here's your classic sporty frat-boy strip-club vibe, small and cheesy but also friendly. Not as up-to-the-minute wow as newer places, but a lot

You Are What You Wear

We may all be taught not to judge a book by its cover, but that's what pretty much every nightclub (and even the strip clubs) in town is going to do. Most of the clubs have precise dress codes, banning the obvious gang attire, but also, in some cases, collarless shirts, sneakers, baseball caps, shorts, jeans, sandals, and more. When in doubt, call ahead, but you might want to pack something fashionable and metrosexual just to be sure.

less pressure because of it. *2121 Western Ave.* ☎ *702/384-0074. Topless. $30 cover after 8pm until early morning. Map p 100.*

★★ **Déjà vu Showgirls** NORTH STRIP In addition to the "totally nude" draw, dancers here tend to do actual routines rather than just languidly stroll about the stage. *3247 Industrial Rd.* ☎ *702/894-4167. Unescorted women allowed. Totally nude. Cover $15. No alcohol. Map p 100.*

★ **Glitter Gulch** DOWNTOWN The last bastion of Old Vegas, though an updated version of it. Not great for the bashful, but perfect for the merely curious. *20 Fremont St.* ☎ *702/385-4774. Topless. 2-drink minimum (drinks $7 & up) before 8pm; cover is $20 (includes 1 drink) after 8pm. Map p 100.*

★ **The Palomino** NORTH STRIP Smart owners of this all-nude facility gave the lower level a minor face-lift (farewell, red flocked wallpaper; hello, flatscreen monitors), and then turned the upstairs over to male strippers on weekends. (Yes, they get totally naked as well.) Expect a very gender-mixed crowd with an urban vibe. *1848 Las Vegas Blvd. N.* ☎ *702/642-2984. Totally nude. $20 cover. Map p 100.*

★★★ **Sapphire Gentleman's Club** NORTH STRIP This modern and friendly facility is billed as the largest strip club in the world. The girls are less clad than the Strip's ubiquitous go-go dancers, but really just by a scant degree. Oh, and ladies have their very own male strippers to leer at. *3025 S. Industrial.* ☎ *702/796-0000. Unescorted women allowed. Topless. $30 cover after 6pm. Map p 100.*

★★★ **Seamless** WEST OF STRIP Here's where the already blurred line between dance club and strip club disappears—at 4am, to be precise. Prior to that, this is a high-tech strip club, with a futuristic interior. When the clock strikes four, the strippers turn into regular go-go dancers (p 105). The transition is indeed "seamless," and it does make for one-stop nightlife shopping. *4740 S. Arville St.* ☎ *702/227-5200. $20 cover. Map p 99.*

★★★ **Treasures** WEST OF STRIP A mélange of Victorian sporting house—the way a real "gentlemen's club" should look, if you ask me—and high-tech accouterments (look at the effects on the stage, including the neon stripper pole). You pay for this comfort and style, but its class also makes it a comfortable first-time strip-club experience. *2801 Westwood Dr.* ☎ *702/257-3030. No unescorted women. Topless. Cover $30. Map p 100.* ●

Arts, Entertainment & Weddings Best Bets

Best **Cirque Production**
★★★ *KÀ, MGM Grand, 3799 Las Vegas Blvd. S. (p 112)*

Best **Cirque Production Set on Water**
★★★ *O, Bellagio, 3600 Las Vegas Blvd. S. (p 113)*

Best **Cirque Bargain**
★★★ *Mystère, TI Las Vegas, 3300 Las Vegas Blvd. S. (p 113)*

Best **Classy Nudie Show**
★★ MGM Grand's *Crazy Horse Paris, MGM Grand, 3799 Las Vegas Blvd. S. (p 116)*

Smartest Show in Town
★★★ Penn & Teller, *The Rio, 3700 W. Flamingo Rd. (p 116)*

Best **Comedy Club**
★★★ The Improv, *Harrah's Las Vegas, 3475 Las Vegas Blvd. S. (p 112)*

Best **High-Tech Performance Art**
★★★ Blue Man Group, *The Venetian, 3355 Las Vegas Blvd. S. (p 112)*

Best **Traditional Magic**
★★★ Lance Burton, *Monte Carlo Resort & Casino, 3770 Las Vegas Blvd. S. (p 115)*

Best **Celebrity Impersonators**
★ Legends in Concert, *Harrah's, 3475 Las Vegas Blvd. S. (p 115)*

Funniest Show
★★ Rita Rudner, *Harrah's, 3475 Las Vegas Blvd. S. (p 116)*

Best **Afternoon Show**
★★★ Mac King, *Harrah's, 3475 Las Vegas Blvd. S. (p 115)*

When you just can't wait to get down the aisle, head for the 24-hour drive-up window at the Little White Wedding Chapel.

Best **for Broadway Fans**
★★ Disney's The Lion King, *Mandalay Bay, 3950 Las Vegas Blvd. S. (p 114)*

Best **Old-Fashioned Vegas Revue**
★★★ Jubilee!, *Bally's Las Vegas, 3645 Las Vegas Blvd. S. (p 115)*

Best Chapel for **Kitsch**
Little White Wedding Chapel, *1301 Las Vegas Blvd. S. (p 118)*

Best Place to **be Married by an Elvis Impersonator**
★ Graceland Wedding Chapel, *619 Las Vegas Blvd. S. (p 118)*

Best for a **Traditional Wedding**
★ A Special Memory Wedding Chapel, *800 S. 4th St. (p 118)*

Previous Page: Cirque du Soleil has become a Vegas entertainment juggernaut; and its very first show in town, Mystère, is still going strong.

A&E on the Strip

American
  Superstars 1
Blue Man Group 5
Cirque du Soleil's
  KÀ 13
Cirque du Soleil's
  LOVE 6
Cirque du Soleil's
  Mystère 4
Cirque du Soleil's
  O 10
Cirque du Soleil's
  Zumanity 12
Criss Angel
  Believe 14
Disney's The
  Lion King 15
The Improv 7
Jersey Boys Vegas 3

Sahara ..... Monorail
          & station

Jubilee! 9
Legends in Concert 7
Le Rêve 2
Lance Burton:
  Master Magician 11
Mac King 7
MGM Grand's Crazy
  Horse Paris 13
Mr. Cook E. Jar 7
Penn & Teller 8
Phantom of
  the Opera 5
Rita Rudner 7

Las Vegas A&E A to Z

Comedy Clubs

★★ **The Improv** MID-STRIP One of the many U.S. offspring of the famed NYC comic institution (which opened in 1963). The top comics on the circuit usually cycle through here. You might see the next Robin Williams or Jerry Seinfeld, who both worked their way up through the Improv. *In Harrah's Las Vegas, 3475 Las Vegas Blvd. S. ☎ 800/392-9002 or 702/369-5111. Tickets $40. Map p 111.*

Live Shows

★ **kids American Superstars** NORTH STRIP The celebrity-impersonator show where the performers sing live (pretty rare!) and aren't half bad. The faux-celebs are closer in voice than appearance, but none of the appreciative (and youngish) crowds seem to mind that. *In the Stratosphere Casino Hotel & Tower, 2000 Las Vegas Blvd. S. ☎ 800/998-6937 or 702/380-7711. www.stratospherehotel.com. Tickets $43 adults, $33 kids 5–12. Map p 111.*

The Blue Man Group didn't start out in Vegas, but their performance art antics have found a welcome home here.

It's not the best of the Cirque du Soleil gang, but LOVE might tickle the fancy of Fab Four fans.

★★★ **kids Blue Man Group** MID-STRIP Three men coated in blue paint play with more paint, marshmallows, and musical instruments made out of PVC pipe while the audience howls. It's middlebrow performance art, and no less enjoyable for all that. *In The Venetian, 3355 Las Vegas Blvd. S. ☎ 877/833-6423. www.venetian.com. Tickets $82–$142. Map p 111.*

★★★ **kids Cirque du Soleil's KÀ** SOUTH STRIP Factor in the actual story line (separated royal siblings battle various forces in their efforts to reunite), the special effects, the incredible moving stage, and the overall artistry of Cirque, and this is probably the best show in the city. *In MGM Grand, 3799 Las Vegas Blvd. S. ☎ 866/774-7117 or 702/531-2000. www.cirquedusoleil. com. Tickets $69–$150 (plus tax). Map p 111.*

★ **Cirque du Soleil's LOVE** MID-STRIP Largely just a bunch of interpretive dances set to remixed Beatles tunes, with the usual Cirque arty and weird set design floating through. It's pretty, but even Beatles fans might be disappointed at the lack of substance. *In The Mirage, 3400 Las Vegas Blvd. S.* ☎ *800/963-9637 or 702/792-7777. www.cirquedusoleil.com. Tickets $94–$150 (plus tax). Map p 111.*

★★★ **kids** **Cirque du Soleil's Mystère** MID-STRIP The first big Cirque production in Vegas and still one of the best. Don't come looking for a story line; just settle back and let the imagery and acrobatics of this world-class show wash over you. *In TI Las Vegas, 3300 Las Vegas Blvd. S.* ☎ *800/963-9634 or 702/796-9999. www.cirquedusoleil.com. Tickets $60–$95 (plus tax & service fee). Map p 111.*

★★★ **Cirque du Soleil's O** MID-STRIP The action in this dreamy and moving piece takes place in, around, and above a 1.5-million-gallon pool. It's as if Dali and Magritte

These rubber-jointed contortionists are only one of the many delights found in Cirque du Soleil's sublime O.

collaborated on an Esther Williams show. So beautiful, it might make you cry. *In Bellagio, 3600 Las Vegas Blvd. S.* ☎ *888/488-7111 or 702/693-7722. www.cirquedusoleil.com. Tickets $94–$150 (plus tax). Map p 111.*

High-End Headliners

The days when top-notch commercial talent regarded Vegas as a cheesy step in the wrong career direction are over. Céline Dion—who returns to Vegas in 2011—blazed a trail with her old run at Caesar's Palace that other headliners are traveling. Cher, Bette Midler, Barry Manilow, and the Osmonds all have high-profile gigs. The bad news: They're playing on limited contracts (and only go onstage a limited number of days each year)—and when they do perform, it'll cost you an arm, a leg, and who knows how many other body parts to see them. But if you have the cash to burn, here's how to spend it:

- ★★ **Donny and Marie:** In the Flamingo, 3355 Las Vegas Blvd. S. (☎ **702/733-3333**); tickets $85–$250.
- ★★ **Barry Manilow:** In Paris Las Vegas, 3655 Las Vegas Blvd. S. (☎ **877/603-4386**); tickets $127–$225.
- ★★★ **Bette Midler:** In Caesars Palace, 3570 Las Vegas Blvd. S. (☎ **877/7BETTEM** [723-8836]); tickets $45–$227.
- ★★★ **Cher:** In Caesars Palace, 3570 Las Vegas Blvd. S. (☎ **866/510-2437**); tickets $87–$228.

The Best A&E & Weddings

Folksy Mac King does a first-rate magic/comedy act for a reasonable price—a Vegas miracle.

Cirque du Soleil's *Zumanity*

SOUTH STRIP   This ode to sexuality is a rare near-total miss by the otherwise reliable Cirque brand. Not so much erotic as it is trying too hard. *In New York–New York, 3790 Las Vegas Blvd. S. ☎ 866/606-7111 or 702/740-6815. www.zumanity.com. Age 18 & over only. Tickets $125 (sofas), $85–$99 (theater seats), $69 (cabaret stools, partial views), $129 per person (duo sofas, sold in pairs), plus tax and service fee. Map p 111.*

Criss Angel *Believe* SOUTH

STRIP   This anything but blessed union of the famous illusionist with Cirque du Soleil was legitimately savaged when it debuted. Ongoing tweaks have at least thrust this incoherent melding of magic, set pieces, and admittedly inventive choreography into mediocrity. There are better places to spend your money. *In the Luxor, 3900 Las Vegas Blvd. S. ☎ 800/557-7428. Tickets $70–$181. Map p 111.*

Buying Tickets

Many Vegas shows sell discounted tickets through local brokers. For information on getting these discounts, see p. 174.

★★ kids Disney's The Lion King

SOUTH STRIP   A nearly complete version of the original Broadway show, with superior staging, puppetry, dramatic set pieces, costumes, and special effects that magnificently distract from the slight story. A nice change of pace from generic Vegas. *In Mandalay Bay, 3950 Las Vegas Blvd. S. ☎ 877/623-7400 or 702/632-7777. www.mandalaybay.com. Tickets $53–$169. Map p 111.*

★★ *Jersey Boys Vegas* MID-STRIP

The time-tested songs of the Four Seasons are the central draw of this enthusiastic and compelling Tony-winner, which should satisfy both the theater veteran and the vacationing family. *In The Palazzo, 3325 Las Vegas Blvd. ☎ 866/641-7469. Tickets $64–$235. Map p 111.*

The topless Vegas revue may be dying, but Jubilee!, *with its signature showgirls, lives on.*

The performers in MGM Grand's Crazy Horse Paris tease as they artfully take it all off.

★★★ **Jubilee!** MID-STRIP   The last of the sadly dying Vegas topless showgirl revues. Thanks to terrific production values, which include the story of Samson and Delilah and the sinking of the *Titanic* (no, I'm not making this up), not to mention enormous Bob Mackie wigs, this is camp perfection. *In Bally's Las Vegas, 3645 Las Vegas Blvd. S. ☎ 800/237-7469 or 702/739-4567. www.ballys.com. Ages 18 & over only. Tickets $63–$110 (plus tax). Map p 111.*

★★★ kids **Lance Burton: Master Magician** SOUTH STRIP   Burton's folksy demeanor and sardonic wit are fine accompaniments to his genuine magic skills. Forget the big splashy sequences and focus on the close-up magic that is Burton's specialty. His comedy juggler, Michael Goudeau, is the town's most valuable supporting player. *In the Monte Carlo Resort & Casino. ☎ 877/386-8224 or 702/730-7160, 3770 Las Vegas Blvd. S. www.montecarlo. com. Tickets $67–$73 (plus tax). Map p 111.*

★ **Le Rêve**   nally a Cirque rip-off, including ing a tank of water for a set, this spectacle underwent a major revamp to give it its own identity. It's not a bad extravaganza . . . but still more copy than original. *In Wynn Las Vegas, 3131 Las Vegas Blvd. S. ☎ 888/320-110. www.wynn lasvegas.com. Ages 13 & older. Tickets $113–$200. Map p 111.*

★★★ kids **Mac King** MID-STRIP   Given Vegas's sky-high ticket prices, this is possibly the best value in town. The affable King adroitly mixes comedy and magic (of the mind-blowing, close-up variety), and

The famous magical duo of Penn & Teller show off their skills and sense of humor at the Rio.

Enjoy Phantom of the Opera in a custom-built theater at The Venetian.

but Cook isn't going down without a fight. He's so terrible, he's good; he's actually pretty good, with a startlingly flexible voice to go along with his stage posturing. A must-do Vegas experience. *In Harrah's Carnaval Court Lounge, 3475 Las Vegas Blvd. S.* ☎ *702/369-5222. www.cookejarr.com. Free admission. Map p 111.*

★★★ Penn & Teller MID-STRIP
The smartest show in town, as the famous duo gleefully skewer the very magician tradition they happen to excel at. *In the Rio Hotel, 3700 W. Flamingo Rd.* ☎ *888/746-7784. www.riolasvegas.com. Ages 5 & over only. Tickets $85–$96 (plus tax). Map p 111.*

★ *Phantom of the Opera* MID-STRIP
An abridged version (90 min., no intermission) of the famous Andrew Lloyd Webber musical, with even more special effects. *In The Venetian, 3355 Las Vegas Blvd. S.* ☎ *866/641-7469 or 702/414-7469. www.venetian.com. Tickets $80–$175 (plus tax). Map p 111.*

★★ Rita Rudner MID-STRIP
The stand-up comedienne comes off as Every Woman, not to mention the audience's Best Friend Forever, as she wryly and dryly tosses out one-liners that cut to the heart of gender relations. And she's funny as heck doing it. *In Harrah's, 3475 Las Vegas Blvd. S.* ☎ *702/369-5222. www.harrahs.com. Tickets $54–$90. Map p 111.*

Making it Legal

Going to the chapel in Vegas isn't hard, but even spur-of-the-moment nuptials require Uncle Sam's approval. For details on getting a marriage license in Vegas, see p 28, ⑥.

is an excellent choice for an afternoon break. *In Harrah's, 3475 Las Vegas Blvd. S.* ☎ *800/427-7247. www.harrahs.com. Tickets $25 (plus tax and service fees). Discount coupons are almost always available in local magazines & handouts. Map p 111.*

★★ MGM Grand's *Crazy Horse Paris* SOUTH STRIP
Inspired by the Parisian institution, this erotic burlesque nudie show is artfully done, as beautifully proportioned performers gracefully doff their clothes in clever ways. It's what "adult entertainment" ought to be, and puts *Zumanity* to shame. *In MGM Grand, 3799 Las Vegas Blvd. S.* ☎ *877/880-0880. www.mgmgrand.com. 18 & over only. Business casual attire required. Tickets $50–$60 (including tax and fees). Map p 111.*

Mr. Cook E. Jarr MID-STRIP
Lounge singers are a dying breed,

Best **Wedding Chapels**

Wedding Chapels A to Z

★ **Chapel of the Flowers** This slick operation is your best bet for a traditional wedding (though no rice or confetti throwing—bummer!). Choose among the friendly complex's five chapels (I like the Victorian best), use the drive-through, or opt for an outdoor ceremony. *1717 Las Vegas Blvd. S. (at E. Oakey Blvd.).* ☎ *800/843-2410 or 702/735-4331. www.littlechapel.com. Map p 117.*

★ kids **Cupid's Wedding Chapel** The self-described "little chapel with the big heart" lives up to its rep, and not only because it doesn't churn out ceremonies quite as fast as the other places in town (weddings are by appointment only). It also rolls out the red carpet to couples blending

preexisting families, making it a great option for those with kids. *827 Las Vegas Blvd. S. (btw. Gass & Hoover aves.).* ☎ *800/543-2933 or 702/598-4444. www.cupidswedding.com. Map p 117.*

Cupid's Wedding Chapel is a great option for those blending families.

An Elvis-themed wedding at Viva Las Vegas.

★ Graceland Wedding Chapel

Elvis never slept here and he didn't get married here, but this mom-and-pop joint has catered to a number of rock stars over the years (and you can get an Elvis impersonator if you want the King to officiate). It's not the nicest in town, but the tiny chapel (only 33 seats) is a pretty friendly place to get hitched. *619 Las Vegas Blvd. S. (at E. Bonneville Ave.).* ☎ *800/824-5732 or 702/382-0091. www.gracelandchapel.com. Map p 117.*

Little White Wedding Chapel

Are there better and friendlier places in town to tie the knot? Yes. But for pure Vegas kitsch, you can't beat this 24-hour wedding factory, which is little, is white, and has a really famous drive-through window, where many a celeb has embarked on a path to 48 hours of wedded bliss. Just avoid the noisy gazebo. *1301 Las Vegas Blvd. S. (btw. E. Oakey & Charleston blvds.).* ☎ *800/545-8111 or 702/382-5943. www.alittlewhitechapel.com. Map p 117.*

★ Mon Bel Ami Wedding Chapel

This pretty church-style building does frilly and fancy ceremonies (though you can still get Elvis if you want him). Weddings aren't of the rushed variety, making it less popular with the walk-in set and better for those who like to plan ahead. *607 Las Vegas Blvd. S. (at E. Bonneville Ave.).* ☎ *866/503-4400 or 702/388-4445. www.monbelami.com. Map p 117.*

★ A Special Memory Wedding Chapel

Want a traditional, non-tacky, big-production wedding? Here's the place. The pretty interior of the main New England–style chapel actually looks like a church, it holds up to 115, and there's even a cool staircase from which a bride can make a grand entrance. Of course, if you want that drive-through option, it's still there (this is Vegas). *800 S. 4th St. (at Gass Ave.).* ☎ *800/962-7798 or 702/384-2211. www.aspecialmemory.com. Map p 117.*

★★★ Viva Las Vegas Wedding Chapel

Want to star in your own theatrical wedding production? This fun spot specializes in theme weddings—in addition to the eponymous Elvis, they've done everything from *Star Wars* to *Camelot* to James Bond! The southwestern-style chapel holds up to 100. *1205 Las Vegas Blvd. S.* ☎ *800/570-4450 or 702/384-0771. www.vivalasvegas.com. Map p 117.*

★ Wee Kirk O' the Heather

Though it's the oldest wedding chapel in Vegas (opened in 1940), the decor at this veteran is fresh, the service is warm, and the whole package strikes just the right balance between kitsch and classic. *231 Las Vegas Blvd. S. (btw. Bridger & Carson aves.).* ☎ *800/843-2566 or 702/382-9830. www.weekirk.com. Map p 117.* ●

9 The Best **Hotels**

Hotel Best Bets

Most **Luxurious**
★★★ Four Seasons $$$$ *3960 Las Vegas Blvd. S. (p 126)*

Best **Business Hotel**
★★ Las Vegas Hilton $$ *3000 Paradise Rd. (p 127)*

Best **Views**
★★ Palms Casino Resort $$$ *4321 W. Flamingo Rd. (p 131)*

Best **Room on the Strip**
★★★ THEhotel at Mandalay Bay $$$ *3950 Las Vegas Blvd. S. (p 134)*

Best **Classic Vegas Hotel**
★★ Caesars Palace $$$ *3570 Las Vegas Blvd. S. (p 124)*

Best **Use of Wacky Theme**
★★ New York–New York Hotel & Casino $$ *3790 Las Vegas Blvd. S. (p 130)*

Best **Moderately Priced Strip Rooms**
★★ Luxor Las Vegas $$ *3900 Las Vegas Blvd. S. (p 128)*

Most **Improved Rooms**
★ Paris Las Vegas $$ *3655 Las Vegas Blvd. S. (p 132)*

Best **for Families**
★ Circus Circus $ *2880 Las Vegas Blvd. S. (p 124)*

Best **Bathrooms**
★★ The Venetian $$$ *3355 Las Vegas Blvd. S. (p 135)*

Best **Downtown Bargain**
★★ Main Street Station $ *200 N. Main St. (p 128)*

Best **Gym**
★★ The Venetian $$$ *3355 Las Vegas Blvd. S. (p 135)*

Best **Swimming Pool**
★★ The Mirage $$ *3400 Las Vegas Blvd. S. (p 130)*

Best **Resort**
★★★ M Resort Spa & Casino $$ *12300 Las Vegas Blvd. S. (p 128)*

Best **Lobby**
★★ New York–New York $$ *3790 Las Vegas Blvd. S. (p 130)*

Best **Beds**
★★★ Red Rock Resort $$$ *10973 W. Charleston Rd., Summerlin (p 132)*

Best **Rock 'n' Roll Hotel**
★★ Hard Rock Hotel & Casino $$$ *4455 Paradise Rd. (p 127)*

Best **Strip Bargain**
★ Stratosphere Las Vegas Hotel & Casino $ *2000 Las Vegas Blvd. S. (p 135)*

Best **Non-Casino Hotel**
★★★ Vdara Hotel & Spa $$$ *2600 W. Harmon Ave. (p 135)*

Best **"Locals" Hotel**
★★ South Point $$ *9777 Las Vegas Blvd. S. (p 133)*

The Venetian has the best bathrooms in Vegas.

Previous Page: The lobby of the Red Rock Resort.

South Strip Hotels

Excalibur 5

Four Seasons Hotel Las Vegas 10

Hooters Casino Hotel 6

Luxor Las Vegas 7

Mandalay Bay 9

MGM Grand Hotel & Casino 4

Monte Carlo Resort & Casino 1

New York-New York Hotel & Casino 2

Orleans 3

THEhotel at Mandalay Bay 8

Mid-Strip Hotels

ARIA Resort & Casino 14

Bally's Las Vegas 10

Bellagio 11

Caesars Palace 7

The Flamingo Las Vegas 6

Harrah's Las Vegas 5

Mandarin Oriental Las Vegas 15

The Mirage 4

The Palazzo 2

Palms Casino Resort 9

Paris Las Vegas Casino Resort 12

Planet Hollywood Resort & Casino 16

Rio All-Suite Hotel & Casino 8

Treasure Island 1

Vdara Hotel & Spa 13

The Venetian 3

The Westin Casuarina Las Vegas Hotel, Casino & Spa 17

Las Vegas Hotels

Best Western
   Mardi Gras Inn 7

Circus Circus
   Hotel & Casino 4

Clarion Hotel & Suites—
   Emerald Springs 11

Courtyard by Marriott 6

Desert Rose Resort 15

Encore Las Vegas 9

Green Valley Ranch
   Resort 18

Hard Rock Hotel
   & Casino 13

Las Vegas Hilton 5

Motel 6 14

M Resort Spa
   & Casino 17

Red Rock Resort 1

Sahara Hotel & Casino 3

South Point Hotel &
   Casino 16

Stratosphere Las Vegas
   Hotel & Casino 2

Terrible's 12

Trump International
   Hotel Las Vegas 8

Wynn Las Vegas 10

Downtown Hotels

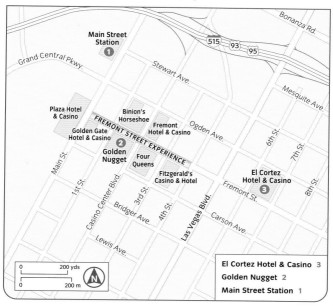

El Cortez Hotel & Casino 3
Golden Nugget 2
Main Street Station 1

Las Vegas Hotels A to Z

★★ ARIA Resort & Casino MID-STRIP   Cutting-edge decor mixes with high-tech wizardry in this luxe hotel's two curved glass towers. The plush guest rooms feature all manner of cool techno gizmos—and floor-to-ceiling windows. A soaring 3-story lobby, vast pool area, fab spa, and more restaurants and bars than you could probably handle in a single visit round out the first-class offerings. *3730 Las Vegas Blvd. S. (at Harmon Ave.).* ☎ *866/359-7757. www.arialasvegas.com. 4,004 units. Doubles $179 and up. AE, DC, MC, V. Map p 121.*

★ Bally's Las Vegas MID-STRIP   Bally's has one of the best locations on the Strip (dead center,

and on the monorail line), but not much of a wow factor in a city where that means a lot. Still, you

The rooms at ARIA Resort & Casino offer marvelous views.

One of Bellagio's posh guest rooms; some rooms overlook the hotel's famous fountains.

can get a large, very comfy, and modern room for a ridiculously low rate. It's a very pleasant place to stay for value seekers. *3645 Las Vegas Blvd. S. (at Flamingo Rd.).* ☎ *800/ 634-3434 or 702/739-4111. www. ballyslv.com. 2,814 units. Doubles $99 & up. AE, DC, MC, V. Map p 121.*

★★ **Bellagio** MID-STRIP The first of the "luxury resort"–style Vegas casino hotels, which in this case means posh rooms, a classy Euro-style pool area, and access to some of the best restaurants in town. Accommodations feel a little small compared to some of the even newer resorts, but they are still handsome. Though the size can be daunting (it's a nice trek to the pool and spa from most rooms), the grown-up atmosphere makes up for it. *3600 Las Vegas Blvd. S. (at the corner of Flamingo Rd.).* ☎ *888/987-6667 or 702/693-7111. www.bellagio. com. 3,933 units. Doubles $169 & up. AE, DC, DISC, MC, V. Map p 121.*

★★ **Caesars Palace** MID-STRIP Though they've toned down the cheese factor, and upped this veteran to a ridiculous and often impossible-to-navigate size, no hotel is more Vegas spectacle than Caesars. Rooms vary from tower to tower in terms of size, and no

longer have that goofy romance that once characterized the place, but all are generically handsome and comfortable. The spa, Qua, is a sybaritic stunner, as is its heavenly Garden of the Gods pool complex. Toss in The Forum Shops (p 69), and a variety of bars and excellent restaurants, leaving here isn't necessary—which is good, because it's so hard to find the door. *3570 Las Vegas Blvd. S. (just north of Flamingo Rd.).* ☎ *877/427-7243 or 702/731-7110. www.caesarspalace. com. 3,348 units. Doubles $129 & up; suites $549 & up. AE, DC, DISC, MC, V. Map p 121.*

kids **Circus Circus Hotel & Casino** NORTH STRIP The circus acts still fly above the casino action and families still stay here, but its days as an attraction are long gone. Now it's the place to come for cheap rooms, though note that its Manor rooms are a bargain (or should be) for a reason. A dump-your-bags-and-head-to-more-interesting-climes location. *2880 Las Vegas Blvd. S. (btw. Circus Circus & Convention Center drives).* ☎ *877/ 434-9175 or 702/734-0410. www. circuscircus.com. 3,774 units. Doubles $59 & up. AE, DC, DISC, MC, V. Map p 122.*

A petite suite in the Augustus Tower at Caesars Palace.

The rooms at Circus Circus may not be much to write home about, but the resort is still a great place to stay if you're traveling with kids.

★ kids Clarion Hotel & Suites— Emerald Springs EAST OF STRIP

Housed in three peach-stucco buildings, the Emerald Springs offers a friendly, low-key alternative to the usual Vegas glitz and glitter, though it's only 3 blocks from the Strip. Public areas and rooms here are notably clean and well kept (if dated), and even the smallest accommodations (studios) offer small sofas, desks, and armchairs with hassocks. *325 E. Flamingo Rd. (btw. Koval Lane & Paradise Rd.).* ☎ *800/732-7889 or 702/732-9100. www.clarionlasvegas.com. 150 units. Suites $99 & up. AE, DC, DISC, MC, V. Map p 122.*

★ Courtyard by Marriott EAST OF STRIP

A good-looking hotel (in a chain-establishment kind of way), this complex of three-story buildings in an attractively landscaped setting has pleasant-looking rooms (all with balconies or patios) and a location right across the street from a monorail station. *3275 Paradise Rd. (btw. Convention Center Dr. & Desert Inn Rd.).* ☎ *800/321-2211 or 702/791-3600. www.courtyard.com. 149 units. Rooms $149 & up (for up to 4 people). AE, DC, DISC, MC, V. Map p 122.*

★★ kids Desert Rose Resort

EAST OF STRIP   The suites here are bland, but they come with full kitchens and balconies (a rarity in Vegas, where windows rarely open). It's really a lifesaver for families looking for a comfortable place that is not too far off the beaten path (it's a block from the Strip) and won't break the bank. *5051 Duke Ellington Way.* ☎ *800/811-2450 or 702/739-7000. www.desertroseresort.com. 278 units. Suites $99 & up, including breakfast. AE, DC, DISC, MC, V. Map p 122.*

★★ El Cortez Hotel & Casino

DOWNTOWN   This Downtown veteran has been transformed into an unusually cool and contemporary place to stay, even while retaining its Old Vegas cred. And it's ultra-affordable, too. The traditionally furnished rooms (some quite large) have some useful modern features (minifridges, flatscreen TVs, and so on); the Cabana Suites are especially desirable. *600 Fremont St. (btw. 6th & 7th sts.).* ☎ *800/634-6703 or 702/385-5200. www.elcortez hotelcasino.com. 428 units. Doubles $35 & up. AE, DISC, MC, V. Map p 123.*

★★ Encore Las Vegas NORTH STRIP   This aptly named second

A suite at the Flamingo Las Vegas, whose pool is still one of the best in the city.

act of Steve Wynn's scores on all the luxe fronts. The whimsically decorated public areas (Moroccan, red, and butterflies mix to good effect) are more fun than the guest rooms, which are nevertheless grand, modern, and richly appointed (especially those marble bathrooms!). Prices are stratospheric. *3121 Las Vegas Blvd. S. (near Spring Mountain Rd.).* ☎ *888/320-7125 or 702/770-7171. www.encorelasvegas.com. 2,034 units. $159 and up double. AE, DC, DISC, MC, V. Map p 122.*

★ **kids** **Excalibur** SOUTH STRIP No longer the sword-and-sorcery fantasy escape it once promised to be, this is the place to go either if you simply must stay in an oversized cartoonish castle (whose theme has been sadly downsized of late) and/or if you must stay on the Strip and need a bargain room— stick to the newer Widescreen rooms and avoid the Standard ones. The pool area might help make the stay feel a little more special. *3850 Las Vegas Blvd. S. (at Tropicana Ave.).* ☎ *800/937-7777 or 702/597-7700. www.excalibur.com. 4,008 units. Doubles $59 & up. AE, DC, DISC, MC, V. Map p 121.*

The first-rate pool area at the plush Green Valley Resort is great for lounging.

★ **kids** **The Flamingo Las Vegas** MID-STRIP This Strip veteran is (slowly) turning what were rather forgettable rooms into snazzy, kinda-now, kinda-wow eye-poppers. Thanks to hot pink walls and accents, black-and-white photos of its heyday as Bugsy Siegel's hangout, and TVs embedded in the bathroom mirrors, you clearly want to stay in the new rooms. The rest of the hotel is scruffy, though the pool area, complete with live birds, is one of the city's best. Good for families who cover an age range. *3555 Las Vegas Blvd. S. (btw. Sands Ave. & Flamingo Rd.).* ☎ *800/732-2111 or 702/733-3111. www.flamingolv.com. 3,999 units. Doubles $85 & up. AE, DC, DISC, MC, V. Map p 121.*

★★★ **kids** **Four Seasons Hotel Las Vegas** SOUTH STRIP Situated at the top of Mandalay Bay, and accessed through its own entrance, this is your home away from Vegas (though the Strip action is right at your door if you need a fix). This grown-up oasis (though kids are warmly welcomed) has posh yet quietly tasteful accommodations, plus the service the Four Seasons is renowned for. And unlike most of the other big-name hotels, there are no extra charges for such amenities as gym use. *3960 Las Vegas Blvd. S.* ☎ *877/632-5000 or 702/632-5000. www.fourseasons.com. 424 units. Doubles $450 & up. AE, DC, DISC, MC, V. Map p 121.*

★★ **Golden Nugget** DOWNTOWN The finest hotel in Downtown is currently on an upswing, with public areas sporting a fresh mix of the best of new and old Vegas. Rooms are attractive and comfortable (not quite at the level of similar Strip hotels, but comparatively bargain priced), and the snazzy pool is a major plus. *129 E. Fremont St. (at Casino Center Blvd.).* ☎ *800/846-5336 or 702/385-7111.*

The pool at the Hard Rock Hotel is one of the city's biggest hangouts.

www.goldennugget.com. 1,907 units. Doubles $69 & up. AE, DC, DISC, MC, V. Map p 123.

★★ Green Valley Ranch Resort

HENDERSON   Mash the Ritz-Carlton and W styles together and you have this greatly appealing resort. Its spacious rooms have supremely plush beds. The modern pool area, complete with sandy "beach" and mattresses for serious lounging, plus a bocce ball court, is terrific. The casino is small and a bit of a walk from the main hotel action, but the trendy Whiskey Beach bar is a nighttime draw. The long drive from the Strip and the none-too-low prices are the only detriments. *2300 Paseo Verde Pkwy. (at I-215).* ☎ 866/782-9487 or 702/617-7777. www.green valleyranchresort.com. 200 units. Doubles $129 & up. AE, DC, DISC, MC, V. Map p 122.

★★ Hard Rock Hotel & Casino

EAST OF STRIP   Still the place to stay if you sport tattoos or Pamela Anderson on your arm, but its hipster cred has been somewhat eclipsed by newer kids in town. The beach-party pool area remains a happening hangout, but the rooms try so hard for style that they

sometimes forget comfort. Expanding and transitioning may help the latter, and rock 'n' roll is always here to stay—but you shouldn't stay here if you need to ask, "Who was Kurt Cobain and why is there a glass case of his stuff over there?" *4455 Paradise Rd. (at Harmon Ave.).* ☎ 800/HRD-ROCK (473-7625) or 702/693-5000. www.hardrockhotel. com. 657 units. Doubles $109 & up. AE, DC, MC, V. Map p 122.

★ Harrah's Las Vegas MID-STRIP

A dated but adequate facility, best occupied if you can get a good rate, and ultimately acceptable because of its superconvenient mid-Strip location. Upgrades are improving the pedestrian rooms with better-quality beds and the like. *3475 Las Vegas Blvd. S. (btw. Flamingo & Spring Mountain rds.).* ☎ 800/ HARRAHS (427-7247) or 702/369-5000. www.harrahs.com. 2,579 units. Doubles $79 & up. AE, DC, DISC, MC, V. Map p 121.

★ Hooters Casino Hotel SOUTH

STRIP   A South Florida theme and "party all the time" atmosphere pervade the famous (or is that infamous?) restaurant chain's first-ever hotel, housed in the old San Remo building. The public areas are crammed with things to see (yes, there are Hooter Girls) and do, but are somewhat claustrophobia-inducing. The rooms, though smaller and less luxurious than the modern Vegas norm, are still fun and comfortable. *115 E. Tropicana Ave.* ☎ 866/584-6687 or 702/739-9000. www.hooterscasinohotel.com. 696 units. Doubles $39 & up. AE, DC, DISC, MC, V. Map p 121.

★★ Las Vegas Hilton EAST OF

STRIP   Still a top choice for the businessperson, because, unlike most other hotels in town, this one is more about business than pleasure. Rooms are somewhat more

One of the handsome guest rooms inside the huge MGM Grand, one of the largest hotels in the world.

geared to working customers than playing customers, though the smallish casino is a good retreat. There is plenty of on-site recreation, but the hotel's main draw is its proximity to the Convention Center. It's also a good fallback during nonconvention times, when prices can be pretty low. *3000 Paradise Rd. (at Riviera Blvd.).* ☎ *888/732-7117 or 702/732-5111. www.lvhilton.com. 3,174 units. Doubles $49 & up. AE, DC, DISC, MC, V. Map p 122.*

★★ kids Luxor Las Vegas

SOUTH STRIP   The inexplicable decision to turn what was formerly a deliciously goofy, Egyptian-themed paradise into a generic cookie-cutter resort sent me into mourning. Rooms inside the pyramid (they couldn't get rid of that!) are small and shower-only (and not great if you're tall, thanks to the slanted glass walls). Best of all are the corner rooms, where they plant a Jacuzzi tub right where those slanted windows meet. I prefer the Tower rooms, which are larger and have better bathrooms. *3900 Las Vegas Blvd. S. (btw. Reno &*

Hacienda aves.). ☎ *888/777-0188 or 702/262-4000. www.luxor.com. 4,400 units. Doubles $69 & up. AE, DC, DISC, MC, V. Map p 121.*

★★★ M Resort Spa & Casino

SOUTH OF STRIP   Famous for hosting Bravo's *Top Chef: Las Vegas*, M Resort is a hike from the Strip, but if you don't mind the commute this sophisticated "boutique" property (in Vegas that means 400 rooms) has everything you could ask for in a casino resort: large comfortable rooms, floor-to-ceiling views, giant tubs, two flatscreen TVs (one in the bathroom mirror!), and reasonable rates. *12300 Las Vegas Blvd. S., Henderson.* ☎ *877/673-7678 or 702/797-1000. www.themresort.com. 390 units. Doubles $120 & up. AE, DISC, MC, V. Map p 122.*

★★ Main Street Station

DOWNTOWN   One of the best deals in town, this pretty hotel is clean, comfortable, and even kind of sweet, with a late-Victorian San Francisco style. Superior air circulation makes the public areas much less smoky than those at its counterparts.

The pretty rooms inside The Mirage are small, but the hotel itself impresses thanks to a vast array of amenities.

The Monte Carlo's posh boutique Hotel 32 is worth the extra bucks.

Rooms are unexpectedly stylish and cozy, though the location next to the freeway means that noise can be an issue for some. It's only a couple of blocks from the action on Fremont Street. *200 N. Main St. (btw. Fremont St. & I-95).* ☎ *800/713-8993 or 702/387-1896. www.mainstreet casino.com. 406 units. Doubles $59 & up. AE, DC, DISC, MC, V. Map p 123.*

★★ kids **Mandalay Bay** SOUTH STRIP It doesn't really live up to its South Asian theme, but this beauty is one of my personal favorites. It's oddly kid-friendly, thanks to the big rooms and bathrooms (dig those marble bathtubs), its famous pool area (including beach, wave pool, and lazy river), and the ability to access your room without traversing the casino. A great assortment of restaurants, clubs, and bars will please adults, thus rounding out the demographic appeal. *3950 Las Vegas Blvd. S. (at Hacienda Ave.).* ☎ *877/632-7800 or 702/632-7000. www.mandalaybay.com. 3,309 units. Doubles $99 & up. AE, DC, DISC, MC, V. Map p 121.*

★★★ **Mandarin Oriental Las Vegas** MID-STRIP The Four Seasons has a worthy Strip competitor in this luxe boutique hotel. The public areas' sleek and subtle Asian theme carries over into the state-of-the-art and large guest rooms (the bathrooms notably have freestanding tubs). Toss in gourmet dining, a bi-level spa, and you have a welcome respite smack in the middle of the Strip. And if you must gamble, there's a casino next door. *3752 Las Vegas Blvd. S. (at Harmon Ave.)* ☎ *888/881-9578 or 702/590-8888. www.mandarinoriental.com/las vegas. 392 units. Doubles $375 & up. AE, DC, DISC, MC, V. Map p 121.*

★★ kids **MGM Grand Hotel & Casino** SOUTH STRIP Dauntingly big (it's the largest hotel in the U.S.), but with handsome though blandly upscale rooms that you can often get for a decent price. The West Wing rooms are smaller but have a hip flair and comfort that give them their own significant style. MGM also has a variety of restaurant options and the largest pool area

A chic Red Room at Paris Las Vegas.

apart from Mandalay Bay, complete with a lazy river. *3799 Las Vegas Blvd. S. (at Tropicana Ave.).* ☎ *800/880-0880 or 702/891-7777. www.mgmgrand.com. 5,034 units. Doubles $99 & up. AE, DC, DISC, MC, V. Map p 121.*

★★ **The Mirage** MID-STRIP Its pretty rooms are now running with the Vegas generic upscale pack (though the bathrooms are small), but the rest of the hotel is chic and Asian sleek. The rainforest entrance is still one of the most impressive hotel welcomes in town, and the pool area is a tropical marvel complete with water slide. Good restaurants, terrific bars, and hot clubs complete the mix. *3400 Las Vegas Blvd. S. (btw. Flamingo & Spring Mountain rds.).* ☎ *800/627-6667 or 702/791-7111. www.mirage.com. 3,044 units. Doubles $109 & up. AE, DC, DISC, MC, V. Map p 121.*

★ **Monte Carlo Resort & Casino** SOUTH STRIP Though its name evokes classic and classy, beyond the crystal chandelier–filled lobby this is a fairly generic hotel. Rooms are merely average, though the Hotel 32 boutique level is worth the splurge. The touted pool area

allows for frolicsome fun, but is now overshadowed by other versions on the Strip. Affordable rates and a great location may make the general lack of sparkle unimportant. *3770 Las Vegas Blvd. S. (btw. Flamingo Rd. & Tropicana Ave.).* ☎ *800/311-8999 or 702/730-7777. www.montecarlo.com. 3,002 units. Doubles $99 & up. AE, DC, DISC, MC, V. Map p 121.*

Motel 6 EAST OF STRIP The biggest Motel 6 in the country is a great budget choice and quite close to major Strip casino hotels (the MGM is nearby). The rooms are clean and attractively decorated (though some have shower-only bathrooms and the blankets are a bit rough). *195 E. Tropicana Ave. (at Koval Lane).* ☎ *800/4-MOTEL-6 (466-8356) or 702/798-0728. www.motel6.com. 607 units. Doubles $45 & up. AE, DC, DISC, MC, V. Map p 122.*

★ kids **New York–New York Hotel & Casino** SOUTH STRIP This chaotic location was a bit more tolerable when the heavy Manhattan theme made it more of an attraction. Now that the spectacle is in the process of being toned down into more of the new Vegas

The lobby of the sophisticated M Resort Spa & Casino; a stay here is worth the commute to the Strip.

The Vegas Hotel Experience

Vegas hotels are not your average hotel experience. Most hotels are content to be located near attractions. Vegas hotels *are* the attraction. Or they bring the attractions into the hotel. Or both. Expect access to all kinds of unusual goodies, from happening night-clubs to roller coasters to, oh yes, casinos. But hotel size brings its own issues; 3,000-room (or more) resorts simply do not have the kind of service one expects at a true resort. Personal attention can be spotty, maintenance can be a bit slow (that stain on the carpet will likely stay there for some time), and it's highly likely you will hear plumbing and other noises emanating from nearby rooms. The final caveat is the hidden price. Most hotels charge extra for almost every-thing beyond bed and bath, including gym use, Wi-Fi use, pool cabana use—it all adds up. Many casino hotels now audaciously automatically add that charge in as a mandatory "resort fee." Only true resorts such as the Four Seasons have inclusive room prices. Factor that in when making your decision.

blandness, the inconveniences are starting to outweigh the pleasures. The guest rooms are middlebrow sophisticated, but nothing startling, and can vary dramatically in size and shape; they're also overpriced when compared with what you get at other spots on the Strip. *3790 Las Vegas Blvd. S. (at Tropicana Ave.).* ☎ *800/693-6763 or 702/740-6969. www.nynyhotelcasino.com. 2,023 units. Doubles $79 & up. AE, DC, DISC, MC, V. Map p 121.*

★ kids **Orleans** SOUTH STRIP Easily overlooked because it's sort of in the middle of nowhere off the Strip, the Orleans has no fancy reputation to help draw attention (and a sometimes lackluster staff doesn't help). It's still worth considering because you can often find bargain rates on the surprisingly roomy accommodations, which sport the occasional sweet Victorian touch. Free shuttle services to the Strip help with the isolation, as do the 70-lane bowling alley (open really late) and 18-screen multiplex. *4500*

W. Tropicana Ave. (west of the Strip & I-15). ☎ *800/ORLEANS (675-3267) or 702/365-7111. www.orleanscasino. com. 1,886 units. Doubles $59 & up. AE, DC, DISC, MC, V. Map p 121.*

★★ **The Palazzo** MID-STRIP This expansion of the Venetian functions as its own hotel, with its own massive grand lobby, own restaurants, and own (pricey) rates. Its "suites" are a wee bit better than those at its sister property, but it's even more expensive for roughly the same experience, so unless money's no object (lucky you!), a splurge stay here isn't a must. *3325 Las Vegas Blvd. S.* ☎ *877/883-6423 or 702/607-7777. www.palazzo lasvegas.com. 4,027 units. Doubles $199 and up. AE, DC, DISC, MC, V. Map p 121.*

★★ kids **Palms Casino Resort** MID-STRIP Still one of the hipper hotels, and a bit daunting because of that. But look past the zero-body-fat types lining up to get into one of the many happening clubs and bars, and you will find a good, cheap food

A palazzo bedroom at the Rio, whose accommodations are among the largest in Vegas.

court; a multiplex; and a fine child-care facility. It's not the first place I would suggest for a family, but those elements might sway you. Rooms have especially comfortable beds and lots of pizzazz. Try to get a high-level unit for some of the best views of the city. *4321 W. Flamingo Rd. (just west of I-15).* ☎ *866/942-7777 or 702/942-7777. www.palms.com. 664 units. Doubles $99 & up. AE, DC, DISC, MC, V. Map p 121.*

★★ Paris Las Vegas Casino Resort MID-STRIP Now here's a

hotel that remains dedicated to its French theme—an element of Vegas that is vanishing, to my despair. Merci! It's also perfectly located on the Strip. Regular rooms are a little generically pretty (though the bathtubs are satisfyingly deep), but the Red Rooms are done up in sort of a masculine French bordello and are worth the extra price. *3655 Las Vegas Blvd. S.* ☎ *888/BONJOUR (266-5687) or 702/946-7000. www. parislv.com. 2,916 units. Doubles $119 & up. AE, DC, DISC, MC, V. Map p 121.*

★★ Planet Hollywood Resort & Casino SOUTH STRIP Those

hoping for kitsch will be disappointed in this centrally located hotel's classy and clubby design, which has obliterated all traces of its previous incarnation as the Aladdin. And the chain's memorabilia angle works well in the very comfy rooms, which all have a movie or entertainment theme (needless to say, the Judy Garland room has a very different vibe than the *Pulp Fiction* one). *3667 Las Vegas Blvd. S.* ☎ *877/333-WISH (9474) or 702/785-5555. www.planethollywood resort.com. 2,567 units. Doubles $99 & up. AE, DC, DISC, MC, V. Map p 121.*

★★★ Red Rock Resort SUM-

MERLIN A fantastic resort—right across from the eponymous red rocks themselves—that's not that many minutes from the Strip, giving you both privacy and ready access. It's one of the best settings in Vegas. Rooms are striking, and the comfy beds will make you disinclined to get up (especially with the big flatscreen TV in front of you), and the bathrooms are positively sprawling. The pool attracts celebrities pretending they want to keep a low profile. The gym and spa are not worth the mandatory additional price. *10973 W. Charleston Rd.* ☎ *866/767-7773 or 702/797-7625. www.redrocklasvegas.com. 800 units. Rooms $139 & up (up to 4 people). AE, DC, DISC, MC, V. Map p 122.*

★ Rio All-Suite Hotel & Casino

MID-STRIP Still some of the largest rooms in Vegas, though no more "suites" than at the Venetian (you just get a living/sitting area along with your bedroom area) and outstripped in style by so many others. Because the place is hectic—it feels like spring break all the time and bringing kids is not encouraged—and located off the Strip, it's not a first-choice venue. *3700 Las Vegas Blvd. S. (just west of I-15).* ☎ *888/752-9746 or 702/777-7777. www.playrio.com. 2,582 units. Doubles $99 & up. AE, DC, DISC, MC, V. Map p 121.*

Sahara Hotel & Casino NORTH STRIP One of the few venerable old casino hotels still standing in Vegas (it opened in 1952), the Sahara has a solid Moroccan theme, a roller coaster (though it mystifyingly discourages children), and budget-friendly rates. Rooms are motel bland (though windows actually open!), but if all you're looking for is four walls and a mattress, this isn't a bad choice. *2535 Las Vegas Blvd. S. (at E. Sahara Ave.).* ☎ *888/ 696-2121 or 702/737-2111. www. saharavegas.com. 1,720 units. Doubles $45 & up. AE, DC, DISC, MC, V. Map p 122.*

★★ **kids** **South Point Hotel & Casino** SOUTH OF STRIP This "locals" joint is lower profile and south of the Strip. But given the size of the rooms here, the frills (squishy beds, flatscreen TVs), and the access to plenty of on-site entertainment (movie theaters, bowling alley, a first-rate equestrian center, budget food choices)—all for a much lower price than its on-the-Strip competition—the (rather minor) distance from the main action hardly matters. *9777 Las Vegas Blvd. S.* ☎ *866/796-7111 or 702/796-7111. www.southpointcasino.com. 650 units. Doubles $79 & up. AE, DC, DISC, MC, V. Map p 122.*

★ **kids** **Stratosphere Las Vegas Hotel & Casino** NORTH STRIP Think of this place as a motel, with prices to match, and the difference between its humble yet adequate rooms and the much more lavish numbers down the Strip won't bother you a bit. The very friendly service makes it that much more

One of the sleek suites at THEhotel at Mandalay Bay, arguably the best place to stay in Las Vegas.

attractive. You will need a car if you stay here because it's much too far to walk to the main Strip action or to Downtown. *2000 Las Vegas Blvd. S. (btw. St. Louis & Baltimore aves.).* ☎ *800/99-TOWER (998-6937) or 702/380-7777. www.stratosphere hotel.com. 2,444 units. Doubles $49 & up. AE, DC, DISC, MC, V. Map p 122.*

★ **Terrible's** EAST OF STRIP This unexpected bargain isn't terrible at all (its owner is convenience store and gas station magnate Ed "Terrible" Herbst). And it's near the Strip! Rooms are as basic as can be, though accommodations in the newest hotel tower have fresh furnishings and flatscreen TVs. The pool area is particularly nice for a budget operation. *4100 Paradise Rd. (at Flamingo Rd.).* ☎ *800/640-9777 or 702/733-7000. www.terrible herbst.com. 325 units. Doubles $39 & up. AE, DC, DISC, MC, V. Map p 122.*

The Westin Casuarina's lack of pizzazz makes it a somewhat bland option, but the "Heavenly Beds" do make for a good night's sleep.

★★★ THEhotel at Mandalay

Bay SOUTH STRIP   Quite possibly the best hotel on the Strip. It's certainly the most sophisticated, with its Manhattan-style sleekly contemporary lobby; and it certainly has the largest rooms, each a dark-wood and gleaming black one-bedroom suite, complete with two flatscreen TVs and a deep soaking tub. Its separate-from-but-attached-to Mandalay Bay location means you can have your getaway and gamble too. *3950 Las Vegas Blvd. S.* ☎ *877/632-7800 or 702/632-7777. www.hotelatmandalaybay.com. 1,120 units. Suites $160 and up. AE, DC, DISC, MC, V. Map p 121.*

★★ Treasure Island MID-STRIP

Strip away the TI's original theme (pirates and treasure) and what you have left is a very nice albeit bland upscale hotel. Good-sized rooms with some unexpected careful details (including decent art on the walls and large soaking tubs in the

bathroom) are superior to those at the neighboring Mirage, even if that hotel is more interesting overall. The pool is a disappointment. *3300 Las Vegas Blvd. S. (at Spring Mountain Rd.).* ☎ *800/944-7444 or 702/ 894-7111. www.treasureisland.com. 2,885 units. Doubles $89 & up. AE, DC, DISC, MC, V. Map p 121.*

★ Trump International Hotel

Las Vegas NORTH STRIP   This huge, non-gaming tower parlays the opulence that The Donald is known for, with gilded windows, lots of marble, and ubiquitous crystal chandeliers. Plush and sizable studio "suites" boast Jacuzzi-style tubs, two flatscreen TVs, and small kitchens, complete with coffeemakers—a Sin City rarity. And if you find yourself missing a casino, there are plenty within walking distance. *2000 N. Fashion Show Drive (at Las Vegas Blvd.).* ☎ *702/982-0000. www.trump lasvegashotel.com. 1,282 units. Studio suites start at $99. AE, DISC, MC, V. Map p 122.*

The huge guest rooms inside The Venetian are among the best in the city.

Playing the Hotel Rate Game

Hotel rates in Las Vegas fluctuate more wildly than the stock market, and can be just as hard to predict. Rates in this chapter are the listed minimum rack rates (without the 9%–10% hotel tax included), but the same room at the same hotel can range from $50 to $300 to a lot more (or a lot less), depending on when you book. You will, for example, always pay top dollar around New Year's, on weekends, and when a major convention is in town. Take the prices I list with a grain of salt and always do your homework. Check out the going rates on the major hotel booking sites (Expedia, Travelocity, and Travelaxe.com) and always check the websites of the hotels themselves for available discount packages and rates.

Also note that rates listed here are for double occupancy only; most Vegas hotels usually charge extra (sometimes as much as $35 per person, per night) for another person in the room, even if the extra guest happens to be your child. If you're bringing kids along, always ask about the hotel's policy when booking.

★★★ **Vdara Hotel & Spa** MID-STRIP A luxury, non-smoking, non-gaming all-suite hotel right in the middle of the Strip. And it's seriously committed to sustainability? It's a winner in my book. The earth-toned suites come in various sizes, all with minikitchens (stove tops and dishwashers!), deep soaking tubs, and the high-tech wizardry one expects in the latest crop of Vegas hotels. It just might be the most restful of the CityCenter properties, though it's right on Bellagio's back doorstep if you need a Vegas fix. *2600 W. Harmon Ave. (at Las Vegas Blvd. S.).* ☎ *866/745-7767 or 702/590-2767. www.vdara.com. 1,495 units. Suites from $159. AE, DISC, MC, V. Map p 121.*

★★ **The Venetian** MID-STRIP Some of the largest and best rooms on the Strip, though not precisely the "suites" they advertise. Instead, it's one big space encompassing both bedroom and sunken living room, with plenty of stately touches and marble bathrooms with double

sinks. The Venezia tower (worth the extra cash) has its own entrance and more of a Ritz-Carlton vibe. The immense property can be hard to navigate. *3355 Las Vegas Blvd. S.* ☎ *877/883-6423 or 702/414-1000. 4,029 units. Doubles $149 & up. AE, DC, DISC, MC, V. Map p 121.*

Sign Up!

Most Vegas hotels offer discounted packages and room rates to those who friend them on Twitter, Facebook, etc. It's a friends with benefits arrangement that you should definitely take advantage of.

★ **The Westin Casuarina Las Vegas Hotel, Casino & Spa** MID-STRIP Brand-name reliability means those Westin Heavenly Beds—though, oddly, not the best beds in town—and various features that make this more business traveler–friendly than pleasure seeker–appropriate. The gym is free, the casino dated and forgettable. It has more pizzazz than other chain hotels in town, but so much less than the powerhouse hotels that the prices seem a bit of a cheat. *160 E. Flamingo Rd.* ☎ *866/837-4215 or 702/836-9775. www.starwoodhotels. com. 825 units. Doubles $139 & up. AE, DC, DISC, MC, V. Map p 121.*

★★ **Wynn Las Vegas** NORTH STRIP An adult luxury resort on steroids. While the enormous rooms are full of nifty touches—high-thread-count linens, Warhol silk-screens, curtains that operate with a push button, long tubs in the bathroom, fancy amenities—the overall experience is just too big to offer the kind of service one would expect after all the hype this place generated. For these prices, you can do better. *3131 Las Vegas Blvd. S. (at the corner of Sands Ave.).* ☎ *888/320-9966 or 702/770-7100. www.wynnlasvegas.com. 3,933 units. Doubles $199 & up. AE, DC, DISC, MC, V. Map p 122.* ●

The lobby at CityCenter's Vdara Hotel & Spa.

The nifty rooms inside the Wynn Las Vegas come with all sorts of bells and whistles, but they're also very pricey for what you get.

Hoover Dam & Lake Mead

Hoover Dam

Boulder City

- 1 Boulder City
- 2 Nevada Southern Railway Station
- 3 Milo's
- 4 Boulder Dam Hotel/ Hoover Dam Museum
- 5 Hoover Dam
- 6 Visitor's Center
- 7 Winged Figures of the Republic
- 8 Elevator Towers
- 9 Coffee Cup Diner
- 10 Alan Bible Visitors Center
- 11 Lake Mead

LAKE MEAD NATIONAL RECREATION AREA

- Unpaved road
- Marina/Boat launch
- Picnic area
- Ranger station

Previous Page: One of the magnificent rock formations found in the Valley of Fire.

The architectural and engineering marvel that is Hoover Dam is probably the major reason there is a Vegas today (those lights on the Strip need lots of power). It's one of the world's major electrical-generating plants, but it's also a wonder of Art Deco design and a remarkable combination of beauty and function. It's responsible for the creation of the 110-mile-wide (177km) Lake Mead, an unexpected recreational oasis smack in the middle of the desert. START: **From Las Vegas, take U.S. 93 South. U.S. 93 becomes U.S. 93/95 South, which then becomes the Nevada Highway.**

1 ★★ **Boulder City.** This charming small town (originally built by the Bureau of Reclamation to house the workers building Hoover Dam, originally called Boulder Dam) is all the more unexpected because it's only 20 miles (32km) from Vegas. It doesn't hurt that this is the only place in Nevada where it's not legal to gamble. Wander through the adorable downtown area (construction and growth are strictly regulated to maintain its character) as a Mayberry antidote to the "bright lights, big city" atmosphere, which despite its proximity seems another lifetime away. ⏱ *30 min. Off Nevada Hwy. www.bouldercity.com.*

2 ★ kids **Nevada Southern Railway Station.** This seasonal train ride offers visitors the chance to take a 3-mile (4.8km) journey along a historic train route (built in 1931 as a supply route for the Hoover Dam) aboard refurbished 1911 Pullman cars. A can't-miss for train buffs and a sweet outing for everyone else. ⏱ *45 min. Reservations are unnecessary, but allow 15 min. before departure time to buy tickets & choose a seat. 600 Yucca St., Boulder City. ☎ 702/486-5933. www.nevadasouthern.com. Admission $8 adults, $7 seniors 65 & up, $4 kids 12 & under. Trains depart 10, 11:30am, 1 & 2:30pm from Boulder City Sat–Sun Feb–Dec.*

Recharge your own dam power with a healthy salad, cheese plate, or glass of wine at **3** **Milo's.** Dine indoors or alfresco and soak in Boulder City's small-town charm. *538 Nevada Hwy., Boulder City. ☎ 702/293-9540. $.*

4 **Boulder Dam Hotel/Hoover Dam Museum.** This still-active hotel is set in a Dutch-colonial-style building built to house VIPs visiting the Dam construction. The structure also holds a museum that neatly explains why the dam and related construction projects represented virtually the only economic possibility for the area during the Depression. The great emphasis on the human-interest element of construction makes this a good counterpart to the more engineering-oriented

Charming Boulder City is unusual in that it's the only place in Nevada where you can't gamble.

exhibit at the Dam itself. *1305 Arizona St., Boulder City. Hotel ☎ 702/293-3510. www.boulderdam hotel.com. Hoover Dam Museum ☎ 702/294-1988. www.bcmha.org. Admission $2 adults, $1 children & seniors. Open 10am–5pm Mon–Sat, noon–5pm Sun. Closed Jan 1, Easter Sunday, Mother's Day, Thanksgiving & Christmas Day.*

Take U.S. 93 South to the Nevada–Arizona border. Pass the turnoff for Lake Mead, and as you near the dam you'll see the parking structure on your left. Parking fee is $7, cash only. Note that this drive can get very backed up on Sundays and the end of holiday weekends, so if you must visit on those days, go early in the morning or late in the day.

5 ★★★ **Hoover Dam.** The star of the show and a wonder of the modern, engineering world. You may not realize how beautiful a monolithic structure can be until you behold the dam. Note how the design reflects the Art Deco period so influenced by the post–King Tut–tomb–discovery Egyptian revival. Construction on this National Historic Landmark lasted from 1931 to 1936 and, once completed, the face of the southwest was changed forever. Anytime someone turns on a light switch in California or Nevada, they can thank the Hoover Dam engineers and the workers who gave so much (more than 100 people died during construction) to make it come true. *See* **6**.

6 **Visitor's Center.** All the information you could possibly want about Hoover Dam is contained in this three-level exhibition and information center. Videos, interactive displays, photos, and more help illustrate what a massive feat this was. Two tours are available. **The Powerplant Tour** is a partly

guided, partly self-guided tour of the Dam, including a 500-foot (152m) elevator ride down to one of the generators, a journey through a tunnel drilled through rock, and a trip to the observation deck overlooking Lake Mead. **The Hoover Dam Tour** (worth the extra time and expense) travels deeper into the dam's rocky hallways to view its inner workings. ⏱ *2 hr. Off U.S. 93 South. ☎ 866/730-9097 or 702/494-2517. www.usbr.gov/lc/hooverdam. Powerplant Tour: $11 adults; $9 seniors, military & dependents; $6 children 7–16; free for kids under 7. Hoover Dam Tour: $30. Open 9am–6pm, last admission at 5:15pm.*

7 ★★ **Winged Figures of the Republic.** Should you opt to walk the Dam on your own, stop on the Nevada side to pay homage to these 30-foot-high (9.1m) winged mythological figures representing the higher nature of all humankind (they were designed by sculptor Oskar J. W. Hansen). The bronze-shelled statues were originally erected, along with an astrological star chart, as a memorial to higher intelligence, but after World War II were rededicated to the men who built the dam, plus

The huge Winged Figures of the Republic guard the entrance to Hoover Dam on the Nevada side.

Lake Mead is known both for its scenery and for its outdoor recreational opportunities.

their little mascot dog. *Off U.S. 93 South. Free admission.*

8 ★ Elevator Towers. Exhibits on local flora and fauna are found on the dam's elevator towers, thus combining nature and industry. Note how the clock on the tower on the Nevada side gives one time, and the one on the Arizona side another; the latter is on Mountain Standard Time, 1 hour ahead of the former—except during daylight saving time, because Arizona does not observe it. *See 5 above; just viewing the exterior is free.*

Get a cup of joe or a burger at the classic greasy spoon **Coffee Cup Diner.** *512 Nevada Hwy., Boulder City. www.worldfamouscoffeecup.com. ☎ 702/294-0517. Open daily 6am–2pm. $.*

Take U.S. 93 North to Lakeshore Dr./NV 166.

10 Alan Bible Visitors Center. Staffed by eager, knowledgeable locals, Lake Mead's main visitor center is a great place to pick up information on area recreational activities. Do explore its small but interesting exhibits on local nature and history. It's also here that you pay your fee for the Lake Mead scenic drive (see 11). ⏱ *20 min. 4 miles (6km) northeast of Boulder City, on*

U.S. 93 at NV 166. ☎ 702/293-8990. Open 8:30am–4:30pm daily, except Thanksgiving, Christmas & New Year's Day.

Follow the scenic Lakeshore Dr./ NV 166 into Lake Mead National Recreational Area.

11 ★★★ Lake Mead. Created in 1935 by the building of Hoover Dam (and named for the commissioner of the Bureau of Reclamation at the time), Lake Mead is the largest man-made lake in the United States. The best way to view the lake (whose beauty isn't lessened by its artificial origins) is to take its 30-mile (48km) scenic drive. Expect colorful desert landscape, panoramic views, and mountain vistas. There are several beaches and campgrounds along the way, with plenty of opportunities for various recreational activities. The water is a bit chilly and the beaches are rocky; so it's used more for fishing and sailing purposes than swimming. ⏱ *1½ hr.; more if you indulge in the recreational facilities. www.nps.gov/lame. Entry fee $5 per vehicle, $3 per person walking or biking. Open daily, 24 hr., though some spots in the park have shorter hours (inquire at visitor center, 10).*

The scenic route becomes Northshore Rd. and from here you can head to the Valley of Fire or take U.S. 93/95 North back to Las Vegas.

Valley of Fire State Park

1 Valley of Fire State Park Entrance
2 Visitor's Center
3 Rainbow Vista
4 Mouse's Tank
5 Seven Sisters
6 Cabins
7 Petrified Logs
8 Elephant Rock
9 Lost City Museum
10 Inside Scoop

••••• Unpaved road
----- Hiking trail (approximate route)

0   2 mi
0   2 km

Overton
169

VALLEY OF FIRE STATE PARK

Duck Rock
White Domes
Rainbow Vista 3
Silica Dome
Baseline Mesa
Mouse's Tank 4
Petrified Log
Natural Arch
Visitor Center 2
Cabins 6 7
Elephant Rock 8
Pinnacles
Atlatl Rock
Petrified Logs
Seven Sisters 5
Clark Memorial
Charlie's Spring
Beehives
169
← To 15

LAKE MEAD NAT'L RECREATION AREA

To Overton Beach & Lake Mead →

Northshore Dr.

For those who think a desert is brown, flat, and feature-less, the Valley of Fire comes as a shock. This almost other-worldly tundra of brilliant red sandstone formations was created 150 million years ago as wind twisted and shaped the landscape into what could be called a Jurassic zoo of creaturelike configurations. The man-made structures that make Las Vegas a marvel have noth-ing on what nature can do, given enough time. START: **From Las Vegas, take I-15 North to exit 75 (Valley of Fire turnoff); trip time is 1 hour. For a more scenic route, take I-15 North, then take Lake Mead Boulevard East to Northshore Road/NV 167 and proceed to the Valley of Fire exit; trip time is 1½ hours. Be sure to bring plenty of water.**

1 **Valley of Fire State Park Entrance.** As you enter the 25,000-acre (10,117-hectare) park (Nevada's oldest state park) on a windy little road, the first major sight will be on your left. The Atlatl Rock was a basic training camp for Native American tribes in the area (an *atlatl* was a stick used to throw spears) and is full of old petroglyphs. Men came here

for coming-of-age ceremonies and to learn hunting and survival skills. ⏲ *5 min. 60 miles (96km) NE of Las Vegas, Overton, NV. http://parks.nv.gov/ vf.htm. Admission $6 per car. Open daily, sunrise to sunset.*

2 **Visitor's Center.** Accessed from the Old Arrowhead road (the first car road running from Los

Valley of Fire State Park is filled with beautiful and eerie rock formations, and is home to some of the best scenery in the state.

Angeles to Salt Lake City), this is where you can purchase various materials concerning information on the park, talk to park rangers, and check out some small displays on the local landscape. Be sure to pick up a map before you head into the park. ⏲ *15 min. NV 169, 6 miles (10km) west of Northshore Rd.* ☎ *702/397-2088. Open daily 8:30am–4:30pm, except for Christmas Day.*

③ **Rainbow Vista.** From the visitor's center, drive through this palette of multicolored sandstone, all the colors of the spectrum splashed down to earth. The drive dead-ends at the pure white silica domes. At this point, you can take a hiking trail to a movie site where they filmed the bawdy western *The Professionals* (1966) with Burt Lancaster and Lee Marvin. A bit of the set is still there. ⏲ *1 hr. round-trip for gardens; 1 hr. for hike.*

④ **Mouse's Tank.** Take a hike down a deep sandy wash (no sandals, shoes only) with many well-executed petroglyphs lining the way. The glyphs are the most ancient and historic in the Southwest, thousands of years old—even the local Paiute people don't know who did them. The titular Mouse's Tank (named for a fugitive who hid out here in the 1890s) lies at the end of the hike and is a natural sandstone bowl *tanaha,* which is a hole in the desert that fills up when it rains (don't come here after a storm), but it's something of a letdown post-petroglyphs. ⏲ *30 min.*

⑤ **Seven Sisters.** Named after an Indian legend describing how the seven stars of the big Dipper were created, these girls are seven huge red rock formations of Mesozoic sandstone. It was originally an ancient sand dune that hardened and cracked over the years, and erosion has separated it into seven distinct shapes with one little brother in the middle.

From Valley of Fire, follow NV 169 southeast toward Scenic Loop Rd. Make a left to stay on NV 169 into Overton. NV 169 becomes S. Moapa Valley Blvd. 30 min.

Heat Alert

Daytime temperatures in the Valley of Fire can reach 120°F (49°C) in the height of summer. This tour is best done in late fall, early spring, and winter, when the climate is more tolerable. Even during those times, carry at least a gallon of water per person.

Some of the detailed petroglyphs found on the hiking trail to Mouse's Tank.

An ancient pueblo village is one of the top attractions at the Lost City Museum.

6 Cabins. These native stone structures are now used for picnicking (bring fixings along with you to the park), but were originally constructed in the 1930s by the Civilian Conservation Corps to provide nighttime shelter for weary travelers. It's a good location for taking a breather before hitting the road again.

7 Petrified Logs. These prime examples of fossilized wood have been fenced off to prevent treasure hunters from walking off with them. It's believed that the colorful trunks are the remnants of a forest, whose trees were washed into this area about 225 million years ago.

8 Elephant Rock. This red stone formation is easily accessed via a short trail from the main park road. And it really does look like the head of a giant pachyderm. Can we say prime photo op?

9 Lost City Museum. A sweet little museum focusing on an ancient Anasazi village (named Pueblo Grande de Nevada because the Pueblo Indians occupied it after the Anasazi disappeared) discovered in the area in 1924. Along with exhibits whose contents date back some 12,000 years, there are some displays on the area's 19th-century Mormon settlers. ⏱ *30 min. 721 S.*

Moapa Valley Blvd./NV 169, Overton, NV. ☎ *702/397-2193. www. comnett.net/~kolson. Admission $4 adults, $3 seniors 65+, free for kids 18 & under. Open 8:30am–4:30pm daily. Closed Thanksgiving Day, Dec 25 & Jan 1.*

A sweet old-fashioned ice-cream parlor, **10 Inside Scoop** also offers soups, sandwiches, and box lunches for picnics inside the park. *395 S. Moapa Valley Blvd.* ☎ *702/ 397-2055. $.*

To get back to Vegas, head northeast on S. Moapa Valley Blvd./NV 169 toward S. Pioneer Rd. Merge onto I-15 South to Las Vegas. ●

One of the immense Seven Sisters, giant rock formations set inside the Valley of Fire.

The
Savvy Gambler

Playing the **Games**

As you walk through the labyrinthine twists and turns of a casino floor, your attention will likely be dragged to the various games and, your interest piqued, your fingers may begin to twitch in anticipation of hitting it big. Before you put your money on the line, it's imperative to know the rules of the game you want to play.

Most casinos offer free gambling lessons at scheduled times on weekdays. This provides a risk-free environment for you to learn the games that tickle your fancy. Some casinos follow their lessons with low-stakes game play, enabling you to put your newfound knowledge to the test at small risk. During those instructional sessions, and even when playing on your own, dealers in most casinos will be more than happy to answer any questions you might have. Remember, the casino doesn't need to trick you into losing your money . . . the odds are already in their favor across the board; that's why it's called gambling.

Another rule of thumb: Take a few minutes to watch a game being played in order to familiarize yourself with the motions and lingo. Then go back and reread this section—things will make a lot more sense at that point. Good luck!

Players Clubs

If you gamble, it definitely pays to join a players club. These so-called clubs are designed to attract and keep customers in a given casino by providing incentives: meals, shows, discounts on rooms, gifts, tournament invitations, discounts at hotel shops, VIP treatment, and (more and more) cash rebates. Join a players club (it doesn't cost a cent to sign up), and soon you too will be getting those great hotel-rate offers—$20-a-night rooms, affordable rooms at the luxury resorts, even free rooms. (This is one way to beat high hotel rates in Vegas.) Of course, your rewards are often greater if you play in just one casino, but your mobility is limited.

When you join a players club (inquire at the casino desk), you're given something that looks like a credit card, which you must insert into an ATM-like device whenever you play. Yes, many casinos even have them for the tables as well as the machines. (Don't forget to retrieve your card when you leave the machine, as I sometimes do.) The device tracks your play and computes bonus points.

Which players club should you join? Actually, you should join one at any casino where you play because even the act of joining usually entitles you to some benefits. It's convenient to concentrate play where you're staying; if you play a great deal, a casino hotel's players-club benefits may be a factor in your accommodations choice. Consider, though, particularly if you aren't a high roller, the players clubs Downtown. You get more bang for your buck because you don't have to spend as much to start raking in the goodies.

Previous page: There are a myriad number of card games that you can play in Las Vegas.

Another advantage is to join a players club that covers many hotels under the same corporate umbrella. For example, MGM MIRAGE runs The Mirage, Bellagio, MGM Grand, and more, and their players club offers discounts and point awards at all of their properties.

One way to judge a players club is by the quality of service you receive when you enroll. Personnel should politely answer all your questions (for instance, is nickel play included, and is there a time limit for earning required points?) and be able to tell you exactly how many points you need for various bonuses.

Maximizing your players club profits and choosing the club that's best for you is a complex business. To get into it in depth, see www.lasvegasadvisor.com. Also visit the sites for the individual casinos, many of which allow you to join their clubs online.

Baccarat

The ancient game of baccarat, or chemin de fer, is played with eight decks of cards. Firm rules apply, and there is no skill involved other than deciding whether to bet on the bank or the player. No, really—that's all you have to do. The dealer does all the other work. You can essentially stop reading here. Oh, all right, carry on.

Any beginner can play, but check the betting minimum before you sit down, as this tends to be a high-stakes game. The cards are shuffled by the croupier and then placed in a box called the "shoe." Players may wager on "bank" or "player" at any time. Two cards are dealt from the shoe and given to the player who has the largest wager against the bank, and two cards are dealt to the croupier, acting as banker. If the rules call for a third card, the player or banker, or both, must take the third card. In the event of a tie, the hand is dealt over. **Note:** The guidelines that determine if a third card must be drawn (by the player or banker) are provided at the baccarat table upon request.

The object of the game is to come as close as possible to the number 9. To score the hands, the cards of each hand are totaled and the last digit is used. All cards have face value. For example: 10 plus 5 equals 15 (score is 5); 10 plus 4 plus 9 equals 23 (score is 3); 4 plus 3 plus 3 equals 10 (score is 0); and 4 plus 3 plus 2 equals 9 (score is 9). The closest hand to 9 wins.

Size Counts . . . Sort Of

For those who desire a more informal environment in which to play baccarat, casinos offer minibaccarat, played on a normal-size table no larger than a blackjack table. There is no substantive difference between baccarat and its little brother. It's simply a matter of size and speed—the size of your bankroll and the speed with which you may build it (or lose it). Table stakes in minibaccarat tend to be lower, and the hands proceed at a much faster pace.

Each player has a chance to deal the cards. The shoe passes to the player on the right each time the bank loses. If the player wishes, he or she may pass the shoe at any time.

Note: When you bet on the bank and the bank wins, you are charged a 5% commission. This must be paid at the start of a new game or when you leave the table.

Big Six

Big Six provides pleasant recreation and involves no study or effort. The wheel has 56 positions on it, 54 of them marked by bills from $1 to $20. The other two spots are jokers, and each pays 40 to 1 if the wheel stops in that position. All other stops pay at face value. Those marked with $20 bills pay 20 to 1, the $5 bills pay 5 to 1, and so forth. The idea behind the game is to predict (or just blindly guess) what spot the wheel will stop at and place a bet accordingly.

Blackjack

The dealer starts the game by dealing each player two cards. In some casinos, they're dealt to the player faceup, in others facedown, but the dealer always gets one card up and one card down. Everybody plays against the dealer. The object is to get a total that is higher than that of the dealer without exceeding 21. All face cards count as 10; all other number cards, except aces, are counted at their face value. An ace may be counted as 1 or 11, whichever you choose it to be.

Starting at his or her left, the dealer gives additional cards to the players who wish to draw (be "hit") or none to a player who wishes to "stand" or "hold." If your count is nearer to 21 than the dealer's, you win. If it's under the dealer's, you lose. Ties are a push and nobody wins. After all the players are satisfied with their counts, the dealer exposes his or her facedown card. If his or her two cards total 16 or less, the dealer must "hit" (draw an additional card) until reaching 17 or over. If the dealer's total exceeds

21, he or she must pay all the players whose hands have not gone "bust." It is important to note here that the blackjack dealer has no choice as to whether he or she should stay or draw. A dealer's decisions are predetermined and known to all the players at the table.

If you're a novice or just rusty, do yourself a favor and buy one of the small laminated cards available in shops all over town that illustrate proper play for every possible hand in blackjack. Even longtime players have been known to pull them out every now and then, and they can save you from making costly errors.

How to Play
Here are eight "rules" for blackjack:
1. Place the number of chips that you want to bet on the betting space on your table.

2. Look at the first two cards the dealer starts you with. If you wish to "stand," then wave your hand over your cards, palm down (watch your fellow players), indicating that you don't want any

additional cards. If you elect to draw an additional card, you tell the dealer to "hit" you by tapping the table with a finger (watch your fellow players).

3. If your count goes over 21, you are "bust" and lose, even if the dealer also goes "bust" afterward.

4. If you make 21 in your first two cards (any picture card or 10 with an ace), you've got blackjack. Blackjack should ideally pay off at 3:2 (you make 3 dollars for every two dollars bet), but many casinos now pay out at the less stellar 6:5, especially if you're playing a single deck. Note that you won't be paid at all if the dealer also has blackjack, in which case it's a push and nobody wins.

5. If you find a "pair" in your first two cards (say, two 8s or two aces), you may "split" the pair into two hands and treat each card as the first card dealt in two separate hands. You will need to place an additional bet, equal to your original bet, on the table. The dealer will then deal you a new *second* card to the first split card and play commences as described above. This will be done for the second split card as well. **Note:** When you split aces

you will receive only one additional card per ace and must "stand."

6. After seeing your two starting cards, you have the option to "double down." You place an amount equal to your original bet on the table and you receive only one more card. Doubling down is a strategy to capitalize on a potentially strong hand against the dealer's weaker hand. **Tip:** You may double down for less than your original bet, but never for more.

7. Anytime the dealer deals himself or herself an ace for the "up" card, you may insure your hand against the possibility that the hole card is a 10 or face card, which would give him or her an automatic blackjack. To insure, you place an amount up to one-half of your bet on the "insurance" line. If the dealer does have a blackjack, you get paid 2 to 1 on the insurance money while losing your original bet: You break even. If the dealer does not have a blackjack, he or she takes your insurance money and play continues in the normal fashion.

8. **Remember:** The dealer must stand on 17 or more and must hit a hand of 16 or less.

Look, but Don't Touch!

1. **Never touch your cards (or anyone else's),** unless it's specifically stated at the table that you may. While you'll only receive a verbal slap on the wrist if you violate this rule, you *really* don't want to get one.

2. **Players must use hand signals to indicate their wishes to the dealer.** All verbal directions by players will be politely ignored by the dealer, who will remind players to use hand signals. The reason for this is the "Eye in the Sky," the casino's security system, which focuses an "eye" on every table, and must record players' decisions to avoid accusations of misconduct or collusion.

Professional Tips

Advice of the experts in playing blackjack is as follows:

1. Do not ask for an extra card if you have a count of 17 or higher, ever.

2. *Do not* ask for an extra card when you have a total of 12 or more if the dealer has a 2 through 6 showing in his or her "up" card.

3. *Ask* for an extra card or more when you have a count of 12 through 16 in your hand if the dealer's "up" card is a 7, 8, 9, 10, or ace.

There's a lot more to blackjack strategy than the above, of course. So consider this merely as the bare bones of the game. Blackjack is played with a single deck or with multiple decks; if you're looking for a single-deck game, your best bet is to head to a Downtown casino.

A final tip: Avoid insurance bets; they're sucker bait!

Craps

The most exciting casino action is usually found at the craps tables. Betting is frenetic, play is fast-paced, and groups quickly bond while yelling and screaming in response to the action.

The Possible Bets

The craps table is divided into marked areas (Pass, Come, Field, Big 6, Big 8, and so on), where you place your chips to bet. The following are a few simple directions.

PASS LINE A "Pass Line" bet pays even money. If the first roll of the dice adds up to 7 or 11, you win your bet; if the first roll adds up to 2, 3, or 12, you lose your bet. If any other number comes up, it's your "point." If you roll your point again, you win, but if a 7 comes up again before your point is rolled, you lose.

DON'T PASS LINE Betting on the "Don't Pass" is the opposite of betting on the "Pass Line." This time, you lose if a 7 or an 11 is thrown on the first roll, and you win if a 2 or a 3 is thrown on the first roll.

If the first roll is 12, however, it's a push (standoff), and nobody wins. If none of these numbers is thrown and you have a point instead, in order for you to win, a 7 will have to be thrown before the point comes

up again. A "Don't Pass" bet also pays even money.

COME Betting on "Come" is the same as betting on the Pass Line, but you must bet after the first roll or on any following roll. Again, you'll win on 7 or 11 and lose on 2, 3, or 12. Any other number is your point, and you win if your point comes up again before a 7.

DON'T COME This is the opposite of a "Come" bet. Again, you wait until after the first roll to bet. A 7 or an 11 means you lose; a 2 or a 3 means you win; 12 is a push, and nobody wins. You win if 7 comes up before the point. (The point, you'll recall, was the first number rolled if it was none of the above.)

FIELD This is a bet for one roll only. The "Field" consists of seven numbers: 2, 3, 4, 9, 10, 11, and 12. If any of these numbers is thrown on the next roll, you win even money, except on 2 and 12, which pay 2 to 1 (at some casinos 3 to 1).

BIG 6 AND 8 A "Big 6 and 8" bet pays even money. You win if either a 6 or an 8 is rolled before a 7. Mathematically, this is a sucker's bet.

ANY 7 An "Any 7" bet pays the winner 5 for 1. If a 7 is thrown on the first roll after you bet, you win.

A typical craps table.

The Savvy Gambler

DICE PROBABILITIES

NUMBER	POSSIBLE COMBINATIONS	ACTUAL ODDS	PERCENTAGE PROBABILITY
2	1	35:1	2.8%
3	2	17:1	5.6%
4	3	11:1	8.3%
5	4	8:1	11.1%
6	5	6.2:1	13.9%
7	6	5:1	16.7%
8	5	6.2:1	13.9%
9	4	8:1	11.1%
10	3	11:1	8.3%
11	2	17:1	5.6%
12	1	35:1	2.8%

"HARD WAY" BETS In the middle of a craps table are pictures of several possible dice combinations together with the odds the casino will pay you if you bet and win on any of those combinations being thrown. For example, if double 3s or 4s are rolled and you had bet on them, you will be paid 7 to 1. If double 2s or 5s are rolled and you had bet on them, you will be paid 9 to 1. If either a 7 is rolled or the number you bet on was rolled any way other than the "Hard Way," then the bet is lost. In-the-know gamblers tend to avoid "Hard Way" bets as an easy way to lose their money.

ANY CRAPS Here you're lucky if the dice "crap out"—if they show 2, 3, or 12 on the first roll after you bet. If this happens, the bank pays 7 to 1. Any other number is a loser.

PLACE BETS You can make a "Place Bet" on any of the following numbers: 4, 5, 6, 8, 9, and 10. You're betting that the number you choose will be thrown before a 7 is thrown. If

you win, the payoff is as follows: 4 or 10 pays at the rate of 9 to 5; 5 or 9 pays at the rate of 7 to 5; 6 or 8 pays at the rate of 7 to 6. "Place Bets" can be removed at any time before a roll.

Some Probabilities

The probability of a certain number being rolled at the craps table is not a mystery. As there are only 36 possible outcomes when the dice are rolled, the probability for each number being rolled is easily ascertained. See the "Dice Probabilities" chart in this section to help you in case you decided it was more fun to pass notes or sleep during your math classes.

So 7 has an advantage over all other combinations, which, over the long run, is in favor of the casino. You can't beat the law of averages, but if you can't beat 'em, join 'em. (Play the "Don't Pass" bet.)

Poker

Poker is the game of the Old West. There's at least one sequence in every Western where the hero faces off against the villain over a poker

hand. In Las Vegas, poker is a tradition, although it isn't played at every casino.

Traditional Poker

There are lots of variations on the basic game, but one of the most popular is Hold 'Em. Two cards are dealt facedown to the players. After a betting round, five community cards (everyone can use them) are dealt faceup on the table. The player makes the best five-card hand, using their own cards and the "board" (the community cards), and the best hand wins. The house dealer takes care of the shuffling and the dealing and moves a marker around the table to alternate the start of the deal. The house usually rakes around 10% (it depends on the casino) from each pot. Most casinos also provide tables for playing Seven-Card Stud, Omaha High, and Omaha Hi-Lo. A few will even have Seven-Card Stud Hi-Lo split. To learn how these variations are played, either read a book or take lessons.

Warning: If you don't know how to play poker, don't attempt to learn at a table. Card sharks are not a rare species in Vegas; they will gladly feast on fresh meat (you!). Find a casino that provides free gaming lessons and learn, to paraphrase Kenny Rogers, when to hold 'em, and when to fold 'em.

Table Games

Beyond the traditional poker games, Vegas is also home to a number of table games that capitalize on the popularity of poker, everything from a variation on Texas Hold'Em to three-card poker. The biggest difference between these games and the real thing? You play against the house, not other players (some people find this less intimidating). And the house usually holds a serious advantage in these games, though many of them feature bonus or progressive payouts should you manage to hit a given hand (a flush, for example).

It's actually more difficult to explain many of these games than it is to play them (though I do cover Pai Gow, Caribbean Stud, and Let it Ride later in this chapter). For this reason, I recommend watching a table for a while or taking a lesson (when offered). Note that many of the poker-related table games often have explanation cards in a small dispenser on the side of the table—if you're interested in a game, take one and read it. If you have questions, feel free to ask the dealer.

Warning: The table games can be lots of fun, but do not assume that you will learn strategy that you can use later on at a real poker table. The poker hands might be the same, but the approach is very different. Hands that you routinely play at a table game because you aren't playing against a slew of opponents will often leave you dead in the water in an actual game.

Pai Gow Poker

Pai Gow poker (a variation on poker) is a popular table game that is played with a traditional deck plus one joker. The joker is a wild card that can be used as an ace or to complete a straight, a flush, a straight flush, or a royal flush. Each player is dealt seven cards to arrange into two hands: a two-card hand and a five-card hand. As in standard poker, the highest two-card hand is two aces, and the highest five-card hand is a royal flush. The five-card hand must be higher than the two-card hand (if the two-card hand is a pair of 6s, for example, the five-card hand must be a pair of 7s or better). Any player's hand

Poker Hands

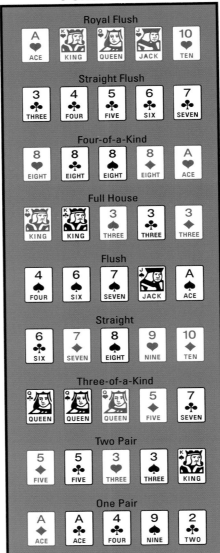

All the major poker hands.

that is set incorrectly is an automatic loser. The object of the game is for both of the players' hands to rank higher than both of the banker's hands. Should one hand rank exactly the same as the banker's hand, this is a tie (called a "copy"), and *the banker wins all tie hands*. If the player wins one hand but loses the other, this is a "push," and no money changes hands. The house dealer or any player may be the banker. The bank is offered to each player, and each player may accept or pass. Winning hands are paid even money, less a 5% commission.

Caribbean Stud Poker

Caribbean Stud poker is yet another variation of poker that is gaining in popularity. Players put in a single ante bet and are dealt five cards facedown from a single deck; they play solely against the dealer, who receives five cards, one of them faceup. Players are then given the option of folding, or may call by making an additional bet that is double their original ante. After all player bets have been made, the dealer's cards are revealed. If the dealer doesn't qualify with at least an ace/king combination, players are paid even money on their ante and their call bets are returned. If the dealer does qualify, each player's hand is compared to the dealer's. On winning hands, players receive even money on their ante bets, and call bets are paid out on a scale according to the value of their hands. The scale ranges from even money for a pair, to 100 to 1 on a

royal flush, although there is usually a cap on the maximum payoff, which varies from casino to casino.

An additional feature of Caribbean Stud is the inclusion of a progressive jackpot. For an additional side bet of $1, a player may qualify for a payoff from a progressive jackpot. The jackpot bet pays off only on a flush or better, but you can win on this bet even if the dealer ends up with a better hand than you do. Dream all you want of getting that royal flush and taking home the jackpot, but the odds of it happening are astronomical; so don't be so quick to turn in your resignation letter. Most veteran gamblers will tell you this is a bad bet (from a strict mathematical standpoint, it is), but considering that Caribbean Stud already has a house advantage that is even larger than the one in roulette, if you're going to play, you might as well toss in the buck and pray.

Let It Ride

Let It Ride is another popular game that involves poker hands. You place three bets at the outset and are dealt three cards. The dealer is dealt two cards that act as community cards (you're not playing against the dealer). Once you've seen your cards, you can choose to

pull the first of your three bets back, or "Let It Ride." The object of this game is to get a pair of 10s or better by combining your cards with the dealer's. If you're holding a pair of 10s or better in your first three cards, you want to let your bets ride the whole way through. Once you've decided whether to let your first bet ride, the dealer exposes one of his or her two cards. Once again you must make a decision to take back your middle bet or keep on going. Then the dealer exposes the last of his or her cards; your third bet must stay. The dealer then turns over the hands of the players and determines whether you've won. Winning bets are paid on a

scale, ranging from even money for a single pair up to 1,000 to 1 for a royal flush. These payouts are for each bet you have in play. Like Caribbean Stud, Let It Ride has a progressive jackpot that you can win for high hands if you cough up an additional dollar per hand, but be advised that the house advantage on that $1 is obscene. But hey, that's why it's called gambling.

Roulette

Roulette is an extremely easy game to play, and it's really quite colorful and exciting to watch. The wheel spins and the little ball bounces around, finally dropping into one of the slots, numbered 1 to 36, plus 0 and 00 (on American wheels, which is what you'll find mostly in Vegas; European wheels eschew the 00 so they lower the house advantage—not a beloved prospect for the casinos in Vegas). You can place bets "Inside" the table and "Outside" the table. Inside bets are bets placed on a particular number or a set of numbers. Outside bets are those placed in the boxes surrounding the number table (see picture below). If you bet on a specific number and it comes up, you'll be paid 35 to 1 on your bet. Bear in mind, however, that the odds of a particular number coming up are actually 38 to 1 (don't forget 0 and 00!) so the house has a 5.26% advantage the moment you place an Inside bet. For payoffs on Outside bets, such as Red/Black, Odd/Even, and so

forth, see the drawing below. The methods of placing single-number bets, column bets, and others are fairly obvious. The dealer will be happy to show you how make many interesting betting combinations, such as betting on six numbers at once. Each player is given different-colored chips so that it's easy to follow the numbers you've bet on.

Some typical bets are indicated by means of letters on the roulette layout depicted in the figure. The winning odds for each of these sample bets are listed. These bets can be made on any corresponding combinations of numbers.

Tip: The latest trend in Vegas is "electronic" roulette, where you bet electronically (no need to manually distribute all of those chips) on the spin of an actually wheel. The biggest difference in games that use this technology is that they go a lot faster, which (given the large house advantage on this game) means you can lose your money even more quickly.

Slots

You put the coin in the slot and pull the handle. What, you thought there was a trick to this?

Actually, there is a bit more to it. But first, some background. Old-timers will tell you slots were invented

A typical roulette table.

to give wives something to do while their husbands gambled. Slots used to be stuck at the edges of the casino and could be counted on one hand, maybe two. But now they are the casino. The casinos make more from slots than from craps, blackjack, and roulette combined. There are some 140,000 slot machines (not including video poker) in the county. Some of these are at the airport, steps from you as you deplane. It's just a matter of time before the planes flying into Vegas feature slots that pop up as soon as you cross the state line.

But in order to keep up with the increasing competition, the plain old machine, where reels just spin, has become nearly obsolete. Now, they are all computerized and have added buttons to push, so you can avoid getting carpal tunnel syndrome from yanking the handle all night. (The handles are still there on many of them.) Many don't even have reels any more, but are entirely video screens, which offer a number of little bonus extras that have nothing to do with actual play. The idea is still simple: Get three (sometimes four) cherries (clowns, sevens, dinosaurs, whatever) in a row and you win something. Each machine has its own combination. Some will pay you something with just one symbol showing; on most, the more combinations there are, the more opportunities for loot. Some will even pay if you get three blanks. Study each machine carefully to learn what it does. **Note:** The **payback** goes up considerably if you bet the limit (from 2 to as many as 90 coins).

Progressive slots are groups of linked machines (sometimes spread over several casinos) where the jackpot gets bigger every few moments (just as lottery jackpots build up). Bigger and better games keep showing up; for example, there's Anchor Gaming's much-imitated **Wheel of Gold,** wherein if you get the right symbol, you get to spin a roulette wheel, which guarantees you a win of a serious number of coins.

Other gimmick machines include the popular **Wheel of Fortune** machines; slots that have a gorilla attempt to climb the Empire State Building, heading up as you win; and machines with themes like *Star Trek* or *I Dream of Jeannie*. And, of course, there are always those giant slot machines, gimmicky devices found in almost every casino. They may not win as often as regular slots (though there is no definite word on it one way or the other), but not only are they just plain fun to spin, they often turn into audience-participation gambling, as watchers gather to cheer you on to victory.

Nickel slots, which for a long time had been overlooked, relegated to a lonely spot somewhere by a back wall because they were not as profitable for the casinos as quarter and dollar slots, are now everywhere. Many machines now offer a 45-nickel maximum (meaning a larger bet on those machines than on the five-quarter-maximum slots), and gamblers have been flocking to them. As a result, more cash is pocketed by the casino (which keeps a higher percentage of cash off of nickel slots than it does off of quarter slots), which is happy to accommodate this trend by offering up more and more nickel slots. (See how this all works? Are you paying attention?) Ultratightwads will be pleased by the increased presence of the humble penny slot, but few, if any, allow for only a penny bet—in fact, the maximum bet is $3!

The most important recent move in Vegas gambling, however, was the transition to cashless machines. When gambling with these machines, players insert their money, they play, and when they cash out, they get—instead of the comforting sound of coins cascading out into the tray—a little paper ticket with their total winnings on it. (Those of us who find the sound of the coins pouring out a comfort are only slightly pleased to learn that the noise plays, as a computer-generated audio effect, when the ticket is disgorged.) Hand in your ticket at a cashier's window (or use the omnipresent ATM-style redemption machines) and you get your winnings. It's not nearly as viscerally satisfying, but the future is now. As a result of the cashless machine trend, the casinos are much quieter, as many of the formerly chatty machines have been largely silenced, and that famous Vegas clang-clang is somewhat dimmed.

Are there surefire ways to win on a slot machine? No. But you can lose more slowly. The slot machines use minicomputers known as random number generators (RNGs) to determine the winning combinations on a machine, but though each spin may indeed be random, individual machines are programmed to pay back different percentages over the long haul. As a result, a machine programmed to return a higher percentage might be "looser" than others. A bank of empty slots probably (but not certainly) means the machines are tight. Go find a line where lots of people are sitting around with trays full of money. (Of course, yours will be the one that doesn't hit.) A good rule of thumb is that if your slot doesn't hit something in four or five pulls, leave it and go find another. It's not as though you won't have some choice in the matter. Also, each casino has a bank of slots that they advertise as more loose or with a bigger payback. Try these. It's what they want you to do, but what the heck.

Tip: For a pretty good explanation of slot odds, check out http://wizardofodds.com/slots. The site also has a wealth of information on gambling in general.

Sports Books

Most of the larger hotels in Las Vegas have sports-book operations, which look a lot like commodities-futures trading boards. In some, almost as large as theaters, you can sit comfortably, occasionally in recliners and sometimes with your own video screen, and watch ballgames, fights, and, at some casinos, horse races on huge TV screens. To add to your enjoyment, there's usually a deli/bar nearby that serves sandwiches, hot dogs, soft drinks, and beer. As a matter of fact, some of the best sandwiches in Las Vegas are served next to the sports books.

Sports books take bets on virtually every sport (and not just who'll win, but what the final score will be, who'll be first to hit a home run, who'll be MVP, who'll wear red shoes, you name it). They are best during important playoff games or big horse races, when everyone in the place is watching the same event—shrieking, shouting, and moaning, sometimes in unison. Joining in with a cheap bet (so you feel like you too have a personal stake in the matter) makes for bargain entertainment.

Video Poker

Rapidly gaining on slots in popularity, video poker works the same way as regular poker, except you play against the machine. You are dealt a hand, you pick which cards to keep and which to discard, and then you get your new hand. And, it is hoped, you collect your winnings. This is somewhat more of a challenge and more active than slots because you have some control (or at least the illusion of control) over your fate, and it's easier than playing actual poker with a table full of folks who probably take it very seriously.

There are a number of varieties of this machine, with **Jacks or Better, Deuces Wild, and so forth.** Be sure to study your machine before you sit down. (The best returns are offered on the **10/7 Double Bonus Poker** machine, where, theoretically, if you play perfectly, you can, in fact, beat the house.) The Holy Grail of general video-poker machines is the 9/6 (it pays nine coins for a full house, six coins for a flush), but you'll need to pray a lot before you find one in town. Some machines offer **double down:** After you have won, you get a chance to draw cards against the machine, with the higher card the winner. If you win, your money is doubled and you are offered a chance to go again. Your money can increase nicely during this time, and you can also lose it all very quickly, which is most annoying.

Technology is catching up with video poker, too. Now they even have touch screens, which offer a variety of different poker games, blackjack, and video slots—just touch your screen and choose your poison.

Tip: The key to winning at video poker (where the strategy is very different than playing actual poker) is playing your cards perfectly at each individual machine. To do that, a little study time is in order. I suggest perusing the video poker books in the ShopLVA section of the website for the very reputable Las Vegas Advisor (www.lasvegasadvisor.com). If, like me, you like a more hands-on tutorial, Bob Dancer's Video Poker for Winners software is a real champ when it comes to teaching proper strategy for video poker; it's also for sale at the Las Vegas Advisor site. ●

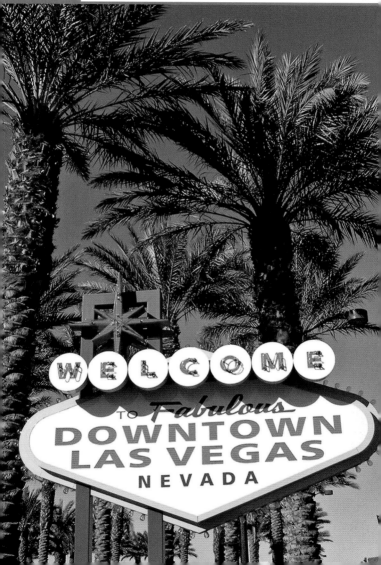

The
Savvy Traveler

Before You Go

Government Tourist Offices

For advance information, call or write the Las Vegas Convention and Visitors Authority, 3150 Paradise Rd., Las Vegas, NV 89109 (☎ 877/VISIT-LV [847-4858] or 702/892-0711; www.visitlasvegas.com).

For information on all of Nevada, including Las Vegas, contact the Nevada Commission on Tourism (☎ 800/638-2328; www.travelnevada.com).

The Best Times to Go

Most of a Las Vegas vacation is usually spent indoors, so you can have a good time here year-round. That said, the most pleasant seasons in this area are spring and fall (when crowds are everywhere and prices are high), especially if you want to experience the great outdoors. Summers here mean ultrahigh temps, but also fewer crowds and lower prices. Winters can get downright cold, so you can forget about using the hotel pool (almost all are outdoors and many close from Labor Day to Memorial Day); but prices in mid-December and mid-January usually descend into good-value territory.

Holidays (especially New Year's) in Vegas are a mob scene—and for Vegas, "holiday" includes Super Bowl Sunday, anytime during the NCAA Basketball Championships (especially the Final Four), boxing matches, and all other important pro and college sporting events. Hotel prices skyrocket not only during the holidays, but also when big conventions and special events take place. If a major convention is to be held during your trip, you might want to change your date. You can check convention dates by contacting the Las Vegas Convention and Visitors Authority (☎ 877/VISIT-LV [847-4858] or 702/892-0711; www.visitlasvegas.com).

Festivals & Special Events

Before you arrive, contact the **Las Vegas Convention and Visitors Authority** (☎ 877/VISIT-LV [847-4858] or 702/892-0711; www.visitlasvegas.com), or the **Chamber of Commerce** (☎ 702/735-1616; www.lvchamber.com), to find out what other events are scheduled during your visit. Once you're in town, check *Las Vegas Weekly* (www.lasvegasweekly.com), the free magazines you'll find in your hotel room, or **www.lasvegasevents.com**.

MAR. The start of spring sees the running of two of the most important **NASCAR/Winston Cup** races in the country. Held at the **Las Vegas Motor Speedway,** 7000 Las Vegas Blvd. N. (☎ 800/644-4444; www.lvms.com), the Sam's Town 300 and the UAW-DaimlerChrysler 400 attract thousands of racing fans each year.

JUNE. The annual **CineVegas Film Festival** (☎ 702/992-7979; www.cinevegas.com), usually held in early June, is growing in popularity and prestige, with film debuts from both independent and major studios, plus lots of celebrities hanging around for the big parties. The **World Series of Poker,** held at **The Rio All-Suite Hotel & Casino** (3700 W. Flamingo Rd.; ☎ 800/PLAY-RIO [752-9746]) in June, July, and August, is *the* gambling event in Vegas, featuring high-stakes gamblers and showbiz personalities. There are daily events with entry stakes ranging from $125 to $5,000. For a chance at the main event's $12-million purse, players must ante

Previous page: The Strip might be more famous today, but Downtown Las Vegas is where it all began.

LAS VEGAS'S AVERAGE TEMPERATURES (°F/°C) & PRECIPITATION					
	JAN	FEB	MAR	APR	MAY	JUNE
High °F	57	63	69	78	88	99
High °C	14	17	21	26	31	37
Low °F	37	41	47	54	63	72
Low °C	3	5	8	12	17	22
Avg. Precip. (in.)	.59	.69	.59	.15	.24	.08
(cm)	1.5	1.8	1.5	.4	.6	.2
	JULY	AUG	SEPT	OCT	NOV	DEC
High °F	104	102	94	81	66	57
High °C	40	39	34	27	19	14
Low °F	78	77	69	57	44	37
Low °C	26	25	21	14	7	3
Avg. Precip. (in.)	.44	.45	.31	.24	.31	.40
(cm)	1.1	1.1	.8	.6	.8	1.0

up $10,000. You can crowd around the tables and watch for free, or if you want to avoid the throngs you can catch a lot of it on TV. For more informat.on visit **www.worldseries ofpoker.com**.

OCT. Pro golf's best players hit the greens at the televised 4-day **Justin Timberlake Shriners Hospitals for Children Open** (☎ **702/873-1010**), which is played at TPC Summerlin and TPC at the Canyons in October.

NOV. Some of the world's top comics and comedy troupes laugh it up at **The Comedy Festival** (☎ **800/ 634-6001**; www.thecomedyfestival. com). The event also includes workshops, film festivals, and more. Held in mid-November, its primary host casino is Caesars Palace.

DEC. The **National Finals Rodeo** (☎ **866/388-3267** [for tickets]; www.nfrexperience.com) is the Super Bowl of rodeos, attended by about 200,000 people each year, suddenly turning Vegas into Cowboy Country. Order tickets as far in advance as possible.

In mid-December, the winners of college football's Pac-10 Conference and the Mountain West conference square off against each other in

the **Maaco Bowl Las Vegas.** The action takes place at the 32,000-seat Sam Boyd Stadium. Call **702/ 732-3912** or visit www.lvbowl.com for ticket information.

New Year's Eve is the biggest day of the year on the Vegas calendar; reserve your hotel room early (and be prepared to pay top dollar). Downtown, at the Fremont Street Experience, there is a big block party with two dramatic countdowns to midnight at 9pm (midnight on the East Coast) and midnight. The Strip is usually closed to street traffic and hundreds of thousands of people pack the area for the festivities.

Weather

Vegas isn't always hot, but when it is hot, it's melting. Still, the humidity averages a low 22% and even on hot days there's apt to be a breeze. Also, except on the hottest of summer days, there is relief at night, when temperatures drop by as much as 20°F. Keep in mind, however, that this is the desert and it's not hot year-round; it can get quite cold, especially in the winter. That summer breeze can become a cold, biting, strong wind of up to 40 mph

(64kmph) and more in winter. And there are entire portions of the year when you won't be using your hotel pool at all (even if you want to, because many of the hotels close huge chunks of their fabulous pool areas for "the season," which can be as long as from Labor Day to Memorial Day). If you aren't traveling at the height of summer, bring a jacket. Also remember sunscreen (apply it often!) and a hat—even if it's not all that hot, you can burn easily and very quickly.

Useful Websites

- **www.vegas4visitors.com**: A sweeping and comprehensive site on Las Vegas, with lots of practical advice and strong opinions.

- **www.lvchamber.com**: The Chamber of Commerce's official website has a calendar of events, lots of practical tips, info on getting married in Vegas, and more.

- **www.vegas.com**: Using resources from the city's free weeklies, this site features plenty of locally written reviews and opinions.

- **www.lasvegasadvisor.com**: Veteran Vegas bargain hunter Anthony DeCurtis gives out all sorts of valuable tips, plus trivia, gambling advice, and lots of cool info.

- **www.visitlasvegas.com**: The Convention and Visitor Bureau's official site is well-organized by subject matter and offers lots of information and practical tips on hotels, dining, entertainment, and more. There's also information on discount vacation packages.

Cellphones

It's a good bet your phone will work in Las Vegas, but take a look at your wireless company's coverage map on its website before heading out.

I've had problems with reception every now and then (using two different providers), especially inside some of the casino hotels.

Car Rentals

If you stick to one section of the Strip, or concentrate solely on Downtown, then you technically don't need a car. I used to strongly recommend getting one anyway because a car does make it easier to get around, parking doesn't cost you anything beyond the valet tip, and if you want to do some serious touring off the Strip, it's almost a must. But that was before rental car taxes and fees in Vegas rose to 27.5%, plus a $3-per-day fee if you rent out of McCarran. On my last trip I figured out it would have been cheaper if a little less efficient to use public transport and some cabs than the bill I got at the rental counter. So now I say that if you're not planning on venturing off the Strip and you have no mobility issues, a car is more of a maybe than a must.

National companies with outlets in Las Vegas include **Alamo** (☎ 877/227-8367; www.alamo.com), **Avis** (☎ 800/230-4898; www.avis.com), **Budget** (☎ 800/527-0700; www.budget.com), **Dollar** (☎ 800/800-3665; www.dollar.com), **Enterprise** (☎ 800/261-7331; www.enterprise.com), **Hertz** (☎ 800/654-3131; www.hertz.com), **National** (☎ 800/227-7368; www.nationalcar.com), **Payless** (☎ 800/729-5377; www.paylesscarrental.com), and **Thrifty** (☎ 800/847-4389; www.thrifty.com).

If you're visiting from abroad and plan to rent a car in the United States, keep in mind that foreign driver's licenses are usually recognized in the U.S., but you should get an international one if your home license is not in English.

For decent car-rental rates, consult the major travel websites (Travelocity, Expedia) to comparison shop. You should also check out **Breezenet.com** (www.bnm.com), which offers domestic car-rental

discounts with some of the most competitive rates around.

Getting **There**

By Plane

For a list of airlines that have regularly scheduled flights into Vegas see "Toll-Free Numbers & Websites" on p 178.

Las Vegas is served by **McCarran International Airport** (☎ 702/ 261-5211; www.mccarran.com), just a few minutes' drive from the southern end of the Strip, where the bulk of casinos and hotels are concentrated. This big, modern airport is rather unique in that it includes several casino areas with more than 1,000 slot machines.

Getting to your hotel from the airport is a cinch. **Bell Transportation** (☎ 800/274-7433 or 702/739-7990; www.bell-trans.com) runs 20-passenger minibuses daily between the airport (shuttles depart just west of the baggage-claim area) and all major Las Vegas hotels and motels (7:45am–midnight). Several other companies offer similar ventures—just stand outside on the curb, and one will be flagged for you. The cost is $6.50 per person each way to hotels on the Strip or around the Convention Center, $8 to Downtown or other off-Strip properties (north of the Sahara Hotel and west of I-15). Other similarly priced shuttles run 24 hours and can be found in the same place. Buses from the airport leave about every 10 minutes. When you want to check out of your hotel and head back to the airport, call at least 2 hours in advance to be safe (though often you can just flag down one of the buses outside any major hotel).

Even less expensive are **Citizens Area Transit (CAT) buses** (☎ 702/ CAT-RIDE [847-4858]; www.rtcsnv. com/transit). The no. 108 bus departs from the airport and takes you to the Stratosphere, where you can transfer to the no. 301, which stops close to most Strip- and Convention Center–area hotels. The no. 109 goes from the airport to the Downtown Transportation Center (at Casino Center Blvd. and Stewart Ave). Bus fares (depending on the route you take) are $1.75–$3 for adults, 75[ce]–$1.50 for seniors and children 6 to 17, and free for children under 6. It's cheaper than a shuttle, but it might not be enough to put up with the added hassle (buses do not stop in front of hotel main entrances, while shuttles do—you could be in for a long walk if you opt for the bus), especially if you have luggage.

You can also take a taxi from the airport to the Strip (around $15–$23) or Downtown ($18–$25); the maximum number of passengers allowed in a cab is five (infants and kids included).

By Car

The main highway connecting Las Vegas with the rest of the country is **I-15;** it links Montana, Idaho, and Utah with Southern California. From the east, take **I-70** or **I-80** west to Kingman, Arizona, and then **U.S. 93** north to Downtown Las Vegas (Fremont St.). From the south, take **I-10** west to Phoenix and then U.S. 93 north to Las Vegas. From San Francisco, take I-80 east to Reno and then **U.S. 95** south to Las Vegas.

Getting **Around**

By Public Transportation
The **no. 301** bus operated by **CAT** (☎ **702/CAT-RIDE [847-4858];** www.rtcsnv.com/transit) plies a route between the Downtown Transportation Center (at Casino Center Blvd. and Stewart Ave.) and a few miles beyond the southern end of the Strip. The fare is $1.75 for adults, 75¢ for seniors and children 6 to 17, and free for children under 6. A low $4 buys an all-day pass. CAT buses run all day and are wheelchair accessible. Exact change is required.

The Deuce (☎ **702/CAT-RIDE [847-4858];** www.rtcsouthernnevada. com) is a fleet of modern double-decker buses that run the length of the Strip into Downtown and near the airport. A one-way ride is $3 for adults, $1.50 for seniors 62 and older and children 6 to 17, and free for those under 6. A $7 all-day pass lets you get on and off as many times as you like and also lets you ride other RTC buses all day. Exact change is required.

By Taxi
Cabs line up in front of all major hotels and are an easy way to get around town (if not the cheapest). Cabs charge $3.30 at the meter drop and 25[ce] for each additional ⅛ mile, plus an additional $1.80 fee for being picked up at the airport; time-based penalties are assessed when you get stuck in a traffic jam. You can often save money by sharing a cab—up to five people can ride for the same fare. Do not attempt to hail a taxi from anywhere but an approved stand when you're on the Strip; it's illegal for cabs to pick up fares off the street.

Cab companies in the area include **Desert Cab Company** (☎ 702/ 386-9102), **Whittlesea Blue Cab**

(☎ 702/394-6111), and **Yellow/ Checker Cab/Star Company** (☎ 702/873-2000).

By Monorail
The **Las Vegas Monorail** (www. lvmonorail.com) is a rider's best shot at getting from one end of the Strip to the other with a minimum of frustration (though the expense can add up). The 4-mile (6.4km) monorail route runs from the MGM Grand at the southern end of the Strip to the Sahara at the northern end, with stops at Paris/Bally's, The Flamingo, Harrah's, the Las Vegas Convention Center, and the Las Vegas Hilton along the way. Keep in mind that some of the physical stops are not as geographically close as their namesakes, so there can be an unexpected additional (very long) walk from the monorail stop to wherever you intend to go.

Trains can accommodate more than 200 passengers (standing and sitting) and make the end-to-end run in about 15 minutes. Operating hours are Monday through Thursday from 7am to 2am and Friday through Sunday from 7am to 3am. Fares are exceedingly steep $5 for a one-way ride, no matter what distance you travel; discount multiride/multiday passes are sold and can bring the price of a ride down to about $3.50. Kids ages 5 and under ride free.

By Car
If you plan on venturing beyond the Strip (or far from the general area surrounding your hotel), a car is your best bet. The Strip is too spread out for walking (and often Las Vegas is too hot or too cold to make those strolls pleasant), Downtown is too far away for a cheap cab ride, and public transportation is

often ineffective in getting you where you want to go in a timely manner. You should note that places with addresses some 60 blocks east or west of the Strip are actually less than a 10-minute drive—provided there is no traffic.

Having advocated traveling by car, I should warn you that traffic is reaching horrifying proportions, and it's harder and harder to get around town with any certain swiftness. A general rule of thumb is to avoid driving on the Strip whenever you can, and avoid driving at all during peak rush hours (8–9:30am and 4:30–6pm). Notable back roads that can help you access the major hotels while avoiding the Strip include Harmon Avenue, Koval Lane, and Frank Sinatra Drive. Get yourself a good map (most Vegas car-rental agencies hand out excellent ones) and familiarize yourself with chosen routes before you set out.

Parking in Vegas is usually a pleasure because all the casino hotels offer free valet service. That means for a mere $1 to $2 tip you can park right at the door, though valet parking usually fills up on busy nights (or is offered to guests only on busy evenings). In those cases, you can use the gigantic self-parking lots that all hotels have.

On Foot

The best way to navigate Downtown is on your own two feet, especially in the Glitter Gulch area on Fremont Street, which is now pedestrian-only. Walking also makes sense on the Strip, if you're going short distances and want to avoid traffic tie-ups. I know people who walk up and down the Strip as a matter of course, but despite the flat terrain, it can get very tiring (especially when it might very well be a mile from your room to a hotel's entrance). Keep in mind the following:

1. **Distances in Las Vegas can be very deceiving.** That hotel that looks really close to where you're standing may be more than a mile away. And if it's broiling hot outside or freezing cold (and it can get very chilly in winter), that may be the longest mile you've ever walked.

2. **Don't even think of jaywalking.** Pushing your luck in this area will likely result in you getting hurt. Badly. Use the provided escalators and pedestrian walkways to cross the Strip and its major side streets.

3. **Make use of indoor walkways and free shuttles.** A free monorail connects Mandalay Bay with Luxor and Excalibur (and indoor walkways connect all three hotels as well), and a free tram shuttles between The Mirage and TI at the Mirage. Monte Carlo and Bellagio are connected to CityCenter via moving walkways. And you can walk from Paris Las Vegas to Bally's without ever stepping outside. A free shuttle also runs from Paris Las Vegas and Harrah's to the Rio.

Fast Facts

APARTMENT RENTALS Note that most home and apartment rentals in Las Vegas are located off the Strip and that a car becomes a necessity if you go this route. **Las**

Vegas Retreats (☎ 888/887-0951 or 702/966-2761; www.lasvegas retreats.com) is a reputable firm that offers upscale accommodations at decent prices. A pricier (and more upscale) option is **Las Vegas Luxury Home Rentals** (☎ 702/871-9727; www.lasvegasluxuryhome rentals.com).

AREA CODES The area code for Las Vegas is **702.**

ATMS/CASHPOINTS An ATM (automated teller machine) is pretty much right at your elbow no matter where you are in Vegas. Particularly in casinos.

The **Cirrus** (☎ 800/424-7787; www.mastercard.com) and **PLUS** (☎ 800/843-7587; www.visa.com) networks span the globe; look at the back of your bank card to see which network you're on, then call or check online for ATM locations in Vegas.

Be sure you know your personal identification number (PIN) and daily withdrawal limit before you depart. *Note:* Remember that many banks impose a fee every time you use a card at another bank's ATM, and that fee can be higher for international transactions (up to $5 or more) than for domestic ones (which typically run $2–$3 in Las Vegas).

BABYSITTERS Contact **Around the Clock Child Care** (☎ 800/798-6768 or 702/365-1040). In business since 1987, this reputable company clears its sitters with the health department, the sheriff, and the FBI, and carefully screens references. Rates are $75 for 4 hours for one or two children, $15 for each additional hour, with surcharges for additional children and on holidays. Call at least 3 hours in advance.

BANKS Banks are generally open from 9 or 10am to 5 and sometimes 6pm, and most have Saturday hours.

BUSINESS HOURS Casinos and most bars are open 24 hours a day. Stores generally open between 9 and 10am and close between 7 and 8pm Monday through Saturday; on Sunday they usually open around 11am and close by 6pm. Stores in the casino hotels sometimes keep longer hours.

CONSULATES & EMBASSIES All embassies are located in the nation's capitol, Washington, D.C. Some consulates are located in major U.S. cities and most nations have missions to the United Nations in New York City. For addresses and phone numbers of embassies in Washington, D.C., call ☎ 202/555-1212, or log on to www.embassy. org/embassies.

CUSTOMS U.S. airports have considerably beefed up security clearances in the years since the terrorist attacks of 9/11, and clearing Customs and Immigration can take as long as 2 hours, especially on summer weekends.

DENTISTS Hotels usually keep lists of dentists, should you need one. For dental referrals, you can also call the **Southern Nevada Dental Society** (☎ 702/733-8700; www. sndsonline.org) weekdays from 9am to noon and 1 to 5pm; when the office is closed, a recording will tell you whom to call for emergency service.

DINING Vegas is used to all kinds, so unless a restaurant specifies a dress code (and if you're headed to a "name" restaurant, be sure to check in advance), business-casual attire should get you in anywhere. Always make reservations way in advance for higher-end locations (a month early isn't unheard of).

In the budget department, you'll almost always save money by splurging at lunch instead of dinner; prices can be 20% to 50% less at lunchtime in some fancy restaurants. Most restaurants start serving lunch between 11:30am and noon; dinner usually starts at around 5:30pm.

DOCTORS Hotels usually keep lists of doctors, should you need one. For physician referrals, call the **Desert Springs Hospital** (☎ 702/388-4888;

www.desertspringshospital.net).
Hours are Monday to Friday from
8am to 8pm and Saturday from 9am
to 3pm.

DRUGSTORES There's a 24-hour
Walgreen's (which also has a 1-hr.
photo) at 3763 Las Vegas Blvd. S.
(☎ **702/739-9638;** www.walgreens.
com), and a **CVS** at 3758 Las Vegas
Blvd. S. (☎ **702/262-9028;** www.
cvs.com)—both are just across from
the Monte Carlo. **White Cross
Drugs,** 1700 Las Vegas Blvd. S.
(☎ **702/382-1733**), is another
24-hour option.

ELECTRICITY Like Canada, the
United States uses 110–120 volts
AC (60 cycles), compared to 220–
240 volts AC (50 cycles) in most of
Europe, Australia, and New Zealand.
If your small appliances use 220–
240 volts, you'll need a 110-volt
transformer and a plug adapter with
two flat parallel pins to operate
them here. Downward converters
that change 220–240 volts to 110–
120 volts are difficult to find in the
United States, so bring one with
you.

EMERGENCIES Dial ☎ **911** to contact the police or fire department or
to call an ambulance.

EVENT LISTINGS In order to make
sure the show you want isn't dark
during your visit, or to see what
headliner has hit town, you can
check events through the following:
The **Las Vegas Review Journal**
(www.lvrj.com) is the city's daily
paper, and its Friday edition carries
a special "Weekend" section with a
guide to shows and other entertainment options. **City Life** (www.las
vegascitylife.com) and **Las Vegas
Weekly** (www.lasvegasweekly.com)
are free weekly alternative papers
with plenty of club and bar listings.
What's On (www.whats-on.com) is
the free magazine you will usually
find in your hotel room. It's mostly a
rehash of press releases, but often

has discount coupons for some
shows, buffets, and more.

FAMILY TRAVEL Think twice (and
then again) before you bring kids to
Vegas these days. The "Vegas is for
families" concept died ages ago, so
not only is there considerably less
to do with children, but you also
have to do it while constantly distracting them from casinos, booze,
four-story-tall billboards featuring
nearly bare bottoms, and other
adult material. On top of that, some
casino hotels ban children if they
aren't guests of that property—and
they will check your room keys for
proof. If you must bring your children to town, I suggest you look at
my Vegas with Kids tour on p 30.
Another good source of information
is *Frommer's Las Vegas with Kids*.

GAMBLING LAWS You must be 21
years of age to enter, much less
gamble in, any casino. If you look
young, carry your identification with
you as you may be asked to prove
your age. Most casinos are open 24
hours a day.

HOLIDAYS Banks, government
offices, post offices, and many
stores, restaurants, and museums
are closed (but not the casinos!) on
the following legal national holidays:
January 1 (New Year's Day), the third
Monday in January (Martin Luther
King, Jr. Day), the third Monday in
February (Presidents' Day), the last
Monday in May (Memorial Day), July
4 (Independence Day), the first Monday in September (Labor Day), the
second Monday in October (Columbus Day), November 11 (Veterans'
Day/Armistice Day), the fourth Thursday in November (Thanksgiving Day),
and December 25 (Christmas). The
Tuesday after the first Monday in
November is Election Day, a federal
government holiday in presidential-
election years (held every 4 years,
and next in 2012).

For more information on holidays, see "Festivals & Special Events," earlier in this chapter.

HOSPITALS Emergency services are available 24 hours a day at **University Medical Center,** 1800 W. Charleston Blvd., at Shadow Lane (☎ **702/383-2000;** www.umc-cares. org); the emergency-room entrance is on the corner of Hastings and Rose streets. **Sunrise Hospital and Medical Center,** 3186 Maryland Pkwy., between Desert Inn Road and Sahara Avenue (☎ **702/731-8080;** www.sunrisehospital.com), also has a 24-hour emergency room.

For more minor problems, try the **Harmon Medical Urgent Care Center**—the closest to the Strip—at 105 E. Harmon at Koval Lane, near the MGM Grand (☎ **702/796-1116;** www.harmonmedicalcenter. com). It's open 24 hours, it has X-ray machines, and there is a pharmacy on-site.

INSURANCE The cost of travel insurance varies widely, depending on the destination, the cost and length of your trip, your age and health, and the type of trip you're taking, but expect to pay between 5% and 8% of the vacation itself. You can get estimates from various providers through **www.insuremytrip. com**. Enter your trip cost and dates, your age, and other information, for prices from more than a dozen companies.

U.K. citizens and their families who make more than one trip abroad per year may find an annual travel insurance policy works out cheaper. Check **www.moneysupermarket. com**, which compares prices across a wide range of providers for single- and multi-trip policies.

Most big travel agents offer their own insurance and will probably try to sell you their package when you book a holiday. Think before you sign.

Britain's Consumers' Association recommends that you insist on seeing the policy and reading the fine print before buying travel insurance. The **Association of British Insurers** (☎ 020/7600-3333; www. abi.org.uk) gives advice by phone and publishes *Holiday Insurance,* a free guide to policy provisions and prices. You might also shop around for better deals: Try **Columbus Direct** (☎ 0870/033-9988; www. columbusdirect.net).

Trip Cancellation: Trip-cancellation insurance will help retrieve your money if you have to back out of a trip or depart early, or if your travel supplier goes bankrupt. Trip cancellation traditionally covers such events as sickness, natural disasters, and State Department advisories. The latest news in trip-cancellation insurance is the availability of **"any-reason"** cancellation coverage—which costs more but covers cancellations made for any reason. You won't get back 100% of your prepaid trip cost, but you'll be refunded a substantial portion. **TravelSafe** (☎ 888/885-7233; www.travelsafe.com) offers this coverage, and Expedia offers any-reason cancellation coverage for its air-hotel packages.

For details, contact one of the following recommended insurers: **Access America** (☎ 866/807-3982; www.accessamerica.com); **Travel Guard International** (☎ 800/826-4919; www.travelguard.com); **Travel Insured International** (☎ 800/243-3174; www.travelinsured.com); and **Travelex Insurance Services** (☎ 888/457-4602; www.travelex-insurance.com).

Medical Insurance: Although it's not required of travelers, health insurance is highly recommended. Most health-insurance policies cover you if you get sick away from home—but check your coverage before you leave.

International visitors should note that unlike many European countries, the United States does not usually offer free or low-cost medical care to its citizens or visitors. Doctors and hospitals are expensive, and in most cases will require advance payment or proof of coverage before they render their services. Packages such as **Europ Assistance's "Worldwide Healthcare Plan"** are sold by European automobile clubs and travel agencies at attractive rates. **Worldwide Assistance Services, Inc.** (☎ **800/777-8710;** www.worldwideassistance.com), is the agent for Europ Assistance in the United States. Though lack of health insurance may prevent you from being admitted to a hospital in nonemergencies, don't worry about being left on a street corner to die: The American way is to fix you now and bill the living daylights out of you later.

Insurance for British Travelers: Travelers from the U.K. should carry their European Health Insurance Card (EHIC), which replaced the E111 form as proof of entitlement to free/reduced cost medical treatment abroad (☎ **0845/606-2030;** www.ehic.ie). Note, however, that the EHIC covers only "necessary medical treatment," and for repatriation costs, lost money, baggage, or cancellation, travel insurance from a reputable company should always be sought. For other options visit **www.travelinsuranceweb.com**.

Insurance for Canadian Travelers: Canadians should check with their provincial health-plan offices or call **Health Canada** (☎ **866/225-0709;** www.hc-sc.gc.ca) to find out the extent of their coverage and what documentation and receipts they must take home in case they are treated in the United States.

INTERNET ACCESS Most resort hotels in Vegas offer wireless access, but for a hefty daily fee (usually around $17). Some chain hotels offer free Wi-Fi in public areas, while others still offer high-speed access. In Las Vegas, you can find free Wi-Fi at most stand-alone McDonald's, Starbucks, and in the Fashion Show Mall. To find additional public Wi-Fi hotspots, go to **www.jiwire.com**; its Wi-Fi Finder holds the world's largest directory of public wireless hotspots.

Some Vegas hotels still offer Internet service through the television with a wireless keyboard (provided). Figure, on average, that you'll pay about $15 a day for the privilege.

There are usually no easily accessible cybercafes in Vegas, and even those that open tend to close without warning. To check for possibilities, try **www.cybercaptive.com** and **www.cybercafe.com**.

LIMOUSINES Hotels will often provide airport limos for high rollers or VIP guests—in the latter case, that often means someone merely staying in a higher-level room. Ask and see. Otherwise, try **Las Vegas Limo** (☎ **888/696-4400** or 702/736-1419; http://lasvegaslimo.com) or **Presidential Limo** (☎ **800/423-1420** or 702/731-5577; www.presidential limolv.com).

LIQUOR LAWS The legal age for purchase and consumption of alcoholic beverages is 21; proof of age is required and often requested at bars, nightclubs, and restaurants, so it's always a good idea to carry ID when you go out.

Beer, wine, and liquor are all sold in all kinds of stores pretty much around the clock, plus cocktail waitresses are ready to ply you moments after you sit down at a slot machine or gaming table. You won't have a hard time finding a drink in this town.

Do not carry open containers of alcohol in a car or any public area that isn't zoned for alcohol consumption.

Note that it is also forbidden to have an open container of alcohol in a vehicle, even if you're the passenger. The Strip and Fremont Street in Downtown Las Vegas are the only areas in town where you can have open containers on public sidewalks; otherwise, the police can fine you on the spot. And nothing will ruin your trip faster than getting a citation for DUI ("driving under the influence"), so don't even think about driving while intoxicated.

LOST PROPERTY Be sure to tell all of your credit card companies the minute you discover your wallet has been lost or stolen, and file a report at the nearest police precinct. Your credit card company or insurer may require a police report number or record of the loss. Most credit card companies have an emergency toll-free number to call if your card is lost or stolen; they may be able to wire you a cash advance immediately or deliver an emergency credit card in a day or two. Visa's U.S. emergency number is ☎ **800/847-2911** or 410/581-9994. American Express cardholders and traveler's check holders should call ☎ **800/221-7282.** MasterCard holders should call ☎ **800/307-7309** or 636/722-7111. For other credit cards, call the toll-free number directory at ☎ **800/555-1212.**

MAIL & POSTAGE At press time, domestic postage rates were 28¢ for a postcard and 44¢ for a letter. For international mail, a first-class letter of up to 1 ounce costs 98¢ (75¢ to Canada and Mexico); a first-class postcard costs the same as a letter. For more information go to **www.usps.com** and click on "Calculate Postage."

MONEY Vegas runs on money, in all its forms. Most places, except the smallest stores and restaurants, take credit cards. The gaming tables and slot machines run on cold hard cash. If you prefer using traveler's checks, they are accepted in many places in Las Vegas.

American Express (☎ **800/807-6233;** ☎ 800/221-7282 for card holders); **Visa** (☎ **800/732-1322**); and **MasterCard** (☎ **800/223-9920**) all issue traveler's checks.

Be sure to keep a copy of the traveler's checks serial numbers separate from your checks in the event that they are stolen or lost. You'll get a refund faster if you know the numbers.

PARKING Free valet parking is one of the great pleasures of Las Vegas and well worth the $1 or $2 tip (given when the car is returned) to save walking a city block from the far reaches of a hotel parking lot, especially in the summer heat. Valet service can fill up late on weekend nights, but the self-parking lots are vast (*always* write down where you parked if you go this route).

PASSPORTS International visitors should always keep a photocopy of their passport with them when traveling. If your passport is lost or stolen, having a copy significantly facilitates the reissuing process at a local consulate or embassy. Keep your passport and other valuables in your room's safe or in the hotel safe.

POLICE For nonemergencies, call ☎ **702/795-3111.** For emergencies, call **911.**

SAFETY While otherwise quite safe for a big city, in Las Vegas vast amounts of money are always on display, and criminals find many easy marks. At gaming tables and slot machines, men should keep wallets well concealed and out of reach of pickpockets, and women should keep handbags in plain sight (on laps). If you're playing slots, do not forget to take your winnings ticket with you. If you win a big jackpot, ask the pit boss or slot attendant to cut you a check rather than give you cash; it's also perfectly reasonable to ask security to escort you to your car. Outside casinos, popular spots for pickpockets and thieves are restaurants and outdoor shows. Stay alert. Unless your hotel room has an in-room safe, check your valuables in a safe-deposit box at the front desk.

SMOKING Smoking has been banned in Vegas restaurants, and in any bar that serves food. And most poker rooms in Las Vegas do not permit smoking. Otherwise, Las Vegas remains quite smoker-friendly.

SPECTATOR SPORTS Las Vegas isn't known for its sports teams. Except for minor-league baseball and hockey, the only consistent spectator sports are those at UNLV. For the pros, if watching Triple A ball (in this case, a Los Angeles Dodgers farm team) in potentially triple-degree heat sounds like fun, the charmingly named and even-better merchandized **Las Vegas 51s** (as in Area 51, as in alien-themed gear!) are a great bet. This ball team's schedule and ticket info are available by calling ☎ **702/386-7200** or online at **www.lv51.com**. Ice hockey might be a better climate choice; get info for the **Las Vegas Wranglers** at **www.lasvegas wranglers.com** or by calling ☎ **702/471-7825**.

The **Las Vegas Motor Speedway** (p 35) is a major venue for car racing that draws major NASCAR events to Las Vegas.

Because the city has several top-notch sporting arenas, important annual events take place in Las Vegas. The **PGA Tour** (www.pga tour.com) regularly makes a stop in Las Vegas each October. The **National Finals Rodeo** is held in UNLV's Thomas and Mack Center each December. From time to time,

you'll also find NBA exhibition games, professional ice-skating competitions, or gymnastics exhibitions.

Finally, Las Vegas is well-known as a major location for boxing matches. These are held in several Strip hotels, most often at Caesars or the MGM Grand, but sometimes at The Mirage. Tickets are hard to come by and quite expensive.

Tickets to sporting events at hotels are available either through **Ticketmaster** (☎ **702/893-3000;** www.ticketmaster.com) or through the hotels themselves.

TAXES Sales tax is 8.1% (note that it's also levied on show tickets). The Clark County hotel room tax is 12%, and in Downtown it's 13%. The United States has no value-added tax (VAT) or other indirect tax at the national level. Every state, county, and city may levy its own local tax on all purchases, including hotel and restaurant checks and airline tickets. These taxes will not appear on price tags.

TAXIS See "By Taxi" in "Getting Around," earlier in this chapter.

TELEPHONES For **directory assistance** ("information"), dial **411;** for long-distance information, dial **1,** then the appropriate area code and **555-1212.** Generally, hotel surcharges on long-distance and local calls are astronomical. You are often charged even for making a toll-free or phone card call. You're better off using your **cellphone** or a **public pay telephone.** Some hotels are now adding on an additional "resort fee" to the cost of the room, which is supposed to cover local calls (as well as using the pool and other elements that ought to be givens). The fee can range from $1 (Motel 6) to $15 per day. Many convenience groceries and packaging services sell **prepaid calling cards** in denominations up to $50; for international visitors, these can be the least

Getting Discount Tickets

Las Vegas ticket prices keep on climbing every year. The good news is that Vegas has discounters to shop from (though you must purchase tickets in person).

Tix 4 Tonight (www.tix4tonight.com) offers day-of-show discounts (as well as dining discounts at major buffets and restaurants) from 10am to 9pm. It has seven locations scattered throughout the city, including a Downtown branch in the Four Queens Hotel, and a Strip location in the Showcase Mall (next to MGM Grand). It also will sometimes offer a sneak peek of tickets available on its website. **All Access Entertainment** (www.show tkts.com) is another reputable discounter with locations at Circus Circus (10am–8pm) and the Fashion Show Mall (10am–6pm).

Discounts can range from 10% to as high as 50% on between 35 and 50 performances daily (shows that I've seen sold include *Phantom of the Opera, Blue Man Group,* and *Zumanity*). Note that tickets are released for sale throughout the day, so getting there early won't necessarily net you a better selection.

expensive way to call home. Local calls made from public pay phones in Las Vegas cost from 25¢ to 50¢. Pay phones do not accept pennies, and few will take anything larger than a quarter.

Most long-distance and international calls can be dialed directly from any phone. **For calls within the United States and to Canada,** dial **1** followed by the area code and the seven-digit number. **For other international calls,** dial **011** followed by the country code, the city code, and the number you are calling.

TICKETS   To avoid surcharges and obtain better seating options, it's usually best to go through the box office for the show in question (some box offices can be accessed online). Top-draw shows can sell out months in advance, so try to order tickets as early as possible. Ticket agencies generally charge obscene markups and should be consulted

only if you're desperate. For more information on buying discount tickets, see box above.

TIPPING   You can get tip fatigue in Vegas, but try to remember that this city runs on the service sector and tipping is often an important part of certain workers' income. In hotels, tip bellhops at least $1 per bag ($2–$3 if you have a lot of luggage) and tip the chamber staff $1 to $2 per day (more if you've left a disaster area). Tip the doorman or concierge only if he or she has provided you with some specific service (for example, calling a cab for you or obtaining difficult-to-get theater tickets). Tip the valet-parking attendant $1 to $2 every time you get your car.

In restaurants, bars, and nightclubs, tip service staff 15% to 20% of the check, tip bartenders 10% to 15%, tip checkroom attendants $1 per garment, and tip valet-parking attendants $1 per vehicle.

Goes to Paris revue. The most luxurious hotel to date, the Tropicana, opens on the Strip.

1958 The 1,065-room Stardust opens as the world's largest resort complex with a spectacular show from France, the *Lido de Paris*.

1959 The Las Vegas Convention Center goes up, presaging the city's future as a major convention city.

1960 A championship boxing match, the first of many, takes place at the Convention Center. El Rancho Vegas, the Strip's first property, burns to the ground.

1963 McCarran International Airport opens.

1966 The Aladdin, the first new hotel on the Strip in 9 years, is soon eclipsed by the unparalleled grandeur of Caesars Palace. The Four Queens opens in Downtown. Howard Hughes takes up residence at the Desert Inn; he buys up big chunks of Las Vegas and helps erase the city's gangland stigma.

1967 Elvis Presley marries Priscilla Beaulieu at the Aladdin.

1968 Circus Circus gives kids a reason to come to Las Vegas.

1973 The ultraglamorous 2,100-room MGM Grand assumes the mantle of "world's largest resort." Siegfried & Roy debut at the Tropicana.

1976 Pioneer aviator Howard Hughes dies aboard a plane en route to a Houston hospital. Dean Martin and Jerry Lewis make up after a 20-year feud.

1979 A new international arrivals building opens at McCarran International Airport.

1980 McCarran International Airport embarks on a 20-year,

$785-million expansion program. A devastating fire destroys the MGM Grand, leaving 84 dead and 700 injured.

1981 Siegfried & Roy begin a record-breaking run in their own show, *Beyond Belief,* at the Frontier.

1982 A Las Vegas street is named Wayne Newton Boulevard.

1989 Steve Wynn makes headlines with his spectacular Mirage, fronted by an erupting volcano.

1990s The family-friendly medieval Arthurian realm of Excalibur opens as the new "world's largest resort" titleholder with 4,032 rooms, a claim it relinquishes when the MGM Grand's new 5,005-room megaresort/theme park opens in 1993, with a *Wizard of Oz* theme. Other properties geared toward families open in the 1990s, most notably Luxor, with its pyramid and Egyptian motifs, and the pirate-themed Treasure Island. The rock-'n'-roll Hard Rock, Mandalay Bay, Bellagio, New York–New York, The Venetian, and Paris Las Vegas carry concept gaming resorts to new heights. Celebrity chefs come to town.

2004 The Strip Monorail debuts.

2005 Wynn Las Vegas, the first major new casino resort to open in 5 years, debuts on the Strip.

2006 The Red Rock Resort opens off the Strip.

2007 The Stardust is demolished to make way for the new Echelon Place. The Aladdin is renamed Planet Hollywood.

2008 The tanking U.S. economy and plunging real estate values send Las Vegas into a tailspin, causing hotels to discount massively in order to attract visitors.

2009 CityCenter opens on the Strip.

Toll-Free Numbers & Websites

Airlines

AIR CANADA
☎ 888/247-2262
www.aircanada.ca

AIRTRAN AIRLINES
☎ 800/247-8726
www.airtran.com

ALASKA AIRLINES/HORIZON AIR
☎ 800/252-7522
www.alaskaair.com

AMERICAN AIRLINES
☎ 800/433-7300
www.aa.com

ATA AIRLINES
☎ 800/1-FLY-ATA [135-9282]
www.ata.com

CONTINENTAL AIRLINES
☎ 800/525-0280
www.continental.com

DELTA AIR LINES
☎ 800/221-1212
www.delta.com

FRONTIER AIRLINES
☎ 800/432-1359
www.frontierairlines.com

HAWAIIAN AIRLINES
☎ 800/367-5320
www.hawaiianair.com

NORTHWEST AIRLINES
☎ 800/225-2525
www.nwa.com

SOUTHWEST AIRLINES
☎ 800/435-9792
www.southwest.com

UNITED AIRLINES
☎ 800/241-6522
www.united.com

US AIRWAYS
☎ 800/428-4322
www.usairways.com

VIRGIN ATLANTIC AIRWAYS
☎ 800/862-8621 in the continental U.S.
☎ 0870/380-2007 in Britain
www.virgin-atlantic.com

Major Hotel & Motel Chains

BEST WESTERN INTERNATIONAL
☎ 800/528-1234
www.bestwestern.com

COMFORT INNS
☎ 800/228-5150
www.hotelchoice.com

DAYS INN
☎ 800/325-2525
www.daysinn.com

HILTON HOTELS
☎ 800/HILTONS
www.hilton.com

HOWARD JOHNSON
☎ 800/654-2000
www.hojo.com

INTERCONTINENTAL HOTELS & RESORTS
☎ 877/424-2449
www.ichotelsgroup.com

LA QUINTA INNS & SUITES
☎ 800/531-5900 or 1/866-725-1661
www.lq.com

MARRIOTT HOTELS
☎ 800/228-9290
www.marriott.com

MOTEL 6
☎ 800/4-MOTEL6 (800/466-8356)
www.motel6.com

SHERATON HOTELS & RESORTS
☎ 800/325-3535
www.sheraton.com

SUPER 8 MOTELS
☎ 800/800-8000
www.super8.com

Index

Photo **Credits**

p 1 © Ken Ross / Viestiphoto.com; p 3 © Richard Cummins / Lonely Planet Images.; p 4, top © Gail Mooney / Masterfile; p 4, bottom © O'Gara / Bissell Photography / Las Vegas Stock / Digistock.com; p 5, top Courtesy Bally's Las Vegas; p 5, bottom Courtesy Atomic Testing Museum; p 6 © Alise O'Brien / Courtesy M Resort Spa Casino; p 7 © Ross Pictures / Corbis; p 9 Courtesy of MGM Mirage; p 10, top © Paul Cichocki / FremontStock.com; p 10, bottom © Sylvain Grandadam / AGE Fotostock; p 11 © Demetrio Carrasco / AGE Fotostock; p 12, top © Sunny Photography / Alamy; p 12, bottom © Sylvain Grandadam / AGE Fotostock; p 13 © Wendell Metzen / Index Stock Imagery; p 15, middle © Richard Cummins / Lonely Planet Images; p 15, bottom © Paul Cichocki / FremontStock.com; p 16 Courtesy MGM Mirage; p 17, top Courtesy Cirque du Soleil; p 17, bottom Courtesy Wynn Las Vegas; p 19 © Paul Cichocki / FremontStock.com; p 20 © Paul Cichocki / FremontStock.com; p 21 © Neil